THE PARLIAMENT OF SWITZERLAND

THE PARLIAMENT OF SWITZERLAND

BY

CHRISTOPHER HUGHES

*Professor of Politics
at the University of Leicester*

PUBLISHED FOR
THE HANSARD SOCIETY BY
CASSELL · LONDON

CASSELL & COMPANY LTD
35 Red Lion Square · London WC1
and at
MELBOURNE · SYDNEY · TORONTO
CAPE TOWN
JOHANNESBURG · AUCKLAND

© The Hansard Society for
Parliamentary Government 1962

First published 1962

Printed in Great Britain
by Ebenezer Baylis and Son Limited
The Trinity Press, Worcester, and London
F.862

PREFACE

In writing this book I have principally had in mind the reader who has visited Switzerland on holiday, and who has read something about the Swiss Constitution and something about Swiss history. There are, after all, many available books on Swiss government—I myself have written one which is still in print—and there is a modern history available. Switzerland is close to Britain, and the classic holiday country for Britons. For these reasons it did not seem to me worth going over familiar ground again. Nevertheless, I have endeavoured to make the book complete in itself, so that it can be read without previous knowledge, and for this purpose I have prefaced the first chapter with a brief outline of the terms used in describing Swiss government. Even the experienced reader may find this useful, since it is a source of confusion that the term 'Federal Council', which in Germany describes the Senate, in Switzerland describes the Cabinet.

At least two types of book could be written on the Swiss Parliament. The procedure of Parliament could, for example, be put under the microscope. This has never been done effectively, even in Switzerland, and would be both interesting in itself and topical—for procedure is at the moment of writing (1960) under consideration in Switzerland. Nevertheless, it does not seem the subject of discussion which would most interest an English audience. The peculiar structure of the executive (Federal Council) in Switzerland, and the way in which the whole constitution is suffused with the spirit of proportionality, means that no other parliament (except, perhaps, modern Austria's) closely enough resembles the Swiss Parliament to afford a parallel. The Swiss political genius, moreover, has not, as the English has, selected the detail of procedure as its means of expression. Apart from Étienne Dumont, the disciple of our own Bentham, no great thinker or statesman has applied his mind to procedural problems in Switzerland, and it is a subject which the Swiss themselves consider to be of minor importance. The point of interest is in what sort of parliament a 'Federal Council type of cabinet' calls forth.

The other type of book which could be written is a book placing the Swiss federal parliament in the context of Swiss society and of the political situation created by the distribution of social and economic power within Switzerland. Though Swiss society is different at every point from English society, and works, as it were, in a different medium, yet there is a curious way in which it 'adds up to'

v

something rather similar: the same statement can be made also of Swiss government. It seems also to the point, when describing a parliament, to describe what the political conflict is about, and what interests and what ideas are involved in the parliamentary battle—for the purposes of a parliament lie outside the parliament building itself.

What I have tried to do in this book is to reconcile these two approaches, one concerned with the form and the other with the matter, by trying to see how the form of Swiss procedure (the procedure of a Federal Council, not the procedure of an opposition as in Britain) fits into its framework of Swiss society and Swiss ideals. For it seems to me that the approaches are joined at one particular point, the point at which a 'sanction' comes to be applied. This has led me to adopt an unfamiliar interpretation of the Swiss constitution, an interpretation in terms of a concealed doctrine of ministerial responsibility.

The method which has seemed to me most suitable is to deal with actual incidents, and with real persons in specific situations. The first reason for adopting this approach is a scientific one—the laws of political sociology are generalizations from observed incidents, and not *a priori*. The second one is that of timidity. The ground covered by this book is not only entirely new in English, but is unfamiliar even in Switzerland, and the material described has for the most part never appeared between hard covers in any language.

For both these reasons, then, I keep close to actual events—describing the genesis of an actual law, the election of an actual Federal Councillor, an actual general election in three cantons, and so on. I have hoped in this way to carry even the most indignant Swiss reader along with me. The English reader must forgive me for having introduced so many proper names into the narrative. This is a necessary consequence of the method chosen, and I have tried to reduce the number as much as possible by using the same people as often as possible in different contexts. I have also tried to make Swiss institutions intelligible in human terms—rather than in terms of institutions and abstractions—and this is another reason for operating with a cast of named human beings.

The book is sponsored by the Hansard Society for Parliamentary Government. Introductions were often arranged by the Press Department of the Swiss Foreign Office—though I have my own channels also—and by means of these introductions I obtained insights into Swiss administration which would have been denied me as a private scholar. But it must not be thought that the (on the whole, reassuring) results of the investigation were in any way deter-

PREFACE

mined by the sponsors. Indeed when first approached I made it clear that I had no high opinion of the Swiss parliament (whose proceedings I have long followed in the Official Report and, sometimes, from the public gallery). My first sketch was subtitled 'A Study of a Weak Parliament'. It was only with reluctance that I found myself forced by the evidence of what actually happens in committees and in personal contacts to revise and eventually to abandon this view. I finished my investigation with a high respect for both the parliament of Switzerland and its members, but that this would be so was quite unsuspected by me at the outset. The validity of this conclusion depends entirely on the validity of the method adopted (of working from actual typical events to a generalization from them). It is only fair to the reader to say that a 'reassuring' conclusion has never before been reached by those few investigators who have preceded me in this method: there are plenty of books on Swiss constitutional law which depict Swiss government in highly flattering terms—indeed, there are few which do not. There is a distinguished handful of books on Swiss government which, studying things as they actually are, convey the well-documented disillusion of their authors. But those who are bent on flattering the justifiable Swiss satisfaction with their own form of government have, as it were, been afraid to look into the mundane details of committee procedure and the workings of pressure groups. Those bent on investigating pressure groups and the actual workings of politics have been overwhelmed by the contrast with things as they 'should' be. This is the first time that a writer on government has looked at things as they work from day to day in Switzerland, and liked what he has seen. As a foreigner, I have been free from the prejudices of affection or disenchantment. But unsure of my welcome in unexplored territory, I have tried never to stray far from my evidence.

The reputations of certain statesmen have been treated cavalierly in some passages of this book. This is not the custom of political writing in Switzerland, which errs rather on the side of the sanctimonious, but it is essential for my purpose. I must consider whether the choice of cabinet ministers, for example, has been good or bad, whether foreign secretaries have stayed too long in office, whether ministers resign because they are tired or because their associates find them inefficient, and whether the office with which they are consoled after retirement is a bribe or an honour. When things are called by their names, the assessment of institutions may be altered, and I should rather criticize a dead politician than injure (through sheer niceness of mind) a living parliament. But to anyone whom I hurt, I must sincerely apologize.

PREFACE

Date of Survey

The study must be taken as dated 1 September 1960, for institutions change continuously and the careers and prospects of statesmen look very different even after an interval of six months. Details, but not the general picture, have been altered up to 1 August 1961.

Acknowledgements

I have mentioned my debt to the Hansard Society. I owe as great a debt to my University, the University of Leicester, which gave me financial assistance and leave of absence during a part of one term. The burden of this fell on my colleagues, Professor Miller, Mr Hookham, Mr Day and Mr Lyon—to all of whom I owe various debts of gratitude also for advice.

The following have looked critically over the manuscript: my wife, Dr Hans Hubschmid, Dr Hans Lang, Professor Bruce Miller, Herr Fischli. Everyone who has written a book will realize how helpful and thankless a task this is.

The formation as well as the completion of the book owes most to discussions with my friends, Dr Hans Lang of Berne and Dr Hubschmid of the same town. It is based on readings in the three libraries of Berne, and on numerous interviews. In particular I am grateful to:

The Federal Political Department, the Department of Justice, the Department of Finance, the Swiss Embassy in London, the Federal Chancery, the Secretariat of the Federal Assembly, the Foundation Pro Helvetia in Zurich.

Herr Fischli (especially), and Professor Bindschedler, of the Political Department, and Drs Thalmann, Beck, Ries, Leist, Mottier, Hongler and (especially) Drs Brühwiler and Käser, all of them high Federal civil servants.

Professors Giacometti, Freymond and Behrendt, Dr Gruner and his colleague in Basle, Herr Jürg Steiner, Professor von Greyerz and others in Berne.

Dr Hermann Böschenstein. The members of the 'French box' of Press correspondents in the National Council—who were very kind to me.

National Councillors Bringolf (Schaffhausen), Condrau, Duttweiler, Conzett, Akeret, Büchi, Dürrenmatt, Grendelmeier, Oprecht, Vincent, Max Weber.

Councillors of States Buri, Dietschi, Fauquex; Altständerat Dr Emil Klöti (correspondence).

The list is formidable, and incomplete, but the value and intensity of contact varied greatly, from a personal friendship to a single

PREFACE

encounter. In some cases the relationship of hunter and hunted was reversed, and I retain the memory of an interview lasting over an hour with the best informed and least scrupulous of federal politicians, from which I derived only the information that the Assembly was bicameral, and the Swiss flag a white cross on a red ground. My information concerning him is derived from his enemies, but my judgement is based on the interview.

The list refers to my study for this book in 1960. The critical reader will observe obvious gaps in it, some of which are narrowed by other points of contact not listed here, for I have been interested in Swiss public life since 1948. Some people whom I have not met, but of whom I have read, and whom I have only seen in public if at all, I fancy I know better than certain of those I have talked to in private.

My debt to books is acknowledged in the note on Sources.

C. J. HUGHES

University of Leicester

CONTENTS

	Note on the Swiss Constitution	xiii
I	History	1
II	Society	12
III	Parties	21
IV	General Election	37
V	Members and Buildings	52
VI	The Business of the Chambers	64
VII	The Federal Council: Election and Resignation	69
VIII	Other Elections by the Assembly	84
IX	The Federal Council at Work	92
X	Legislation	101
XI	Motions, Postulates, Interpellations and Questions	120
XII	Gestion	128
XIII	Finance	136
XIV	Co-operation	148
XV	The Committee System in General	152
XVI	Interpretations	162
	Appendixes	
	1 Swiss Foreign Policy	167
	2 The Committee Career of a National Councillor	172
	3 The Workings of Proportional Representation (Lucerne, 1959)	175
	4 Sources	179
	5 Note on the Illustrations	184
	Illustrations	187
	Index	197

xi

Note on the Swiss Constitution

Under the present Constitution (of 1874), Switzerland is a *Confederation* of twenty-five *cantons*. Six of these are reckoned as half-cantons, so that there are twenty-two 'whole' cantons.

The Federal Government consists of:

1. A Parliament of two Chambers. In one of these, the *Council of States*, each whole canton is represented by two members—as in the Senate of the U.S.A. In the other Chamber, the *National Council*, the Swiss people are represented by 196 members chosen for a four-year term by proportional representation. The two Chambers sit apart for most business, and are perfectly equal in formal powers. But for some purposes, and in particular, for the election of the Federal Council—the executive—they sit in joint session. The two Chambers together are officially called the *Federal Assembly* or, colloquially, 'the Parliament'.

2. *The Federal Council*, a Cabinet of seven departmental ministers, elected by the Federal Assembly in joint session, for four years immediately after the four-yearly general election of the National Council. Members are re-eligible without limit, and are usually re-elected.

3. A Federal judiciary called the *Federal Tribunal*, which exercises no supervision over *federal* legislation (unlike the U.S. Supreme Court).

4. The Swiss electorate (i.e., most male Swiss citizens of over 20) have certain further rights in the Federal Government, viz:

> (a) *amendments to the Constitution* must be submitted to a referendum, in which there must also be a majority in a majority of cantons;
>
> (b) there is a right to *challenge* laws (and treaties) to a referendum within three months of passing;
>
> (c) there is a right of *initiating* constitutional amendments.

The cantons have unicameral Parliaments (called Great Councils). Five of them have, in addition, traditional annual open-air assemblies of all voters, which are called *Landsgemeinden*.

The cantonal executive councils, which have varying numbers of members, are similar to the Federal Council in that they are executive colleges of departmental ministers, but they differ in the methods of election. They are called Councils of State.

I
History

The Swiss nation is kept together, and kept apart, by history. For this reason alone a book on the modern working of the Swiss State must start by describing the 'Old Confederation', Switzerland as it was before the French invasion of 1798. History also explains why Switzerland is there (for Switzerland is an artificial State that has only rather recently grown into a completely natural organism), and why Swiss government takes its present peculiar form. This is the sort of history—the facts of the past—that would still be history even if no importance were attached to it by the Swiss and even if the writing of history did not have political implications.

It so happens, however, that there is a strong sense of history among the component peoples of Switzerland. Furthermore, it is history of a peculiar sort—for it does not attach itself very much to the Parliament or the central government, but is the history of cantons and towns and districts. It is localized, not national, history. This sense of a living history gives much of the Swiss-ness to Switzerland.

In the third place, the history that is taught as history—the contents of history books, whether true or false—is of considerable current political importance in Switzerland. Contemporary political ideals may, and do, take the form of statements about the past—glorifying the Old Régime, for example, when the aristocracies carried the banners of patriotism, or glorifying the Revolution, after which the new middle class created the Switzerland we know, and gave it an army and an international personality. Much political debate among the classes which create opinion takes this historicizing form in Switzerland, and many political emotions clothe themselves in a historical vocabulary.

For a narrative of Swiss history the reader must look elsewhere: this is a book on the modern Swiss Parliament. All that is necessary to do here is to evoke this sense of history, to describe how history comes to be localized, and how the issues of modern politics may (in some cases) be rooted in history and be argued in historical terms.

THE SENSE OF HISTORY IN SWITZERLAND

The sense of history in Switzerland is most strongly felt when inquiring into the history of a particular place, for most of Swiss history is localized history. Switzerland, like Holland, is (for the most part, and in some sense) a part of the greater Germany. Under the Holy Roman Empire the German-speaking peoples became fragmented, and local communities obtained something very like 'sovereignty'. The Free Imperial Cities were in a very real sense sovereign, the William Tell cantons of 'Inner Switzerland' were in a real sense sovereign also, but even much smaller and more obscure communities obtained a little of the savour of sovereignty. Today the language of sovereignty is used naturally and properly of the cantonal governments—the 'Republic of Geneva', for example, or the 'Free State of Solothurn'—but it is also used in some contexts, and in a more forced sense, of the communes, the parishes we might call them. Thus even today the 'citizenship' of a commune is the necessary preliminary to citizenship of a canton and hence of Switzerland. This citizenship ('*bourgeoisie*') of a commune is a hereditary status following much the same rules as the true citizenship of a nation state.

A community which employs the language of sovereignty, still more a community which really was once sovereign, keeps a more robust sense of history than one whose history is that of local administration. This sense of history has been strengthened in most of Switzerland by the traditions, or the fictions, of republicanism, and by the absence in modern times of wars or inflation of currency. A big difference between modern Switzerland and modern Germany is the loss of this strong local sense of history in Germany, and its preservation in Switzerland.

The mere statistics are impressive; one third of the inhabitants of the modern Swiss communes are hereditary citizens of that commune, while two thirds of the inhabitants of the cantons have the hereditary citizenship of the canton in which they live. But the historical link goes deeper than this. The traditional old families of most ancient towns and many ancient rural communities still live there. For example, the names of the old sovereign patrician families of Berne recorded in the chronicles and archives can for the most part be found in the latest telephone directory, and the same is in general true of the other historic centres of power. Of course, Switzerland is not an aristocracy nor is Swiss society aristocratic, but it is still not possible quite to ignore the old sovereign aristocracies. Among themselves the historic families often (until recent years) refused to

national tradition they are a part of the folklore of democracy throughout the world. The darker historical aspects—the bigotry, the squalid family feuds, the domination by a close aristocracy, the oppression of the subject territories, the reluctance to share citizenship, the support of despotism by mercenary service—are a part only of the domestic traditions of the tiny communities directly concerned.

The towns of Zurich and Berne represent two other significant elements of the Old Confederation. Zurich is the complement of Inner Switzerland, urbane, industrial, civilized, liberal, with a mercantile patriciate. Zurich was the home-town of the Reformation in Switzerland and one of the centres of the Enlightenment in Germany. Zurich represents a tradition which is too little appreciated by the general public in England, for the Swiss contribution to European civilization goes deeper than yodelling and chocolate, deeper even than primitive democracy. It is important to keep Zurich in mind: it is the Athens of Switzerland, and at times has been the Athens of Greater Germany. It has also long been the financial centre of Switzerland, and the importance of Swiss banking and insurance is very great. Its rivals and peers, Geneva and Basle, look outside Switzerland for their economic hinterland and to themselves and to each other for their social life. Zurich makes up for the deficiencies of Urschweiz, economically, culturally and politically, and is a symbol of an important element in the Swiss character.

Berne takes something from Inner Switzerland, and something from Zurich. A walled city, its ruling classes took an interest in country life that only finds its parallel in England; a close hereditary aristocracy, its rulers were leaders rather than tyrants. Stuffy, worthy, self-satisfied, Berne keeps today something in its character from the eighteenth century. There are probably few non-Bernese who have not felt at times that Berne was intolerable, but never that it was contemptible. Berne made Switzerland, in that it provided the element of will, of desire for power, the military and diplomatic backbone, the standard of integrity. Berne (to vary the comparison) was the Prussia of Switzerland and its patricians were the Junkers.

The old Berne, before 1798, governed a much wider area than at the present day. Its former territory included the present canton of Vaud, and some of the Aargau, but as compensation for these losses it received in 1815 the troublesome addition of territories subject to the Prince Bishop of Basle, French-speaking and Catholic (for the greater part). This wide former territory, reaching nearly to Geneva in the south, and nearly to the Rhine in the north, was subject to the sovereign city of Berne. Within this city some two hundred family-

learn or to forget. This is not so today, but by their presence help to keep alive the sense of history in each locality.

THE OLD CONFEDERATION

The area we now call Switzerland had already received that by the end of the eighteenth century, but there was no instit of government ruling it. The concept of neutrality covered (mo less) what we now call Switzerland, but no other political conce which a name can easily be given. Within this geographical three political nebulæ can be distinguished, the Confederation Thirteen Cantons (i.e., the 'Swiss Confederation' or Eidgen(schaft proper), the Republic of Valais, and the Grisons.

1. *The XIII Cantons*

The element of the Thirteen Cantons which is most famil the English reader is the association of the three (or four) communities—Schwyz (from which the Confederation of receives its name), Uri, and Unterwalden—this latter divided time immemorial into Obwalden and Nidwalden, the part 'abo forest' and the part 'below the forest'. The alliance as a lastin stitutional document dates from 1315, but there was an older a of 1291 which modern patriotism prefers to commemorate. The cantons are called Primeval Switzerland, '*Urschweiz*': with L they are called 'Inner Switzerland'.

'Primeval Switzerland' is an essential part of the Swiss that has so much influenced Swiss reality. Peasant[1] (for no towns or castles were permitted to stand), democratic (for the of life and death and all other powers of sovereignty were ulti vested in the Landsgemeinde—the open-air gathering of all fre and very conservative, Urschweiz represents the picture of th as they would like to be seen by others. The mural painting National Council, for example, represents the Spirit of Peace ing over the Rütli, the meadow where the oath of perpetual was taken. The mural in the Council of States represents the gemeinde of Nidwalden. Both are in Inner Switzerland. The aspects of Inner Swiss democracy are a part, the most importa perhaps, of the Swiss national political tradition, and thro

---

[1] In the case of actual Urschweiz the economy was not really agric all, but pastoral and mercantile. The prosperity of the communities v on the transit trade, which made them independent of the towns. The economy was also the basis of military power, for herdsmen are more soldiers than ploughmen.

clans held the citizenship in the years immediately preceding 1798, and of these families some seventy were *regimentsfähig*, qualified by birth for election to the Council of Two Hundred, and of these some dozen were recognized as being in the line of the highest offices of all. Something of this sense of order survives today, in Switzerland as well as in Berne: it provides an element in the Swiss character, the *bourgeois* pride, the solidity, the self-reliance, the self-satisfaction, without which the country would never have survived. One should add that the irritation which the foreigner feels in Berne is very much the same sort of irritation that a foreigner feels in England.

Each of the other of the Thirteen Cantons contributed, and contributes, something distinctive to the Confederation, but it would interrupt the argument too much to consider all of them here: Inner Switzerland, Zurich and Berne are the three main components.

What kept these components together was a common interest, and the most important common interest under the old régime was the joint possession of the Subject Territories. The greater part of the present Canton of Ticino, a third of Aargau, a part of St Gallen and the whole of Thurgau, were subject territories, shared by all or many or some of the thirteen sovereign cantons. This past subjection is still almost a political fact. The discerning eye sees the marks of it in the poverty of the old buildings—there was often a ruthless economic exploitation of the 'subjects', in which the peasant lords of Inner Switzerland obtained a bad pre-eminence. A curious feature of some ex-subject territories is the religious structure, which gave rise to the device known as 'parity' with 'joint-churches' (*Simultankirchen*) that alternate in the course of a Sunday between Catholic and Protestant. But the political structure of the Old Confederation, with its artificial Roman Catholic majority in the Diet, kept many of the subject areas predominantly Catholic. As a further historical curiosity, in two subject communes Jews could, and did, obtain citizenship: in this respect they stood alone in Switzerland until 1866.

The only formal political institution of the Old Confederation was the Federal Diet (*Tagsatzung*, day-session, hence 'diet'). This was a conference of ambassadors, two from each sovereign canton (the divided cantons, Appenzell and Unterwalden, instructing a delegate for each part): a modern version of the system can be seen at work today in the West German Bundesrat. The principle of 'instructed' votes differentiates the old Diet from the modern Council of States, and the lack of a clear recognition of the principle of majority decision differentiates it also from the Diet of the years 1815–48. Nevertheless, some particle of the tradition of the Diet can be said to have survived, and there is a tenuous connexion of legality stretching from the old Diet to the 1815–48 Diet, and from thence through the Constitutions of 1848 and 1874 to the present day.

The Thirteen Cantons were republics, not liberal democracies. The central political link, such as it was, was republican also. This means that the traditional elements in Swiss public life, the aristocratic reactionaries for example, are not in principle opposed to the republican form of government. The Conservatives of blackest clerical dye in Inner Switzerland and the Upper Valais even have the forms of open-air democracy as a part of their tradition. It is a significant contrast between Switzerland and her neighbours that in Switzerland the old right wing consider the form of government as part of their own tradition: it is one of the many paradoxical similarities to Great Britain.

2. *The Allies of the XIII Cantons*

So far, the Thirteen Cantons and their subject territories have been discussed. Included in modern Switzerland are also some of the allies of (some, or all) the Thirteen Cantons, and two sister republics, also formerly allied, the Republic of Valais, and the Republic of Grisons.

The allies were very miscellaneous, and two of them, Rottweil and Mulhouse, are no longer a part of Switzerland. Within modern Switzerland are Neuchâtel (formerly a constitutional monarchy), the town and prince-abbacy of St Gallen, Geneva, and Bienne. These are the most important. But it must be emphasized that the area which is now called Switzerland and neatly divided into twenty-five cantons was a tangle of interlocking alliances, dependencies and liberties to which only rough justice has been done in the foregoing analysis. The political structure of the old régime was of an entirely different texture to the structure after 1815, and it is only by travelling from place to place and inquiring into the history of each place visited, and using the evidence of one's eyes, that it is possible to realize imaginatively a little of the complexity of the old legal and political fabric.

Two of the allies of the Old Confederation of the Thirteen Cantons are of such importance that they can be thought of as independent components of what became included in the eighteenth century under the loose expression 'Switzerland'. These are the Republics of Valais and Grisons, corresponding roughly with the present cantons of that name.

The Valais was nominally the territory of the Prince-Bishop of Sion, but had long ceased in reality to be anything of the sort. The seven jurisdictions of the Upper Valais, acting as so many republics, had formed a miniature confederation. Within this confederation the Prince-Bishop, a member of the local patriciate himself, had a voice (or rather, two votes), and of this territory he acted in some way as titular head. The Lower Valais, including most of the French-speaking part, was (under different titles and in different degrees) subject to the Jurisdictions of the Upper Valais. The accident of history—a mutinous noble had thrust an aged Bishop over the ramparts of the castle that overhangs Sion, and his territory had been wrested from him in consequence—had made the Lötschen valley also subject. The subjection was in many cases a particularly hard and bitter one. The turbulent and bloodstained history of the independent Valais came to an end in 1798, however, and the canton was annexed to France with the status of a *département* in 1810. But in 1814 it returned to Switzerland, where it settled down as a canton among other cantons.

Valais has a *farouche* and peculiar character of its own, a reputation for a bleak and uncompromising Catholicism, and a zealous partisanship in politics.

The Grisons was also in itself a miniature confederation, in fact a federation of three loose confederations complete with subject districts of its own. The three components were: the Grey League (in the upper Rhine valley) that gave its name to the whole alliance; the League of God's House which stretched from Coire, the cathedral city, over the watershed into the Engadine; and the League of the Ten Jurisdictions, of which Davos was the meeting place. The Valtellina (now in Italy) was subject territory to the Three Grey Leagues from 1512 to 1797. Even today, the Grisons has a little of the character of a miniature confederation, with its three languages—German, Italian and Rhaeto-Romansch. The survival of Romansch, as a living language heard in the streets, inns and churches, gives a special interest to the canton.

The history of the Grisons is of exceptional interest also as a case study in democracy and federalism, for each of the communes aspired to something of the dignity of an independent republic.[1] As in Inner Switzerland, a hereditary aristocracy co-existed with a turbulent democracy. The great families of the Grisons, von Salis, von Planta, von Sprecher, and others, play a role as the great families also of Switzerland.

One of the results of local independence was that the choice between the Reformed Faith and Roman Catholicism was largely left

---

[1] See F. Pieth *Bündnergeschichte*, Chur, 1945. It is a strange and often terrible story. Conrad Ferdinand Meyer's novel, *Jürg Jenatsch*, conveys the atmosphere, and some of the mythology, of the old régime in the Grisons.

to the commune, and the confessional map of Grisons is as confused and interlocking as that of the rest of the Confederation. A cantonal government which has to deal with two faiths and three languages has on its hands problems which are usually those of a national government: this gives a certain self-containedness of political interest in the Grisons, though less markedly so than in Valais.

REVOLUTION AND RESTORATION

In 1798, French troops marched into Berne after a brief, ineffectual resistance. The negative work of the revolution which arrived in the train of the invaders was done once for all: the infinitely complex structure of the old régime, the relationships of subjection, the feudal personal relationships, the high and low jurisdictions, disappeared at once and for good. Within two or three years the old régime seemed fantastically archaic, as if it had vanished three hundred years before. The positive work was less well performed. The unitary Constitution of the Helvétique Republic is a landmark in the history of ideas, but was never a living reality as a rule of law. The bold guiding ideas, and a few traces in certain surviving institutions and procedures, survive from the short-lived series of constitutional documents which we call, for convenience, the Helvétique.

From 1803 to 1813 is the period of the 'Mediation Constitution', once again federal. This was a first compromise between the new ideas and the old. It could not survive as an ideal because of its foreign origin: it had been dictated, literally and in the applied sense, by Napoleon and bore his signature. In 1815 we pick up a thread of legality which has never since been quite broken, the Federal Pact of 1815–48.

The Federal Pact was a restoration, but not an integral restoration, of the old régime. The old families returned to their old offices called by their old names. Sovereignty was restored to the old cantons, and granted to the new ones. But within the cantons society had been silently transformed, and in the years after the Revolution of July 1830 in Paris the new middle classes seized, or succeeded peacefully to, power in the leading cantons. This movement is termed the Regeneration by liberal historians. There was, later on, a peaceful counter-revolution of the old aristocracies. The foundations of the modern party system, and the main features of the cantonal constitutions of today, date from this period. The introduction of a democratic form of government was facilitated by the survival, on the village level, of the medieval institutions of self-government.

On the federal level, the Pact set up a 'Federal Diet', which also was the old name applied to a new thing. Like the present Council of States it was composed of two members from each whole canton, but unlike the Council of States (and like the modern West German *Bundesrat*), the votes of the members were 'instructed': this necessitated referring questions back (resolutions 'ad referendum', hence our word 'referendum') to the cantonal governments. Apart from a very small number of federal clerical officials, there was no other permanent federal institution at all. The seat of government revolved in a six-year cycle between Zurich, Berne, and Lucerne (each being the *Vorort* for two years), and the cantonal government of the *Vorort* provided for the administration of federal business.

1848

The difficulties into which the Switzerland of the Federal Pact ran were partly economic and partly political and religious. The economic difficulties were due to the absence of a federal customs duty at the frontier of the Confederation, and the presence of all too many internal customs barriers. A long standing squabble between Berne and Vaud over wine duties proved particularly refractory. Because of the sovereignty of the cantons, there could be no uniform federal postal service or currency, and there was a confusion of weights and measures.

The political and religious difficulties, after 1830, were due to the co-existence of a block of Catholic and Conservative small cantons and the Liberal and (principally) Protestant cantons who held the reality of military and economic power. The old régime in the progressive cantons sympathized with the Catholics, and the Liberals in the Catholic cantons sympathized with their fellow Liberals in power elsewhere. This provided a constant temptation to interfere also in the internal affairs of neighbouring cantons. In 1845, in particular, bands of volunteers invaded Inner Switzerland from the Liberal states, with the connivance and the unofficial support of leaders of the Liberal governments: they met with a resounding defeat at the hands of a small body of cantonal soldiers. Particular issues were the secularization of ancient monasteries by the government of Aargau, and the invitation to the Jesuits to return to Lucerne.

The Catholic Conservative governments felt compelled to enter into a separate league of mutual defence, a Sonderbund, within the Confederation. The Liberals seeing a threat to the Union, demanded the dissolution of the Sonderbund, and on refusal declared military execution. A brisk, ruritanian, civil war ensued, and was won by the Liberals.

The Diet, now with a rather artificial Liberal majority, worked out a new Constitution in committee and in the full House, and submitted it to the votes of the cantons. A majority of cantons accepted. With one exception they all referred the issue of acceptance or rejection to a popular vote (referendum or Landsgemeinde), and from this vote it is possible to see that a great majority of the population accepted it also. But in Fribourg a packed cantonal parliament accepted 'in the name of' its citizens, who most certainly would have rejected it; and there were other irregularities elsewhere.

The Sonderbund war is still current history: popular memory reaches so far and little further. The events of 1848 still determine the nature of the two great historic parties, the Catholic Conservatives and the Liberal Radicals. The Constitution still bears the character (in some of its articles) of a Liberal *Diktat*. Every now and then a strong political wind raises a puff of smoke from the old embers.

In its more important articles, however, the Constitution of 1848 was a true compromise which left the future open for both belligerents. The articles which provide that the agreement of the majority of cantons shall be necessary for a constitutional amendment, and the article which provides that the vote of both chambers shall be required for the passage of a law (with no procedure for reconciling an obstinate dispute) finally settled the Sonderbund conflict. For the Council of States (modelled with an eye on the United States Senate) made the Constitution acceptable also to the Catholics, and it gave the two minorities—French and Catholic—a vested interest in the preservation of the Constitution. In these essentials the present Constitution of 1874 has altered nothing of the Constitution of 1848.

THE OLD CONFEDERATION AS A MODERN POLITICAL PROGRAMME

The old régime in Switzerland is not only, in many districts, part of the modern political and social structure, it is also the political programme of a modern political movement—'the new patriotism' as it might be called. During the 1930s Switzerland had cause to fortify its spiritual defences against threats from Germany and Italy —and especially against 'racialism' based on language. It was natural that even in Liberal circles a new patriotism should grow up, joining hands across the centuries with the older patriotisms, and that history should be taught as a (perfectly justifiable) patriotic propaganda. Conservatives, and traditionalists generally, welcomed for their own purposes the revival of interest in the Old Confederation. The older Liberal view had interpreted Swiss history in terms of a struggle for liberty—the fight against Austria in the early Middle Ages, and then the Reformation, the Enlightenment, the Revolution, the Regeneration, and the final victory of 1848. The newer view rediscovered the virtues of the aristocratic Old Confederation, and regarded the Revolution as a fall from grace, inspired from abroad. Swiss history was rewritten in these terms, and the merits of an aristocratic form of government became the new orthodoxy.

The most recent tendency, however, is for interest in the old régime to work itself out.[1] The techniques of scientific history are at last being applied to the years after 1848. This movement likewise has a political source and a political implication. It derives from a renewed confidence in a sober modern liberalism. Its effect will probably be to relax the Conservative mood induced by the cult of the Old Confederation and the historical romanticism associated with it.

---

[1] The contrast in mood between old and young historians is well seen in the Oxford *Short History of Switzerland* published in 1952. Here the period after 1848 is handled by a Conservative writer of the patriotic school—and is unreadable. The early history of the Confederation, on the other hand, is handled by a sober young historian in a critical manner free from pathos.

II
Society

At the present day, in 1960, statements about the nature and the leadership of Swiss society are guesswork. The existing statistics have not been interpreted, and in most cases even statistics are not there. There are signs that this situation will change very soon and rapidly: the first sociological studies are already appearing or in preparation. But these are not yet available. The situation is made worse by the discretion of the Swiss press, itself significant. Furthermore, biographies of statesmen, soldiers and civil servants are few, and autobiography hardly exists. There is no history of modern Switzerland which takes serious account of social and economic factors, and it is usually true to say of any particular political event since 1848 that there has been no real investigation into what actually happened. The question 'Why did Federal Councillor Musy resign in 1934?' may serve as an example of the sort of question which it is reasonable to ask, but to which it is almost impossible to obtain an answer. Dissertations on remote events, the local history of insignificant towns, and obscure theoretical problems of constitutional law do, indeed, abound, and (to do them justice) display a serious and critical approach to the years before 1848, and face up to difficulties and call them openly by their names. But these are of limited help to the political sociologist. If democracy be described (as it is in Dr Bracher's recent book on the dissolution of the Weimar Republic) as 'social integration through discussion and compromise, and the recognition of certain "rules of the game" ', then something must be said about Swiss society—even if it is based only on the highly personal impressions of a foreigner who (although he has long been interested in Switzerland) is necessarily ignorant of some things which every Swiss child knows. Without a consideration of Swiss society it is not possible to judge the democratic effectiveness of the Swiss Parliament.

GOVERNING CLASS AND SOVEREIGN PEOPLE

Primary education is compulsory throughout the Confederation, and in the primary school all classes meet on equal terms. This is done quite naturally: the children are below the age of caste, and speak the same dialect (with different degrees of robustness) and have the same patriotism and pursuits. In the primary school they acquire a common background, are taught the same history and acquire the same ideals. At this stage the ideals are, by a paradox that runs through Swiss society, of conformity and of liberty at the same time.

At the next stage in the education of the political class, the working class has dropped behind. The *gymnasium* (state grammar school) is a distinctively middle-class institution. At some age during the time at the *gymnasium*, around sixteen it is said, the middle class itself begins to separate into lower, middle, upper, aristocrat (for Swiss aristocrats are of the middle class), and rich. But the school class keeps a certain cohesion, and its members may have an annual or periodic dinner together as 'old boys' throughout their lives. In some provincial towns there are even students' corps for gymnasiasts in their final year.

By the age of sixteen, then, a class system relying to some extent on merit, and much on the status of the parents, is discernible. The universities in this respect are continuations of the *gymnasia*. The leaving examination of the *gymnasium* is the university entrance examination, and most of those who are successful in the *matur* in university towns enter the university as a matter of course. The universities therefore have a distinctly middle-class character; it is a feat of some merit, an achievement that will imprint the character for life, for a working-class student to go through the university to the triumphant conclusion of a doctorate, though it is a feat that is frequently performed.

The student whose parents have means will almost always spend a year, or at least a term, at another university in order to perfect his second language. German-speaking students as a matter of course spend a year or a term at one of the French-speaking universities. Two generations ago all those who could afford it spent time, or graduated, at a university in Germany itself: this is no longer the practice and no longer confers a social advantage.

About twenty per cent of the students are members of a *Verbindung*, a students' corps. The best known Protestant corps, Zofingia, Helvetia, Belles Lettres, each with a different political tinge, are powers in the land. Membership is typical of the inner stronghold of the middle class, the sons of those who have themselves studied. (The Catholic ones have a more religious and a more egalitarian air than the Protestant, and serve rather a different function in the student's life.) These *Verbindungen* are the strongholds of the old middle class, linked together by the *Alt-Herren* (old boys), spanning the frontier between the professions, industry and the Civil Service, and giving a unity and a meaning to the term 'upper middle class'. Though they rank with their German opposite number, they are not to be compared with them: the Swiss *Verbindungen* do not draw harsh boundaries or inculcate illiberal doctrines. But they are clearly of political importance and of social significance: it is difficult to say more in the absence of any scientific investigation. If it is true that Swiss government is a tacit upper-middle class conspiracy, then the student of the sociology of government must investigate carefully the leading *Verbindungen*.

After the university (or during it) comes a stage in middle-class life which is very Swiss, compulsory and genuinely universal military service. Here the classes which have not met since they left primary school are thrown into the melting pot. The comradeship of the ranks is kept up by annual short periods of repeated training, and by the inchoate clubs formed by those who are called for practice in target-shooting, and for an opportunity for drinking together. It is common for some members of the academic middle class to remain as private soldiers, while their classmates fill the commissioned ranks. Military service (apart from the commissioned ranks) cuts across all social distinction of whatever sort, and adds much to the democratic climate of life in Switzerland.

The existence of an academic high *bourgeoisie* has been noticed at some length, because it is the chief, and in a sense the only, truly political class in Switzerland. In the next chapter, the Protestant academic *bourgeoisie* will be connected with a political party, the Radicals. Some words must be added, however, to avoid a false impression. In society as in constitutional matters, Switzerland is a true democracy—that is to say, the social 'climate' is democratic. There is a large measure of deference, a large measure of superiority assumed without self-consciousness and not resented, but what gives Swiss society a peculiar character is a sort of man-to-man democraticness, a savour of equality between those who are not equals, an egalitarianism so pronounced as to approach churlishness but which arises out of a profound respect for the dignity, not perhaps of man as man, but of the citizen as a Swiss.

ARISTOCRACY

Merged in the academic class, but distinct within it, are the remnants of the old sovereign aristocracies of the Swiss towns and countryside. Each old sovereign town has its ancient patriciate still living in its suburbs, and the history of the canton will be written in terms of the family-names of that patriciate. In the great trading

SOCIETY

towns, Zurich, Basle, Geneva, the patricians were quick to obtain a foothold in the new industries and commercial activities of the 1830s. The Bernese, true to tradition, concentrated on the public service—a less fortunate choice economically.

Only in the primitive democratic cantons did patricians remain in public life after 1848. For a long time the urban Swiss patriciates sulked, and indeed are only today being re-absorbed into the ordinary political life of the country: the election of von Steiger, a Bernese patrician, as Federal Councillor in 1940 was, in its way, as much a socio-political landmark as that of Ernst Nobs, the Socialist Burgomaster of Zurich, three years later. It meant in each case that a class outside the Constitution was returning to the fold.

But although the patriciate proper sulked, it is a class that (sharp though its boundaries often are) shades off into the solid commercial and industrial families into which it has married occasionally, and into the numerous old families of patricians of the second and third rank: these second-class patricians, citizens of ancient families who were not within the inner circle, were the discontented class of the old régime—fobbed off with parsonages while the inner circle obtained bailiwicks and high office. These outer circles of aristocracy again merge with the patriciates of non-sovereign towns, with the ancient peasantry also, and, more important, into those families which have as it were ennobled themselves retrospectively by diligent research into the archives. It is typical that when Motta[1] became at last the darling of the right wing he was ennobled in this manner: research revealed that the innkeeper's family could claim a certain feudal glamour. There is no country where amateur genealogy is so seriously pursued as in Switzerland, and every family can attribute to itself, or have attributed to it, a coat of arms, even if it is only a triple-mountain vert, a star and a sickle. From the landlord class to the landlady class a little of the magic of genealogy—often fairly genuine—spreads. It is because of this wide catchment-area of citizen pride and historical feeling that it is necessary to mention the Swiss patriciates even in a book on contemporary Switzerland.[2]

THE LAND

The aristocracy for long regarded itself as being a little above the Constitution. There are two other great interests, the Land, and

[1] Elected Federal Councillor in 1911, and Foreign Minister from 1920 until his death in 1940.
[2] My Swiss friends assure me, however, that I overestimate the aristocratic sentiment in Switzerland.

labour, which until recently were outside the Constitution for a different reason. They were in a sense below the Constitution. The grievances of the Land are ancient ones, and go back to the old régime where (over most of Switzerland) the countryside was ruled by the walled towns. But though ancient, the grievances are rather mild. In the towns today the ownership of industry—of ordinary shares —is still the prerogative of a narrow class. But in the country, ownership of land is very widespread. It is uncommon to farm someone else's land rather than one's own. Most farms are small and tilled by the owner, and the comparatively rare tenant farms are a ladder leading from the life of the labourer to that of the land-owning peasant.

To discuss the social structure of the Swiss countryside, however, requires a greater experience than the present writer possesses, and it would mean considering some two dozen different countrysides separately—the wine areas of Vaud, for example, would give a quite different picture from the pastoral districts of the same canton. Leaving aside some districts which are almost 'distressed areas', one has the impression of a collection of societies which have grown naturally and which have a certain balance. In a society so integrated, politics play an important part—the political man cannot be separated from his other aspects: politics are an expression of personality and status, and almost the most important expression. The veterinary surgeon, the travelling merchant, the priest or minister, the doctor, the schoolmaster, play an important role in formulating opinion, but the big landowner is a rarity.

Some districts are nevertheless in one sense or another very aristocratic in their social atmosphere. The peasant of ancient local family will almost regard himself as being one of the representatives of the old régime. The Schloss may be occupied by a family which no longer owns the land, but whose name retains the power to evoke the history of the district during three centuries. The local member of the Cantonal Great Council may regard that office as almost hereditary in his family—he is as likely to call himself a Radical as a Conservative, however. One often has the impression of a world which Jeremias Gotthelf would recognize, where the electors know accurately the number of cows their member possesses, and vote for him on the basis that 'the important thing is to have Order around the house and in the family'.[1]

[1] Reply given by a Great Councillor to a sociologist investigating the connexion between elector and elected in town and country (Dr Jürg Steiner). This is the only investigation on such a problem that has hitherto been made: it is cited in full in the Appendix on Sources. 'Jeremias Gotthelf' (Albert Bitzius 1797–1854), a pastor in an Emmental village, wrote novels of peasant life which are a classic of the German language.

The landless rural labourer, however, especially in a Protestant countryside, may well feel outside this community, and by voting for a Social Democrat identify himself with the labouring classes of the towns.

Complete in itself, the village society may be more isolated from ordinary social contact with outsiders than is the case in England:[1] the urban professional and middle classes regard themselves as townsmen, and do not retire into the country—and would find it impossible to educate their children if they did. Looked at in one way, the country-dweller can be seen as a separate estate of the realm; looked at in another way, rural society is deeply divided into economic and social classes which are particularly rigid and clearcut. But enough has been said, at any rate, to convey the impression that Swiss rural societies are different from rural society in Britain.

Natural and vigorous though this society appears, in point of fact it survives only because the peasant has been as successful in milking the urban taxpayer as he has been with his own cow: agriculture enjoys enormous subsidies, open and concealed. But the subsidies have not come too late. The old traditions are still there, and the peasantry of Switzerland is a group well worth saving; its traditions are among the noblest attributes of Swiss civilization.

LABOUR. SOCIAL MOBILITY

The political significance of the working class in its own right is through the trades unions and the Social Democratic party. It also has a latent social importance in view of the 'democratic tone' of Swiss life, and in view of social mobility.

The atmosphere of social mobility is more like that of Scotland than of South England. It can be expressed by saying that the barriers to social mobility in Switzerland are not social barriers: this is one of the things meant by a 'democratic tone'. The barriers are there, but they are to be expressed in terms of town and country, poverty and secondary education, rather than in terms of social exclusiveness. Nevertheless, from bottom to top takes three generations in Switzerland, even today.

The typical social ladder is that in the 'first stage' the son of a

---

[1] This is a guess. It must be modified by such factors as the likelihood that some members of the country family will probably be in middle-class positions in the towns and, in some parts, by the annual migration of young workers to the towns at certain seasons.

labourer goes into the post-office or the railways; in the 'second stage' his son goes to *gymnasium* and perhaps, if he has fortunate or devoted parents, to university, and becomes a schoolmaster; and in the 'third stage', *his* son in turn is born free, and goes to *gymnasium* and university as a matter of course. The typical parliamentary career, and the typical *cursus vitae* of a Swiss statesman, occurs in the 'second stage'. It is not the actual class, but the mobility which is typical.[1]

CROSS CURRENTS

It is the good fortune and wisdom of Switzerland that there are many loyalties other than class loyalties which by cutting across class strengthen the nation. Locality is one of these—a strong loyalty to a place and participation in its affairs makes social class irrelevant in one sphere. From the Federal Council to the village council, the Swiss system of the collegiate executive council, in particular, cuts right across class barriers in a way in which few British institutions do (and local government is stronger and busies more volunteers in Switzerland than Britain). The church, especially the Catholic church, is another institution which provides a centre for non-class loyalty and co-operation. The army and the primary school have already been noted. The Guilds (Zünfte) and corporations are, perhaps, to be included among the loyalties of locality, but have an element of exclusiveness which is unconnected with social class: membership is hereditary but spans society.

The impression that this chapter has tried to give is twofold. On the one hand class is very important in Switzerland: in the next chapter the social classes will be linked with the political parties, and this is only one example of how important class is. On the other hand there is a very important element that negates class, and this is the democratic tone of life. Perhaps the easiest way of illustrating the latter, as applied to parliamentary life, is that no Swiss statesman and very few Swiss anywhere have the least difficulty in speaking naturally with working men. Free political institutions give a power to the people at large, and the democratic tone of life is the effect as well as an origin of these free institutions. It is a sign that those who monopolize the daily exercise of power recognize where power (in a way) ultimately lies.

---

[1] At present there is no statistical basis for this assertion. It is an impression gained from a number of individual careers. It would be interesting to establish trends and shifts, and there is a group of investigators in Basle now working on this.

SOCIETY

APPENDIX

Professor Max Huber

The career of one member of the Establishment, untypical only in a personal brilliance which would have ensured success in whatever rank he was born, illustrates the various strands from which the Establishment in Switzerland is spun. It is Professor Max Huber of Zurich.

Max Huber was born in 1874, a second son of the founder of the Aluminium Industries A.-G. He studied at the Universities of Lausanne, Zurich and Berlin, and became Dr jur. Berlin, with a noteworthy thesis on International Law. 'On the advice of his father' he spent two years as Secretary of the *Vorort* of the Swiss Handels- und Industrie-Verein, and then travelled for pleasure and instruction to England, U.S.A., Russia, the East and Australia. A little surprisingly, at the age of 28 his voyages were interrupted by the 'almost unsought-for' offer of the Professorial Chair of Public, International and Ecclesiastical Law at Zurich. 'Very young, and after an education designed rather for a diplomatic career than one in scholarship, I found myself faced with a task too great for me' he later wrote. He held the chair nevertheless until 1921, but 'during the last seven years he did not find time to lecture'. Amateur scholar though he may have been, he found the opportunity to write an excellent book on international law. During the 1914 War he consented to be a Radical member of the Cantonal Council of Zurich and to serve with the rank of a colonel as an adviser to the Judge-Advocate of the army. But after the fall of Hoffmann he became the elbow-rest of successive Heads of the Foreign Department—Calonder, Gustave Ador (a man of his own stamp), and Motta. In 1922 Huber accepted a seat on the International Court at the Hague, and was President of this in 1925–27. He was offered a renewed term but the project did not please him. However, at this moment Gustave Ador died, and Huber succeeded him in the office of President of the International Red Cross, the most honoured place in the patronage of the Swiss Government. 'I thought it my duty to accept this new task,' he said, 'because it was my fatherland which asked this sacrifice of me.'

Professor Huber was from 1915–24 a member and vice-President of the committee of management of the *Neue Zürcher Zeitung* (N.Z.Z.). He was also a member of the board of the Oerlikon Engineering Company, President of his father's firm, the Aluminium Industries A.-G., and of an insurance firm. At the same time he owned a castle and rural estate. His mother was a Werdmüller of Zurich, and his wife an Escher: both names are infinitely evocative in Zurich. He was elected an Honorary Zofingian. As a final honour, as unsought as the others, his death in January 1960 was announced by a leading article covering the whole front page of the N.Z.Z., the Zuricois journal whose high moral tone and Christian sentiments were so close to his own.

III

Parties

The National Council, elected by proportional representation, is divided politically into four groups of about fifty members each. The three great parties, Radicals, Catholic Conservatives, and Socialists, each have one quarter of the Council. Of the remaining quarter half belong to the Farmers' party, and various small parties make up the remainder. The Council of States (Senate), on the other hand, devotes two-thirds of its membership to the Radicals and the Conservatives. The other parties compete for the residue.

That is the broad outline. The figures for 1960 were:

Party[1]	National Council	Council of States	Federal Assembly
Radicals	51	14	65
Catholics	47	18 (incl. one 'independent')	65
Socialists	51	3	54
Farmers	23	3	26
Landesring	10	None	10
Liberals	5	3	8
Democrats (Grisons)	2 ⎫	1	
,, (Zurich)	2 ⎬ 6	None	7 (or 8)
Evangelicals	2 ⎭	None	
Communists	3	None	3
'Non party'	None	2	2 (or 1)
	196	44	240

The party composition of the National Council does not vary much from decade to decade: the Council of States shows more rapid variation. But in both Councils loss of one mandate might lose a

[1] *Names.* There is a great confusion between the official names of the parties in the cantons, the names of the party-groups in the Councils, and the popular names. Under the term 'Radicals' will be recognized the 'Freisinnige Partei'. Under the term 'Catholics', the Conservative People's Party and its local appellations. Landesring is used for the Group of Independents. 'Liberal' is kept for the Conservative-Liberals. The nomenclature is an attempt to rationalize the popular names and to avoid initials.

party a seat on several committees and have wide repercussions. The extent of the under-representation of the Socialists in the Council of States in 1960 is untypical.

THE RADICAL PARTY

As the spiritual heir of the Liberals of the 1830s, the Radical party is the historic party of the Confederation. It is the party (or, strictly speaking, it is a federation of the left wings of the cantonal parties) that carried through the cantonal Regeneration in the years 1830–48, the party that fought and won the Sonderbund War, that created the Confederation of 1848, and carried through the revision of 1874. Until proportional representation was introduced in 1919, the Radical parties had had a majority in the National Council ever since 1848. Until 1943, they had a majority in the Federal Council. The story of the party is of bitter feuds between its right and left wing, but it is the story of the modern Confederation itself.

There is a sense in which even today the Radical party is the only true political party in Switzerland, for it is the only one which habitually thinks in terms of the State. All the institutions of government considered in this book, for example, are Liberal Radical institutions; most were created by that party, and all are to be justified in terms of its doctrines. The law of the Constitution is Liberal Radical, and the commentators upon it in the Swiss universities are Liberal Radical. The civil and criminal law are, by and large, inspired by the same ideas. The federal Civil Service is Liberal Radical in tone. It is a little surprising to find that the parliamentary party is only one quarter of the National Council, and that the Socialists and the Catholics each send as many members.

The Radicals are the liberal party of Switzerland—using those words in the Continental sense. Like other Continental liberal parties, their doctrine centres upon the five concepts, nation, state, law, rights, and property.

The traditional liberal[1] ideal was to create a Swiss Nation with a liberal Constitution out of the confederacy of the Swiss cantons, many of which are irremediably Conservative and clerical. It was this ideal which was attained in 1848. For a long time the liberals retained a monopoly of Swiss-National patriotism. They do not have the monopoly today, but to some extent this is a mark of the success of liberalism. The dissident groups—aristocrats, Catholics, workers,

[1] When talking of the ideals of the Radical party, I am using the term 'liberal', as the more generic term. It here covers the radical–liberals ('radicals') and the liberal–conservatives.

farmers—no longer wait outside in the rain, but are safely brought under the umbrella of the liberal Constitution to work (in non-liberal ways) for the liberal state. This does not mean that the party is anti-cantonal: as a very old party its cantonal roots go deep, and it is the Socialist party which has the least inherent loyalty to the cantonal ideal today. But the liberals do not have that passionate loyalty to the canton which the Catholics have. For the Catholics, as a permanent minority, the Catholic canton is a place where the Church can hold that dignity in public life which is her due: and as the Catholics hold most of the dwarf, grotesquely over-represented, cantons, they have a double vested interest in the federal structure. For the liberals, federalism is a device to bring the government nearer the people; for the Catholics, it is the stronghold of the Church, the guarantee against the possibility of an arrogant Protestant majority.

The liberals have a coherent theory of the State. In its modern form it is a sort of neo-Kantianism, and Professor Hans Kelsen is its great prophet: his English works are the British reader's best introduction to it, but the doctrine in its orthodox form bears a curious resemblance to our own Austinianism. It regards the Constitution as 'a basic norm', an 'ought', and enunciates law in terms of what the citizen 'ought' to do. A book on constitutional law is thus a series of deductions from the text of the Constitution as to what citizens and authorities 'ought' to do: what they actually do, and what they *morally* ought to do from any other reason apart from the positive law, are considerations rigidly excluded. The rigour of the exclusion of natural law and the findings of history and sociology have given this school the name of 'the pure school of law'.

A veneration for the formal technique of law, characteristic of liberalism, is limited by another doctrine, that of the separation of powers. Law is a general rule: its *particular* application is not a proper subject of law at all, but of administration. Many of the statutes of the British Parliament are not 'law' at all, in Swiss eyes: they are examples of Parliament exercising, improperly, executive powers. The Continental 'rule of law' is different to the Diceyan, for it is quite inconsistent with 'the sovereignty of Parliament'. It is the rule of 'law'—precepts in general terms carrying out the higher precepts of the Constitution—not the rule of the legislature. The executive is the executive of the State, not of the Chambers: it is the creature of the Constitution, not of Parliament.

Law, rights, and property are ideas intimately connected in Continental liberalism. The right of property is regarded as that on which civilization depends: infringements of this right (even by governments) arouse a degree of horror with which it is difficult for an Englishman to sympathize. The terror and loathing for Russia and Communism which one finds in Switzerland draw much of their strength from the almost superstitious reverence (among liberals and Catholics) for the sanctity of property. It is curious that the Right to Property is not included in the Federal Constitution, but writers and officials always talk as if it were: it is so basic, that it is understood to be there.[1]

Liberalism is not a philosophy of class, but it has a class appeal, and the class to which it appeals is the upper-middle class, the ruling class of Swiss opinion, Swiss politics, Swiss law and Swiss administration. The other parties, Catholics, Socialists and Farmers, are interest groups hollowed out of the liberal party: they expressly represent sections of the nation, and not the nation itself. This is the historic position of the other parties, and it is the intellectual and emotional position also (in different degrees). They gather the crumbs which fall from the liberal table and ask for more. Radical-liberalism, in short, is the Swiss middle class when the Catholic, the aristocratic (in Berne), the agricultural and the small Socialist-intellectual elements are subtracted from it: in this sense, it is the Swiss nation.

Having said this it is necessary hurriedly to add that the Radical party means something different in every canton—and that it is the only party represented in every canton. In Vaud, for example, it is the natural party of the peasant, especially of the wine-peasant. In Zurich it is the party of the orthodox Protestant, Conservative forces. In Berne (where the Farmers have stolen the peasants and the aristocrats) it is the party of those with fixed salaries. In Lucerne, it is a tenacious minority clan among the more nominal Catholics. The party is very strongly localized, in organization and in ideas. In the broad sweep of history, it may be the only truly National party. In the narrow aspect of a particular general election, it is the party which of all parties has the least doctrinal cohesion: to this its electoral weakness is largely due.

THE CATHOLIC CONSERVATIVE PARTY

This party is inspired by two ideals, which are connected by the Roman Catholic way of life. On the one side is a trust in established social authority (political authority does not enjoy quite the same confidence), and on the other side is a will to carry out the social programme of the popes according to the tenor of the encyclicals.

[1] In its jurisdiction over cantonal law and tribunals the Federal Tribunal applies the rule that there is a guaranteed right to property—even in the cases where the cantonal Constitution also does not mention it.

Both these spring from the same basic Roman Catholic civilization, but they are not found with the same emphasis in the same breast, and the parliamentary party covers the whole spectrum from a Christian social-idealism to a bleak wire-pulling Conservatism devoid of ideas. The right wing is so far from the left that the two groups often submit separate lists in federal elections, but with the lists connected.

The former, or Christian Conservative, wing provides the natural ballot box for the votes of the more isolated, backward or timid peasantry, as well as for the right-wing Catholic intellectual, weaning him (in Fribourg, for example) from more dangerous authoritarian speculation. The left, or Christian Social, wing is used to decoy the Catholic worker from socialism and the intellectual from liberalism. But the parties are not merely decoys: they are genuine moral positions.

In 1959, for the first time a Christian Social cantonal party campaigned (in Schwyz) as a party whose list was not connected with the 'Conservative People's Party', the right wing. This was somewhat of an event: among other things it shows a growing self-confidence among Catholics, a diminution of the minority feeling.

Also for the first time in 1959, the party campaigned under titles which all lacked the word 'Catholic'. The name Catholic Conservative is thus now incorrect in that it is not the name used on the party note-paper, but it is the ordinary name by which the party is called—abbreviated to 'K.K.'. The significance of the change in name is that it opens up the way to a 'C.D.U. solution', a right wing Christian party to which Conservative Protestants will give votes and a few figureheads, as in Western Germany. Basle is the most promising place for such a campaign to win its first battle, for it is close to Germany, and it has an entrenched Protestant Conservative group. Moreover, its Protestants have no feeling that they might be submerged by their confessional enemies.

At the moment, it is doubtful if the party gets a single Protestant vote, while many Catholics in Protestant areas vote Socialist or for the Farmers' party.[1] In Lucerne and Solothurn there is an important Catholic Radical vote, and everywhere there are Catholic families which by tradition vote Radical: as a rule they form their own society, their own sub-caste, and are nominal rather than fervent

[1] If one assumes that the turnout of Catholics is the same as in other religions, then about sixty per cent of Roman Catholic voters must have voted in 1955 for the K.K. party. There is no statistical evidence that non-Catholics voted K.K. See Nationalratswahlen, *Élections au conseil national, 1955*, published by the Bureau fedéral statistique, 1958, for details.

Catholics, transmitting the religion through the mother's side, and the politics on the father's side. The historic reason is that Lucerne and Solothurn are both Catholic cantons which were dominated by a sovereign aristocratic city under the old régime. In Solothurn, especially, the rural areas turned liberal as part of the struggle for political freedom and to rid the land of feudal ground rents. So finely are the constitutional politics of Switzerland balanced (votes in the Council of States, for example) that the liberal Catholic vote in these cantons sometimes seems to be the pivot of federal political life.

Fribourg, the isolated stronghold of Catholic Conservatism, is also a former city-canton, but has taken its own peculiar line of development. In a few years' time it seems likely that it will reach the politically critical stage, when by polling every single man the non-K.K. forces can obtain by a handful of extra votes the absolute majority.

In Inner Switzerland (and Appenzell), universal democracy is part of the tradition of the old régime, and this makes Conservatism democratic and democracy somewhat aristocratic. This ancient freedom colours the whole folklore of Swiss intellectual Catholicism. As a result of democracy the Swiss Roman Catholic parishioners (outside Fribourg) have long been accustomed to control their own religious affairs, for the 'people' was the 'lawful prince' and the seat of civil power. Church organization therefore appeared rather presbyterian under the old régime, with the priests (and in Valais the bishop) designated by the churchgoers in their capacity as sovereign. There was thus a native Swiss opposition to extension of papal power. The last time this came into the open was in 1920, when the Pope desired to appoint a Nuncio in Berne: Protestant Federal Councillors were lobbied by prominent Catholics imploring them to prevent this —they did not want to be too closely supervised by headquarters. This battle, like others, was lost.

In politics, there are two alliances open to the party. On the one hand it might join a '*bourgeois*' block' against materialist and atheist Socialism, defending such values as property and 'the family'. On the other hand it might join an '*étatist*' block defending the community and social values against the corrosion of Protestant (or agnostic) liberalism. Both have been tried, indeed, both are continually being tried, but in recent years as regards the election of persons the tendency has been for a 'black-red-green' alliance (i.e. K.K., Socialist, and Farmers). The turning point was the curiously unimportant occasion of the election of Federal Chancellor Leimgruber, a Catholic, in 1943. Association with the Farmers is understandable, for the Conservatives are the peasants' party in Catholic districts, and the values defended when protecting a peasant society are Catholic values. Alliance with Socialists is not surprising in a republic where a great part of the economy was publicly owned under the old régime, and has been so owned ever since (by Confederation, canton, commune or guild). The actual social policy of the Conservatives as a whole is rather half-hearted: social services are more gratefully received in the town than in the country, and the Conservatives are chiefly a rural party. The idea is welcomed, but the taxation and the secular administration are grudged. The 'family' is the great rallying cry, but what does this mean in terms of practical politics? The only concrete result beyond what is now accepted in Western Europe as the civilized minimum of social insurance, is cheap family railway fares.

Because the possibilities of alliance are so many, and because it is based on small, one-party, cantons where personal issues are more important than truly political ones, the Conservative parliamentary party is tempted to intrigue, indeed not only specializes in it, but almost tends to exhaust itself in personal politics. The late National Councillor Walther of Lucerne, 'the king-maker', was the most eminent example of this, and his most brilliant successes were the election of one second-rate and one fourth-rate Federal Councillor to represent the Radicals in the executive, instead of first-rate candidates. The party's parliamentary influence is thus in one sense very great indeed but in another sense, in the world of ideas, rather small. The character of the party as a whole vacillates between (i) that of a Catholic pressure group, (ii) of a genuine party of ideas, and (iii) of a state within the state, for it alone of Swiss parties covers all social and economic classes within the four walls of its creed and the geographical extent of its power.

THE SOCIALIST PARTY

Before the First World War the Social Democrat Party of Switzerland was a minority sect represented by a handful of National Councillors. The movement had risen out of working men's clubs, such as the Grütliverein, but came in time to compete with them and then to absorb them. Its early history is a part of the early history of Socialism in Europe. The year 1918–19 was a turning point for the party in two respects.

On Armistice Day 1918 the party happed into a general strike, to be the prelude of a workers' revolution and the capture of power on the Russian model. The big strike took place, but the middle classes and the peasants stood together, and the army stood by them.

Allied troops moved to the frontier, ready for the invitation to intervene should the revolution be successful. After two days, the leaders lost their nerve, and the strike was called off.

The next year, 1919, saw the introduction of Proportional Representation. The number of Socialist members rose from nineteen to thirty-eight, and for the first time it seemed feasible for a sincere Socialist to work for democratic power within the parliamentary system. In the early 1930s the Socialists were still an anti-State party, but the attitude was little more than a historical reminiscence: they were basically absorbed within the constitutional structure. The decisive change came in the late 1930s, in the face of the challenge of German fascism. By 1936, the Swiss Socialists were co-operating fully with the *bourgeois* parties, and it was the turn of the extreme right wing to toy with ideas of disloyalty. In 1939 the party voted unanimously for Full Powers for the Federal Council, and in 1943 a Socialist (Nobs, Burgomaster of Zurich) was elected to the Federal Council, for the first time. In December 1959 the Socialist ship berthed within the inner *bourgeois* haven, obtaining the two members of the Federal Council to which their numerical strength in the National Council entitles them. Socialists had, from the 1930s onward, been freely admitted to the collegiate executives of the cantons (i.e., as cantonal ministers) and communes.

In 1937 the trades unions and the employers' organizations in the metal industries signed a 'peace treaty' (*Arbeitsfrieden*), which has given the tone to the whole subsequent history of employer-labour relations in Switzerland. The labour movement has settled down to the position of junior partner in a very prosperous firm, with every sign of contentment. Having given up reliance on the industrial arm, and being a permanent minority of one quarter of the National Council and (at most) one sixth of the Council of States, the Socialist movement has stayed no more than a powerful pressure group in a capitalist society. The language is the language of a party which hopes some time to hold the reins of government, but the tactics and the attitude are not those of opposition, but of pressure within a non-Socialist society.

THE FARMERS' PARTY. (B.G.B. BURGHERS', ARTISANS' AND PEASANTS' PARTY)

As is evident from Chapter Two the term 'farmer' is not really suited to a country where people till their own land. In Switzerland, the word 'farmer' (*Pächter*) conjures up the picture of a farm-servant who has proved himself and has thereby had the opportunity to 'farm' someone else's land. Peasant (*Bauer*) is a word which in English conjures up a picture of wooden shoes and poverty, but in Switzerland suggests a rich and ancient family living under one of those enormous vermilion roofs in the Emmental, with geraniums in front of the windows and a huge manure heap. To conjure up this picture the word 'farmer' is used here in English.

Until 1919 the country population voted for the historic parties, which put up a due proportion of peasant candidates in rural districts, and allowed agricultural interests their approximate share of the fruits of office and of representation in the Council of States. Within the Assembly, there was (and still is) a cross-bench Landowners' Club which acted as a sort of pressure group in the interests, it was said, of the larger landowners. Agriculture had already organized itself outside Parliament as a pressure group, and the Peasants' Secretariat in Brugg had been in continuous existence since 1897: it had been called into being by the prospective revision of the Customs Tariffs in 1903. The year 1919 saw complicated disputes in Berne and Schaffhausen over the division of seats among peasants and non-peasants within the Radical party, and the Farmers' party was started largely because of the accidents of personal rivalry in the cantons: it formed no part of the policy of the *Bauernsekretariat*. The war economy had consolidated the power of the peasant organizations, and the general strike made the Land for a moment the arbiter of the nation's destiny. And 1919 saw the introduction of Proportional Representation.

The Peasant Party (in alliance with the Protestant conservative elements, especially in the city of Berne) obtained at once thirty-one seats, which it increased to thirty-five in 1922 for that legislature-period only. But in 1935 it split over the formation of a Young Peasant Group, a party whose leaders developed a dangerous sympathy with Nazism, and it has never recovered its old position. It now has twenty-one to twenty-three seats at every election (and two or three seats in the Council of States). Since 1929 it has been represented in the Federal Council, claiming always the 'Bernese seat'.

The B.G.B. is very much a cantonal party, with its centre of gravity in Canton Berne. It has made little progress in East Switzerland, and none in Roman Catholic districts. In Thurgau the pre-1919 type of arrangement is still in force: the Radicals and the Peasants campaign as one party, but in the Assembly split into different parliamentary groups, the Peasants who are elected sitting with the Farmers' Party. In social and cultural policy the B.G.B. votes with the Radicals, and in economic policy often finds itself in alliance with the Catholics and sometimes with the Socialists. In some matters, it is a true party of ideas (e.g. in military matters), but more often it is an interest group concerned to get favours for a particular class of landowner or for the Land in general—or for small industry. It is also the natural party of the Protestant die-hard right wing in cantons where the Liberal Conservative Party has disappeared.

THE GROUP OF INDEPENDENTS
(*Landesring der Unabhängigen*)

The Landesring is a party of a very peculiar sort. Herr Gottlieb Duttweiler, a grocer of genius, founded in 1925 a new type of consumers' co-operative, 'Migros'. Existing co-operatives and chain stores made political difficulties for him and promoted cantonal legislation, aimed at, for example, his delivery van service. A man of unlimited imagination and enterprise, Duttweiler decided himself to go into politics, and in the election of 1935 achieved at his first attempt seven mandates, which he has since increased to ten. Five of the seats are in Canton Zurich, two in Berne, and one each in Basle-City, St Gallen and Aargau. The voting support and the finance of the party derive, in a way which it is difficult to discern precisely, from the dividend-book holders of the co-operative. Five of the members are employees of Migros, if one includes Duttweiler himself and Herr Jäckle, the editor of Duttweiler's newspaper, *Die Tat*. The party in fact is linked to the personality of Duttweiler and to the excellence of the services provided by the Migros stores.

Herr Duttweiler himself is now a very vital and quite unpredictable old man, and a line of policy in the group's manœuvres is difficult to discover. But the group disturbs the stuffiness of Swiss political life in Berne, and serves two useful functions in the constituencies. (i) It provides an outlet for discontent with the historical parties, and notably with the Radical party and B.G.B. This is especially necessary because in a big canton the citizen finds it difficult to exert influence on a member of the Assembly under P.R. And (ii) every now and then the Landesring breaks up a too complacent electoral compact made between the party bureaucracies.[1] Duttweiler's presence keeps the other parties on the edge of their chairs.

Duttweiler is a master of referendum tactics, and here the resources of his co-operative enable him to make use of the Initiative and the Challenge—or to exert a decisive influence by threatening to launch one or the other. As a pressure group, the Landesring appears to

[1] For an example, see p. 143.

look more to the consumers' interest than, for example, the Farmers, or the *'Vorort'*, or the trades unions, do. The class represented is perhaps the middle lower and lower middle-class as consumers—though as a chain store Migros constitutes a threat to that class as producers and shopkeepers. But it remains the party of a personality rather than of an idea: in view of Herr Duttweiler's age, the actual (though not the legendary) personality is perhaps now that of Herr Jäckle.

THE LIBERAL PARTY (LIBERAL-CONSERVATIVE, LIBERAL-DEMOCRAT)

While the socially top people of Zurich are traditionally Radicals, in Berne join the B.G.B., and in Catholic Switzerland, of course, are in the Catholic Conservative fold—in Western Switzerland (Basle, Neuchâtel, Vaud, and Geneva) they are in the old Liberal Party. Within this western area circulate three of the four great international newspapers of Switzerland—the *Journal de Genève*, the *Basler Nachrichten*, the *Gazette de Lausanne*. These three all belong to the Liberals: the fourth great paper, the *Neue Zürcher Zeitung* is Radical. For both these reasons, as a party of the social *élite* and as a dominant party in the newspaper world, the Liberal Party has a significance quite out of proportion to its numbers. In numbers it hardly exceeds the Communists—though its geographical concentration enables it to elect five National Councillors to the Communists' three. It is characteristic that with five members in the National Council it has three in the Council of States—as many in 1960 as the Socialists have with fifty-one National Councillors, though the low Socialist figures of this year are due to accident. It is by virtue of the personal weight of its members in the two Councils and to their influence on opinion, and by virtue of the influence of the class they represent, that the Liberal Party is a power in the Confederation. Having such a small membership, the party wisely sends to the Councils its real leaders in person—instead of sending spokesmen of those leaders—and each of its eight members in the Assembly is a personal force to be reckoned with in Swiss public life.

Historically, the Liberal party is the rump of that great party, 'the Centre', which was the first organization of the new high-*bourgeois* class that drove the aristocrats from power in the 1830s. The left wing of this party has become the Radical party, and quite overshadows its parent body. Since that time the old Liberals have shifted rather to the right, and have become the party of the solid men, the great peers of industry and commerce of Basle and Geneva, the large vineyard owners with a long political tradition of Vaud, the dynasties of professors and officials, in a word, 'the establishment', within a limited geographical area.

The five seats in the National Council just qualify the Liberals to be a 'fraction', a recognized parliamentary party with certain rights to a seat in committees. At any election their number might fall to four, and this raises the question with whom they would then ally themselves. The Evangelical Party of Zurich would seem a natural ally on the religious side, but is socially a different sort of party. The more interesting solution would be an alliance with the Catholic Conservatives, an alliance which at a stroke would transform the K.K.s into a C.D.U.-type party (i.e. like Adenauer's Party in West Germany) and for which the K.K.s would no doubt be willing to offer a good political price. At the moment party opinion seems to favour isolation, rather than any incalculable alliance.

THE DEMOCRATIC PARTY

Historically this party was a left wing of the Radicals, which broke off from the main party in East Switzerland towards the end of the last century. It has since lost its hold in Thurgau and St Gallen, but it survives in Zurich, and is a force in cantonal politics in Glarus and the Grisons. Like the Liberal party, it depends on its personalities for its survival in central government politics. In 1955 its Zurich top candidate was the only Councillor who obtained more votes from outside his party than within it, and its Grisons top candidate was the redoubtable Herr Gadient. It now has two members from Zurich and two from Grisons in the National Council, and allies itself with the Evangelical Party to form a 'fraction'. (In Zurich it allied itself for *electoral* purposes with both the Evangelicals and the Farmers.)

Like the Evangelical Party, the Democrats are of more interest in the political psychology of the cantons than in that of the Federation.

THE EVANGELICAL PARTY (*Evangelische Volkspartei*)

This was founded in Berne (a countryside famous for its bizarre Protestant sects) in 1919, but now only exists on the federal level in Zurich. It is a Radical splinter-group with a religious emphasis: it finds itself in a curious sympathy with the Catholic Conservatives on many occasions, but grows in a soil where anti-Catholicism is a living force.

THE COMMUNISTS ('*Popistes*', *Partei der Arbeit, P.d.A.*)

This party is a living political force in Vaud, Neuchâtel and

Geneva, for its presence there determines the local character of the whole Socialist movement: in Geneva it is at present once more the largest political party in the cantonal legislature. In 1960 it had three representatives in the National Council, two from Vaud and one from Geneva, but in 1947 (after having been an illegal party during the war) it obtained seven mandates. But the prestige of the movement suffered, especially in German Switzerland, as a result of the suppression of the revolution in Hungary: it has not yet recovered.

The three members of the National Council are outstanding personalities, and are listened to with respect. But they are too few to be recognized as a 'fraction' and can obtain no allies to make up the number to five, and in consequence are almost outlaws in the Assembly. Swiss middle-class opinion and its press display a hostility to Communism in theory and practice the ferocity of which surprises an English visitor. This hatred is one of the few emotional factors in Swiss foreign policy.

PARTIES AND SOCIAL STRUCTURE

Each Swiss party is an example of a different type of political grouping; the Radicals, the Catholics and the Farmers, for example, are not political parties 'of the same sort' as each other. Each of the parties has a connexion with a social grouping—but these groupings cut across one another; there are Catholic farmers, for example. The relationship of class affiliation to ideas is different in the case of each party, though within any given canton there may be a certain consistency. The parties spring out of the social structure and the climate of ideas in a manner that defies a brief generalization, for though the parties each represent a 'class', the classes they represent are not matched by a counter-class—there is a Catholic faction, but no Protestant one; an agricultural faction but no urban one. The assertions of one party are never quite contradicted all along the line by the assertions of another party. The political structure of the Assembly, and even its procedure, reflect this.

The picture of parties, in fact, needs to be supplemented by a picture of pressures. Proportional Representation in the Swiss manner, and the multi-party executive and multi-party majority in the Assembly, demand and permit an intensive activity of pressure-groups, and the referendum gives them a further implied constitutional sanction (for one cannot will the causes without sanctioning by implication the direct effects). The most important of these pressure-groups is reputed to be 'the *Vorort*'—the *Vorort des schweizerischen*

Handels-und Industrie-Vereins (literally, the 'capital city' of the Swiss Trade and Industry Association)—which is the approximate Swiss equivalent of the Federation of British Industries, though it plays a rather larger part in popular mythology and in the calculations of politicians. It is typical that there is no written study of the *Vorort*, the strongest unofficial political force in Switzerland, and one which calls into question the whole working of Swiss democracy.

The referendum in the form of the Initiative, the Challenge, and the compulsory referendum for Constitutional alterations, is an institution which would call pressure groups into existence if there were none already. A favourite technique is for a group to threaten an Initiative, and then to negotiate under the influence of that threat, or to collect the signatures, and then offer to withdraw the referendum-petition on terms. The referendum calls forth pressure groups in two ways. In the first place, an organization is necessary to arrange and pay for the campaign. To send reply-prepaid postcards to voters in order to collect 50,000 signatures (spread throughout all cantons for preference) needs organization and money. A referendum does not launch itself. In the second place, when the referendum is launched, 'the people' decide the issue. The persons, in other words, who can form 'the people's' opinion decide: forming opinion is an expensive business, and the matter is too important to be left to luck and a chance majority. Swiss democracy is geared to pressure groups: it is a form of government calculated to call such groups into existence and give them power. The system could conceivably continue for a time without parties, but without pressure groups it would not work at all.

The influence of big money does not stop here. The judicial bench is everywhere elective, as are school, and Protestant church, offices. Civil servants, indeed, can dispense with the neutrality or friendship of social power, but many civil servants keep open the possibility of switching over to industry at some time in their lives: they are rather free to do this as the Federal Service thinks in terms of renewable four-year contracts rather than appointment for life. Even (Radical) Federal Councillors retire willingly to a governing board of big industry nowadays. There is no corruption, but there is an informal machinery whereby the realities of social power are harmonized with the location of political power, so as to make a coherent system; and there is a sort of feeling that unless a principle is at stake, it is best not to offend one of the powerful groups until one has secured the sympathy of another interest.

The problem of the student of Swiss government is to find the limits of this system of pressures and the starting point of the other system, the system described in the Federal Constitution of 1874 as amended.

There are two extreme interpretations. One is that the system is entirely in the hands of a certain group or groups. This interpretation at many points seems to fit the facts,[1] but it does not square with the actual personalities involved or the actual course of business. The other interpretation is the one given in the text books, that 'the People' is supreme and so on: this just does not describe the atmosphere of politics. Statesmen do not commune with the soul of a people, they are busy men trying to reconcile perfectly definite demands in practical cases. This theme is taken up again in the concluding chapter.

APPENDIX

The sense of nationality in Switzerland

Political party (and class, vocation and religion) enter deeply into the mental character of many Swiss people, but this must not blind the observer to something which enters still more deeply, the sense of nationality. This is not a very old emotion in Switzerland. In 1914 it was still rather the standpoint of an intellectual. The First World War pulled Switzerland into two camps, French-speaking with French, and German-speaking with German. The feeling of nationality needed to be rather consciously fostered, but the need chimed in with a change of economic climate, a move from trade kept as free as possible to a deliberate and watchful protectionism. A gentle xenophobia helped the feeling of nationality, and the law of citizenship (which is so strictly hereditary that it would seem to assume that there is a Swiss race) was tightened up. In 1914 the New Helvetic Society was launched—the original Helvetic Society had first been the basis for an acknowledgement of a 'Switzerland' which could be a fatherland, in the eighteenth century. It collected support from Catholic intellectuals, from the old Liberal party, from all over Switzerland—to tell the truth, from anti-Socialist circles rather than from Socialists. The Society retains the sympathy of high places: one has the impression it is *bien vu* by industry and by official circles,

---

[1] An interesting example of the power of the old régime was the discussion in 1960 over the retention of horsed cavalry. There is hardly any military or economic case at all, but cavalry provide a substitute form of service for the aristocrat as officer, for the rich—not the poor—peasant as trooper, and for the social powers-that-be as the best form of soldiery for internal use. It has been decided (against the advice of the Government) to retain the cavalry.

that it has become a reunion of the orthodox and an instrument of official policy. Its foundation was something of an event, and it has been ever since a force in the formation of opinion.

This build-up of a national consciousness was abundantly justified in the 1930s. The border between Germany and Switzerland became the frontier of civilization—a frontier which was closed to Jewish refugees,[1] indeed, for nationalism even in a good cause has its own cruelties. The gulf between Swiss-German and Reichs-German became the greatest psychological gulf on the continent of Europe: even today Switzerland and the United Kingdom are the two places where a modern Western German still senses a certain reserve. For twenty years every German Swiss was anxious to emphasize his Swissness, and the revolution in outlook has now become so firmly established that it need no longer be overstated. In the last five years the visitor has the impression that the atmosphere has become more relaxed, more natural, and more liberal.

As an indication of the present feeling, a young sociologist tells me that to the question in an opinion poll 'Are you pleased to be Swiss and only Swiss' ('Ich bin froh, dass ich ausgerechnet Schweizer bin'), only two replies out of 600 were not, unhesitatingly, 'Yes'.

---

[1] See the 'Ludwig Report'; *La politique pratiquée par la Suisse à l'égard des réfugiés de 1933 à nos jours.* Annexe to report of the Federal Council, by Carl Ludwig, Basle. [1957, Federal Chancery.] On one occasion, for example, 'an exhausted family, a man, wife and children, were pushed across the border, begging to be killed rather than to be returned "to that hell" '. One must pay credit to the way in which an official report investigated and published these matters after the War: every nation commits crimes, but not all are sorry for them afterwards.

IV

General Election

Under the Swiss Constitution proportional representation is not a clog on the healthy working of government, nor is it a 'thing indifferent', welcome for its own sake but not organic to the system. In Switzerland, proportionality is bone of the bone and flesh of the flesh of the whole system. The Swiss system of 'the independent collegiate executive' can indeed, and does, work without *forma* proportionality within the executive council being laid down by law. But where this is the case, 'voluntary proportionality' (*freiwilliger Proporz*) is adopted, and in 1960 extended to the Federal Council itself. Proportionality in the Federal Council is the crown, the logical implication, of the system. Because this system is so different from ours, however, Swiss experience cannot be used either to defend or attack projects to introduce 'P.R.' in Great Britain.

Swiss writers sum up the effect of introducing proportional representation for National Council elections in 1919 as 'the removal of the venom from politics'.[1] It can be described in less complacent terms. Not only the venom but much of the life was removed from politics in 1919: it is the apparent lifelessness of the Swiss Parliament which poses a main problem of this book.

Following the method of building up a picture of the whole by examining actual events, the system of election of the National Council by proportional representation is examined here by taking a specific general election (1959) and three examples of specific constituencies. The year and the constituencies are chosen as contemporary and as typical.

THE ELECTORAL SYSTEM[2]

The National Council is elected by proportional representation,

[1] e.g. H.H. Schälchlin *Die Auswirkungen des Proporzwahlverfahrens auf Wählerschaft und Parlament*. Zurich Dissertation, 1946.

[2] The method of election is described in detail in the Federal Law of 1919, while franchise and eligibility are laid down by the Constitution (Article 74) and the Law of 1872, but depend to some extent on cantonal legislation—all males of 20 years of age or more, not disqualified by cantonal law, have the right to vote. The Law of 1919 goes into considerable detail, but the execution of the law is nevertheless cantonal and therefore varies from place to place.

with the cantons as constituencies, on the list system, with connexion of lists and with *panachage* and cumulation, and the results calculated by the d'Hondt method. These terms are explained below.

In a canton large enough for proportional representation to apply, the system works out as follows. Each voter on the register receives (by post, or has to fetch) as many party lists as there are parties, and these lists mostly each contain the names of as many candidates as there are seats: so if there are 8 seats to be filled in the canton, there will be up to 8 names on each party's list. The same name may be printed twice on one list ('cumulation'). The voter also receives an official blank sheet so that he can make up his own list (from among the official candidates) if he likes.

What the voter does with this mass of paper is best described by the instructions issued by the Radical press in Zurich for the benefit of its less intelligent supporters. It should be explained that in this election the Radicals (*Freisinnige*) of Zurich-City and Zurich-Land were submitting separate lists, each with 32 names. So as not to waste fractional votes the two lists were 'connected'. The party therefore did not mind which *Freisinnig* list the voter chose. The instructions (N.Z.Z. 17 Oct 1959, folio 8) were:

> Take the two lists *Freisinnig* Zurich-City and *Freisinnig* Zurich-Land home with you. Destroy the other lists.
>
> You can put either of the lists into the ballot box at the voting station. But you must not change the name of the list.
>
> If you wish to 'cumulate' a candidate, write in his name on the list in ink, and cross out one of the other names on the printed list for every name which you cumulate. There must not be more than 32 names on the list.
>
> You can only put the names of candidates down on the list. If you decide to write in the names of candidates from other parties on your *Freisinnig* list (*panachage*) you weaken thereby the voting strength of the *Freisinnige*. But you do no harm by *panachage* of the names between *Freisinnig* Zurich-City and *Freisinnig* Zurich-Land.
>
> In the voting station you must be sure that the list bears the indication '*Freisinnige* List', and the official rubber-stamp.
>
> For the elections for the Council of States on the separate piece of paper, write on the first line 'Dr Ernst Vaterlaus' and leave the second line blank. Here you cannot cumulate.

GENERAL ELECTION

CALCULATION OF THE RESULT

The following example reveals the superficially somewhat surprising result which may be obtained under the d'Hondt system. It is taken from a pamphlet which has for the last decade been used as a hand-out in Swiss embassies.

If ten National Councillors are to be elected in a canton, and of the 60,000 voters, 36,000 vote for List A, 12,000 for List B, 6,000 for List C, 5,000 for List D, and 1,000 for List E, the distribution of seats will be 6:2:1:1:0.

This seems common sense. The interesting point about it is that it is wrong. List A, surprisingly, would elect 7 members, and List D none.

The calculation is based on the search for a 'Final Quotient', that is to say, a figure which can be divided into each party's total of votes in turn and give as a result the number of seats required. In this case there are 10 seats, and the Final Quotient is 5,142. This goes 7 times into 36,000, twice into 12,000 (the fractional remainder is neglected), once into 6,000 and less than once into 5,000 and 1,000. The distribution is therefore 7:2:1:0:0.

The rule-of-thumb whereby the Final Quotient is discovered has somewhat the appearance of magic, and there is no doubt that voters are confused and find it difficult to reckon whom exactly they are helping by any particular vote if they do not vote the straight party ticket. The method is as follows: Divide the total vote (60,000) by the number of seats *plus* one (11). The result is called the Provisional Quotient (5454). In our example it gives the provisional result of 6:2:1:0:0. But this only adds up to 9, and there are 10 seats to be allocated. The second sum seeks the final quotient. This is obtained by dividing each party's votes by the provisional number of seats it obtains, *plus* one. Thus List A (36,000) is divided by 7 (6 *plus* 1), and gives the result 5,142. This sum is repeated for each seat in turn, and the highest of the results is the Final Quotient; in our example, 5,142 is the highest. It is the number which when divided among each result in turn gives the right number of seats.

An actual example for 1959, the election in Canton Lucerne, is given in Appendix 3.

In real life, from the citizen's point of view there are two points of interest in a general election, namely how many seats the parties each get, and who gets the seat within the party list. The latter choice, the choice of the actual candidate, is made by the minority of voters who take the trouble to write names in and cross names out (*panachage*, or cumulation if the same name is written twice). The effect of *panachage*, voting for the candidates from another list, may be surprising and unwelcome. In the example given, the effect of transferring 1,007 votes from Party A to Party E would have the effect of electing a member from Party D. A vote for Dr X may elect Mr Y from the same, or (rarely) Mr Z from another party. Quite what happens to any particular vote is a matter of guesswork before the election, and of a very complicated calculation when the results are known. The results contain surprises even for the experts. The popular bewilderment is expressed by two words, *Proporzpech* and *Proporzglück*, which have been coined to describe unforeseeable bad and good electoral luck respectively; the element of chance which softens the blow of defeat makes victors modest.

From the point of view of the candidate himself the problem is (i) to get on the party list, preferably near the top—for the candidates crossed off are (it is said) the ones low down on the printed form, and (ii) to acquire enough extra votes by *panachage* and cumulation to get high enough when the results come out, so as to be elected. He needs in fact (a) a party label, and (b) a few thousand extra personal votes to lift him above his party colleagues on the list. The two requirements, taken together, largely determine the type of person who is chosen.

COUNCIL OF STATES

The cantons themselves determine the franchise and the length of tenure for Councillors of States. They even determine who is eligible, and for three French-speaking cantons there is now female suffrage for Councillors of States, and a woman candidate stood, unsuccessfully, for the first time in 1959. In four cantons, of which Berne is the most important, election is by the cantonal parliament: the three parties (in Berne) take their turn for the two seats in the Council of States, so that when a member reaches retiring age he is succeeded by the nominee of another party—or the seat is used as a bargaining counter in a different transaction. Many Council of States elections, however, fall due at the same time as the National Council elections, and the vote is actually cast in the same voting station on the same day.

Elections for the States are (except in the half-cantons) for two candidates, and the usual rule is that each voter casts two votes (for different candidates), and an 'absolute' majority must be obtained by each successful candidate. In the instructions quoted for *Freisinnig* electors in Zurich the second vote was not used in the hope that the Socialist candidate would not get his absolute majority; he did in fact get the majority, but vacated his seat on election to the Federal Council: at the by-election the Socialist who was a candidate for his vacant place was unsuccessful. There is a general feeling that sitting members should not be opposed on seeking re-election, so that it often happens that the election is not contested: the sole interest in such elections is in the 'absolute majority'. If the member does not obtain this on the first round, a second election takes place for that seat—and this time it is very probable that it will be contested.

As will be seen from the descriptions of the Schaffhausen and Lucerne elections, there is often a close connexion between the contests in the Council of States and the National Council.

THE WORKING OF THE SYSTEM

Because the twenty-five cantons (and half-cantons) are the constituencies, and vary greatly in size, tradition, and political character, it is not fruitful to generalize about the character of Swiss general elections without looking into what happens in the various sorts of cantons. While examining particular cantons, the opportunity should be taken to consider the election from the standpoint of particular candidates, each primarily concerned with his own career and the part *he* plays in politics. Very often the candidate's main activity will not be in the federal Parliament: the seat in the Parliament is an item in a personal calculation which perhaps is really concerned with cantonal or pressure politics. The student of elections drops the unsuccessful candidate from his list and troubles with him no longer. But the candidate still lives, and from his point of view the election is just one event in a continuous activity.

There are nine small and very small cantons. There is a very important group of larger or smaller medium-sized cantons, with eight or nine members. Finally there are two very big cantons, Berne and Zurich.[1]

1. A SMALL CANTON. SCHAFFHAUSEN

(Uri, Obwalden, Nidwalden and Appenzell Inner Rhodes are single member constituencies, Glarus, Zug, Schaffhausen and Appenzell Outer Rhodes return two members, and Schwyz returns three.)

For small cantons, an election 'fixed' in advance is usual. In Uri, for example, there has been an arrangement in force for a whole generation whereby a Radical National Councillor is returned unopposed, in return for the unchallenged tenure of two Catholic Conservative members of the Council of States. This is the oldest and most famous of these arrangements which are normally struck from time to time on the basis of electoral strengths known from elections to the cantonal Great Council. The allocation of seats in the cantonal government might enter into the same bargain: 'You take the canton's seat in the National Council, and leave me the seat in the cantonal government.' Sometimes there is a 'silent election', i.e. no election is held. Sometimes there is an election with only the number of candidates corresponding to the number of seats—there may be a poll for another election which can be arranged for that day anyway, or a referendum in the canton. Sometimes there is a 'wild' candidate from outside. And sometimes, of course, the arrangement breaks down and there is a genuine election of the type intended in the Constitution.

In all cantons there is an interaction of cantonal and national politics. There is also regularly a personal union of federal and cantonal political office. This is important for the character of politics: the same gladiators who have fought in the cantonal and perhaps communal arena for many years, and served on the same committees, meet once again on the train for Berne at the beginning of the session. It is natural that they should feel they are colleagues of each other in Berne, perhaps even more than they feel themselves colleagues of members of the same parliamentary party on the federal level. It will be seen that the four members from Schaffhausen, in the two councils, hold the political life of their canton in their hands. This gives them a sort of corporate character in Berne; if they stick together they carry the power of the canton: it is their 'Hausmacht'.

Canton Schaffhausen is a modest area of countryside, in a semicircle around the ancient little town of that name. The town has now become industrialized but retains its ancient centre: the countryside is in some places economically and socially rather backward. The canton sticks out into Germany north of the Rhine, and is Protestant. It returns two National Councillors and two Councillors of States, and elections take place at the same time for both Councils. There are three parties, Socialists, Farmers, and Radicals—until the First World War the canton was entirely Radical. These parties are based on clearly identifiable sections of the population, parties of status rather than parties of opinion. For years there has been no contested election for the National Council. The agreement between the parties was that the Radicals and the Farmers shared the Council of States, and the Radicals and the Socialists shared the National Council. The four existing members were standing again in 1959, and were unassailable. Another silent election was foreseen for the National Council, and an uncontested election (at least on the first round) for the Council of States.

Then, twenty-four hours before nominations for the National Council closed, the Landesring of Independents handed in a list—containing one name printed twice. The Independent relied on the discontent caused by too long a series of fixed elections, and on local political difficulties, echoes of the famous Rheinau scheme.[1] He made a respectable showing, but was not elected. The intervention is an example of the useful function of this party in breaking up too complacent electoral pacts.

National Council:

The elected members were:

(1) *Nationalrat* Bringolf (Socialist), whose parliamentary career is discussed again later on. Salaried Mayor of the Town of Schaffhausen. A member of the cantonal Parliament since 1924, and of the National Council since 1925. He is the best-known representative of Schaffhausen in any field—the Aneurin Bevan of Swiss politics.

(2) *Nationalrat* Scherrer (Radical). An industrialist running the family factory, who made his political career in employers' unions. From 1948, with an interruption, he sat in the cantonal parliament, and from 1947 in the National Council.

Council of States:

The election was held on the same day and in the same polling booth as the other election. The only candidates were the sitting members, so the interest of the election concentrated on whether the members would obtain their absolute majority on the first round. There was some doubt whether the Farmers' candidate would do so: he had made himself unpopular by his courageous attitude during the Rheinau controversy. In the event both candidates did obtain their majority in the first election. They were:

(1) *Ständerat* Schoch (Radical). Dr Schoch is a trained lawyer who

---

[1] A plan for a barrage across the Rhine at Rheinau, to provide electric power, which threatens a quiet landscape. The Rhine is here the international frontier, and the scheme was agreed between the interests concerned and between (Nazi) Germany and Switzerland. Two exciting referendum campaigns were fought against the agreement when it came to be put into effect.

made his career as a stipendiary magistrate ('judge') in the cantonal courts. In the Swiss cantons, the judicial office is a political one, so it is not surprising that in 1944 he was elected to the cantonal government and in 1947 returned to the bench, as President of the Cantonal Supreme Court. He has been a member of the Council of States since 1946. The combination of judicial and political office is quite common.

(2) *Ständerat* Lieb (Farmer). Lieb was at one time a practical farmer, but made his career in the Bauernsekretariat at Brugg—the agricultural lobby—and then as a cantonal civil servant. He has been in the cantonal government since 1931, and in the Council of States since 1947.

Professional Politicians

The careers of all four members are very typical, and should be referred to again by the reader when the question is asked 'Who is a professional politician in Switzerland?' Three out of four (Bringolf, Schoch, Lieb) derive their whole livelihood from politics or from a career which depends entirely on politics. It is only in a rather artificial sense that the often-repeated statement is true, that 'there are no professional politicians in Switzerland'.

The way in which local politics are connected with federal politics should also be noted: it too is typical.

2. A LARGE CANTON: BERNE

Berne and Zurich stand apart from the other cantons by virtue of their size, with (in 1959) thirty-three and thirty-two National Council mandates respectively. The next largest canton, Vaud, has half the number that Zurich has. Berne and Zurich between them contain nearly a third of the population of Switzerland.

Berne has a different character from Zurich. Zurich was the centre from which came the new ideas of German Switzerland—the Reformation, the Enlightenment, Liberalism, Socialism. In Berne, these ideas were adopted, and used in the interests of good government. Berne is the country of administration. In the Old Confederacy, the oligarchy of Berne became a true aristocracy, with many points of similarity to the English patriciate of the eighteenth century. Its members settled in the countryside, planted trees, and governed in the interests of the Republic which their families led in war and peace: they introduced new methods of agriculture and trained their sons in public speaking and military command.

This tradition, in the parts of the old canton which were to remain with Berne, survived the revolution. The old families came back, with the Restoration, and when they abdicated did so with dignity. New families took their place, and were accepted by the people. Today Berne is still the land of government—not of politics. The old governing families have become an important influence in the B.G.B., the Farmers' Party, which is the chief political peculiarity of Berne: the modern officials belong rather to the Radical party. The two parties live side by side in the suburbs of the capital city. Socialism, when it came to the canton, came without doctrinal excitement as the natural party at first of the industrial worker and minor official, and then of the small peasant and agricultural servant; and soon discovered that it had something in common with the traditional paternalism, republicanism, and protectionism of the Conservatives and the B.G.B. The referendum, and the other constitutional devices adopted amid so much excitement in Zurich, have all been adopted in Berne, where the constant drill of voting in favour of every sort of cantonal and communal project, merely adds to the numbing effect of Bernese government. Every Sunday there seems to be a referendum somewhere, and the individual citizen may be called to the urns from four to eight times a year.

But like England in the days of its classic government, Berne has its Ireland—the Bernese Jura. The Powers in 1815, in compensation for the loss of Vaud and the Aargau, allotted Berne the territories of the Prince Bishop of Basle. These territories, being the lands which the Bishop ruled as a Prince of the Empire, were mostly[1] therefore Roman Catholic, and mostly French-speaking.

In the National Council election of 1959 for the thirty-three seats in the canton twelve lists were submitted, containing the names of 259 candidates.

This sounds an unmanageable number, but in point of fact the number is large because the parties attempt to bring the candidates closer to the voters. They do this by each putting up several lists, and 'connecting' the lists so as not to lose votes. Thus the Radicals put up three lists, one for the Emmental and the flat country, one for the Bernese Oberland, and one for the French-speaking districts. Making allowance for these regional lists, there are only four big parties to choose from—Radicals (three lists), Conservatives (two lists), Farmers (two lists), Socialists (two lists). Then the Independents put up a list, an eccentric party put in a list, and the Separatists in the Jura put in a list, which was 'connected' with the Catholic-

---

[1] Berne also absorbed French-speaking territories subject to the town of Bienne and others which, although under the formal sovereignty of the Bishop, were under the protectorship of Berne in the old régime. These are Protestant.

Conservative lists. This makes twelve in all. The individual voter would probably only receive the party lists of his district—the four big parties' local lists and the list of the Independent. In the Jura and the Emmental he might get six. He would skim through his own party's list, adding any candidates whom he knew or admired, and crossing out names to make room for them. This does not represent an impossible task. The task which is impossible is to know exactly whom and what party a particular citizen helped with his vote. The vote disappears into the maw of an extremely complicated arithmetical calculation and comes out transformed, perhaps, into something unexpected.

The Radicals put their full thirty-three names on their first list (for the town of Berne, the lowland country and Emmental). Four of them were already members of the National Council, and those were the four who got in. On their Oberland list they only put thirteen names, and only succeeded in electing one of them, the former National Councillor and Mayor of Thun. On their French list (addressed to the French-speaking officials in Berne, and the town of Bienne, as well as to the Jura proper) they got their only new member in, a Mayor and Cantonal Councillor: he replaced a retired member. Their total representation was thus unchanged and as planned.

The Catholic Conservatives cumulated the name of their sitting member from the Laufental (the small German-speaking Catholic area adjoining Basle), fearing that he would otherwise not be elected: the result shows that the precaution was superfluous. The Separatists' list, connected with the two Catholic lists, elected one member.

The surprising feature of the list which the Farmers submitted was that it gave so little weight to the Protestant Conservative wing in Berne city—an important element in the party. Eleven members were elected, five of them genuine farmers and smallholders, the rest either secretaries of unions or (two) representatives of the 'burghers and artisans' which are the other component of the official title of the cantonal party—'Farmers, Artisans and Burghers: Free Democratic Party of the Middle Classes'. There were no other surprises for the Party in the list of those elected: all the sitting members were successful and, indeed, were placed by the electorate in the right order. No seats were won or lost.

The Socialists, like the Farmers, were misrepresented as regards geographical distribution, but in the antithetical way: all except one of their members came from Berne city, and the single exception came also from a town, Bienne.

In 1950 the Socialists had won a seat from the Independents: this time they lost it back. They had the further misfortune that two of their sitting members failed to be re-elected—one because of the loss of the mandate, and one because of *panachage* by the electorate. 150 more personal votes from other lists would have promoted the failed member into a place on the list above two successful candidates. There seem to have been about 58,000 Socialist voters, but the figure cannot be calculated exactly from the electoral results. Whatever the exact figure, it must have been a mere handful who determined the personal selection of the individual member.

The one genuine worker on the Socialist list took sixteenth place when the results were declared—he lacked the extra votes that the candidates who were already cantonal ministers, or mayors of communes or secretaries of unions, could elicit.

3. CANTON LUCERNE

Zurich and Berne are giants among cantons. Next after them come Vaud, Aargau and St Gallen with sixteen, thirteen and thirteen members. Below these come a block of cantons, represented by a number of members between half a dozen and nine. These are large enough for *Proporz* to work, but not so large that the number of candidates is unreasonable. It is difficult to find a typical example: it would be untypical of Switzerland if the example taken did not have its own peculiarities. The example chosen is Lucerne, with nine members. Further details are in Appendix Three.

The general election of 1955 had made local history. Since 1871, Lucerne had been represented in the Council of States by two Catholic Conservatives. As the historic leader of the Sonderbund, Lucerne had easily assumed the leadership of the Catholic and Conservative cantons of Inner Switzerland. In 1955, one of the two Councillors of States announced his resignation. The Radicals asked for a seat, but it was refused by the Conservatives, as a matter of course. A week before the elections, the Radicals announced their official candidate, Herr Clavadetscher. The Conservatives then realized that their opponents had been making elaborate electoral plans while they slept.

That week saw a campaign of unparalleled bitterness and violence. The Conservatives, sure of themselves, ordered a band to celebrate the victory, but to make doubly sure, called out their last man to vote, with pulpit and with press. They had another card up their sleeve too, a hopeless candidature of a Socialist and a random list of signatures conjured up to support him.

The first count gave a victory to the sitting Conservative candidate: the Radicals and all the parties had voted for him. The conflict was for the second seat. Clavadetscher was ahead of his rival, but the 'wild' candidature had drawn 160 votes in a poll of 28,000, and Clavadetscher was forty votes beneath the 'absolute majority' needed in the first election. (A recount made it to be eighty-seven votes.) The second election a week later drew the last invalid out of bed, with polls in country districts of ninety-eight and ninety-nine per cent. Clavadetscher—a Protestant, a Radical, and from Grisons to boot—got in. The little town went wild with joy and fury for one night.

In 1959, in consequence, the Council of States vote was regarded as the more important: Clavadetscher got in, exceeding the absolute majority by 1,500 votes. Conservatives had been instructed to return blank papers for the second seat.

In the National Council, the left wing of the Conservative party— the 'Christian Socialists'—ran its own list, 'connected' with the right wing. Among other considerations, it was hoped thereby to regain the loyalty of Catholic trades-unionists who were voting with other parties. This was not just a manœuvre: the Christian Social party makes a genuine appeal to the conscience. It put forward five candidates, cumulating Dr Wick, editor of a Catholic newspaper. The intention was that the right wing would give spare votes to Dr Wick, who was a sitting member, previously on the joint Catholic list. The right wing, in return, only put up six candidates. In the election, one of the left wing (Dr Wick) got in, and four of the right. All sitting candidates got in, and two new members, the younger of whom (Leu) comes from a family of rich peasants that has played a distinguished part in Lucerne public life ever since the old patriciate left the scene. He headed the poll.

Two days before the election, a conference of local priests warned against the dangers of liberalism, a warning fully reported in the local press. The Radicals, on their side, also called out the last man to secure the Council of States seat for Clavadetscher. This had an unexpected result: the full turnout for Clavadetscher sent up the National Council poll also to such heights that the Radicals won a seat (by fifty votes) from the Socialists. This was the only Socialist mandate, and they had held the seat since 1922—a severe loss of prestige for them, as it was also their only seat in Inner Switzerland.[1]

---

[1] One Socialist was elected in Schwyz. Though his support was in the more lowland territory towards the Lake of Zurich, strictly speaking he should be reckoned a representative from Inner Switzerland also. The district is politically, but not geographically, Inner Switzerland.

It was also rather unfair, since Socialist voters were indispensable for Clavadetscher's election.

The net result therefore of the hot conflict for the Council of States seat between Radicals and Conservatives was a loss of one seat in the National Council for the Socialists.

ELECTIONEERING

On the surface, in a canton such as Berne (and particularly in the old canton, outside the Jura) there is no detectable activity during an election. At the most, the press will contain advertisements, such as 'Write X's name twice!' with a photograph, put in, not by the candidate himself, but by a group of admirers. In other papers a party may take a page and devote it to photographs of their candidates. The party press will contain articles, and an indication of how to vote, sometimes with an official recommendation from the party to cumulate a particular name.

Beneath the surface, three activities may be mentioned:

(1) *'Vertrauensleute'* (*Party-workers*)

Membership figures for the parties are not published, indeed are a closely guarded secret. An informed guess is 'between eight and fifteen per cent in towns', and in the country 'where quite often all life is politically organized' up to thirty or thirty-five per cent of the voters are party members. The Socialist figure can be guessed from available figures of contributions, and is probably about 60,000 out of 264,000 voters. The Farmers' (B.G.B.) is about 40,000 out of 118,000 voters. In charge of these are party officials, in the Catholic parties and the B.G.B. part-time only (the other part of the time, however, may be in a political newspaper or an agricultural professional organization). The Radicals, Socialists and Landesring have only half a dozen permanent, full-time, officials. Between these and the party members come the 'stalwarts'. The Socialists 'have about 10,000, to make the elections'. The B.G.B. has two grades. In the first are about 7,000 Stalwarts, organized in sections, and in the second about 700 'who are really trustworthy', from the party's standpoint. It is to be presumed that their task is to create public opinion. That is all that seems to be known.[1]

[1] This information, which is almost the only printed description of the institution, is from the *National Zeitung* (Basle) of 15 Oct '59, signed R.E. (Rolf Eberhard). My attention to it was drawn by Dr Gruner, of Basle. Every now and then there is an oblique reference to the system, e.g. in Eugen Steinemann *Die Volkswirtschaft der neuen Schweiz*. S.D.P. der Schweiz, Zurich, 1947. 'Proofs of this book were distributed to 2,000 *Vertrauensleute* of the Party.'

(2) The Press Bureaux

In addition to the *Correspondance politique suisse*, which is anti-Socialist, but otherwise an objective-minded source of political inspiration for the minor press, there are perhaps half a dozen bureaux which supply material for the press, and which are popularly believed not to be so independent of the source of their funds, which exist, in fact, to propagate the views of definite persons and definite organizations. The celebrated *Büro Büchi* was the best known of these. There is also some political advertising, the advertisement of '*Trumpf Buur*' (a political version of Mr Cuthbert's gardening talks) in the interest of certain industrial circles close to the *Vorort*. These, at least, are recognizable. They are, of course, paid for—and many newspapers are short of money.

(3) Public Relations

In 1959 one member was said to have gained his place on the list through his foresight in hiring the services of a public relations firm. In the next year, a group of public spirited army officers hired a public relations firm to propagate views of a certain tendency, which were opposed to those of their official superiors. It is clear that some of the art of influencing public opinion has passed out of the hands of the amateur into the hands of the professional, and of those who can afford to pay him. It is said that some referendums have been influenced by such methods, though an old-fashioned cartoon in *Nebelspalter* may be more effective. On the one hand are these rumours, on the other hand, a vague public fear of the unknown and the subliminal. There is a lack of 'hard' information, as might be expected.

APPENDIX
Representing the People. Dr Räber

In a recent political biography[1] the story is told how the Catholic Conservatives changed the political complexion of Küssnacht. Küssnacht, where Tell slew the Bailiff in the Hollow Lane, was a subject territory of Schwyz under the old régime (a significant paradox). For this reason it was Liberal in politics throughout the nineteenth century. Dr Räber (an ambitious young Conservative) 'regarded it as a matter of honour that Küssnacht should show good

[1] Ludwig Räber. *Ständerat Räber. Ein Leben im Dienst der Heimat. 1872–1934* Einsiedeln, 1950.

results in cantonal and federal referendums and elections, for it was, in a way, "his own" commune. But such political successes are not to be obtained without effort. The smaller party committee met twice monthly, the larger committee whenever necessary. The sections of the village and the hamlets were allotted to precisely determined *Vertrauensleute*. They went from man to man and farm to farm to obtain support . . . And successes were obtained, Küssnacht voted remarkably "well ".'

The biographer adds 'Perhaps these details may seem insignificant, but they are really extremely important. Nothing is more dangerous to a federal politician than to lose his position back home. Every seat in the Council in Berne is a cantonal seat. And ideas are of no use if the people of the canton withdraw their confidence from their representative.

'Dr Räber was never popular in the vulgar sense, but always had the confidence of the common man. On Sunday, after the service in the church, Dr Räber stood a quarter of an hour or longer outside the church door. Here he could speak to everyone, and to everyone he said the right thing. His firm handshake gave confidence, and what he promised was performed as soon as possible. On Sunday evening, towards twilight, he spent an hour in each of the leading inns, taking them in turn, both Liberal inns and Conservative.' Another activity was a 'Pressverein', feeding 'politically neutral' [*sic*] ideas to the local press, to which Räber also contributed weekly articles 'without payment'. The biographer sums up his father's activity as 'tireless detail-work'. Räber died in 1934, and his main work was done 1900–20, but it will be noticed that his methods of 'representing the people' are the modern ones.

V
Members and Buildings

The method of election described in Chapter IV requires the candidate to be on the list of a political party, and favours a particular type of person. The nature of Swiss society determines the big issues in the parliamentary battle, but the character of the contest is much affected by the characteristics of the members and by their interests. This chapter describes the cast and the scenery of this mock-battle, or rather, of this process of social integration in Parliament.

The requirement that the candidate should belong to a political party might seem to be not very onerous, for there are numerous parties and parliamentary discipline is not very strict. But there could well be difficulties for a particular candidate in a particular place: it is, for example, no use standing as a Catholic Conservative in Schaffhausen, or as a Protestant in Urschweiz. It is important to live in the right district and to have the personality that fills the role chosen: there is usually a choice of tides to swim with, but it is important to swim with some tide. However, Switzerland is so varied that a collection of members of parliament who are all orthodox in their own environment would still make a legislature full of variety.

Having got on to a party 'list', the next important thing is to have some characteristic that appeals to the minority of electors who practise 'cumulation' and *panachage*: these are the electors who effectively choose the individual candidate and thereby give the National Council the character that it bears.

There are two obvious ways of obtaining this decisive extra handful of votes. One way is the public career, to become known through local or cantonal political office. The other way is through membership and office in a pressure group, union or society. These associations are called *Verbände* in Switzerland. Whether the public or the Verband career is chosen, it is necessary at the same time to climb within the party, and desirably to hold some position within its hierarchy.

(1) The Public Career

The obvious start to political life, if entering it on the public route, is election to the cantonal Parliament. This may, of course, only be pushing the difficulty a stage further back, for how does one get into the cantonal Parliament? Communal politics may be a start; a popular profession (not schoolmastering, for example), a famous, but not aristocratic, name in the locality, or a well-run farm, or newspaper fame, may be other starts. Almost always it is necessary to represent something tangible, such as the army, the Civil Service, a union, agriculture, labour or industry. It is in a sense a question of choosing 'the best man for the job'—but the job is not legislating but representing.

There are many other political offices other than that of membership of the Great Council. In the countryside most public offices are elective, and all elective offices have a political element. The political element also enters when the appointing authority is itself a political authority. In particular, to be a cantonal judge in Switzerland is to follow a political career—the judge is not corrupt, but he has to fit a particular political bill and then be sponsored by a particular political party, and not lose the confidence of that party before he has acquired a new sponsor.

(2) The *Verband* Career

The other avenue is through a *Verband*. It is clear that watchmakers will vote for a member of the watchmakers' union, and that shoemakers will 'cumulate' shoemakers. The candidate will very often be the paid secretary or employee of the society, but it is difficult to say at a glance which offices are paid and which are honorary. This close connexion gives a distinctive character to the lobby in Switzerland: societies do not have to find an existing member to represent them, the member is a member because he holds a position in the society.

There are of course other avenues. A newspaper-owner or a journalist may have a direct contact with his own public, a man may be famous in his own right, or have a local name as a veterinary surgeon or a solicitor. But what often happens with such people is that their names are on the list, but they are not elected. Their personal votes are reckoned towards the votes of the party—and serve to elect someone else. The citizen votes for a well-loved professor, and elects a compositor.

PROFESSIONAL POLITICIANS

If one takes the official figures for 1955 (which are misleading in detail and quite unscientific) one finds there were no fewer than forty-three National Councillors out of 195 who had chosen the public career approach to a federal political office. There were only twenty-nine officials of *Verbände*, but the number may be understated. If one can add these together and call them professional politicians, they amount together to over a third of the National Council. The real figure, penetrating a little the disguise of terms such as 'Lawyer' and 'Journalist', is probably not less than fifty per cent.

It is thus a little surprising to be continually informed, by full-time politicians, that there are no professional politicians in Switzerland. What is meant by the expression is that no one can subsist only on his day-allowance as National Councillor. This is now seventy francs a day, and the Council meets for about twelve weeks a year. Even counting payment for attendance at committees outside the session, and reckoning the modest profit made when the committees travel for a single day to Schuls or Saas-Fee, this is not a living wage. It covers a very comfortable stay in Berne and a bit more, and that is all: the wage is not despicable and it is not despised, but it keeps no one alive for a year. Whether the fact that members must be paid by someone else is a matter for self-congratulation is doubtful—it has both advantages and disadvantages.

Approaching from the other end one can reckon the number of non-professionals—the banker, the cement manufacturer and so on. The peasants and landowners are the only large group here, and their number is slightly exaggerated by the official figures. The number of genuinely independent members can be built up to about one third, but no further. The majority have lost their amateur status. The whole field, however, needs careful inquiry by a Swiss scholar, for it is necessary to investigate each case. The professions on the voting paper, and even the short biographies in the Year Book, are not wholly reliable.[1]

LENGTH OF EXPERIENCE

As regards length of experience as National Councillor, immediately after an election as a rule a little more than a quarter of the Council are new members, about one quarter have served up to four years, a further quarter from five to ten years, and a quarter more than ten years. Members of the Council of States have very often first served as National Councillors, and this increases the reservoir

[1] Candidates list a profession on the voting paper. They also provide a biography for the *Annuaire des autorités fédérales—Jahrbuch der eidg. Behörden*, a useful publication. But it is very difficult to find out, for example, the directorates held by a member, the register of companies having no index of persons.

of experience. At each election five to fifteen existing Councillors fail to be re-elected: the other new members represent retirements. In 1959, not a quite typical year, ten party mandates changed in nine cantons, thirty-one members retired, and sixteen failed to be re-elected (6 K.K., 6 S.D.P., 2 Radicals, 2 P.D.A.).

COUNCIL OF STATES

The cantons are free to declare the office of member of the cantonal government 'incompatible' with membership of the Federal Assembly, and some of them (e.g. Ticino) do so. Most of the cantons allow two of their ministers to sit in the federal legislature: Berne allows three. The cantons also determine the franchise and the tenure of Councillors of States.

In all cantons except four (Berne, Fribourg, Neuchâtel and St Gallen) members of the Council of States are elected 'by the people'. In Vaud and Geneva this expression now includes women (who cannot elect or be elected to the National Council or vote in federal referenda), but usually the electorate is either the same as that for the National Council, or is the *Landsgemeinde*. In the four cantons which do not have popular election, election is by the cantonal legislature. In either event members of the cantonal government have an electoral advantage, and for this reason alone they dominate the States. The cantonal governments also mostly desire to have one or two of their members in Parliament, so as to keep in touch with what is going on in Berne. Cantonal ministers, for their part, are seldom shy of accumulating offices, each of which adds to their power, and a vote among the forty-four members of the Council of States is worth more than one among the 196 members of the National Council. Moreover the work is lighter and the atmosphere more congenial to the administrative mind.

In 1960 there were twelve *Regierungsräte*[1] (cantonal ministers) in the Council of States, and ten held cantonal political posts (if one includes judgeships) usually given to ex-ministers. Seven were members of cantonal legislatures. Thirteen were ex-members of the National Council.

The typical Councillor of States (*Ständerat, conseiller aux États*) is a man of some senatorial dignity, with power at home, not necessarily government power. If a landlord, he is richer than his counterpart in the National Council; if a minister, he is more powerful.

---

[1] Literally 'Councillors of State' (Ministers) as opposed to 'Councillors of States' (Senators). But the expression is avoided here, as the two are so easily confused.

To be a Councillor of States is more than to be a National Councillor, but an ambitious man will prefer to dominate the National Council than to be important in the Council of States. It is typical that there are three Liberal Conservatives in the Council of States (with five in the National Council) and, by a twist of political fortune, three Socialists, as against fifty-one in the National Council. The Councils are legally absolutely equal, but a little of the air of an upper house is nevertheless detectable in the States.

PARLIAMENT AND THE EXECUTIVE

Though the individual member may often be at the command of other forces than his private conscience, from the standpoint of the Federal Council and the federal Civil Service the Assembly contains a large number of very formidable personages. Even though the real power in society, heavy industry, big finance, and the army leadership in particular, is not personally present there, some very considerable forces are present, in particular members powerful in local government, agriculture, organized labour, and the press.

But members do not only represent the experience they gain outside the federal chambers. A member can amass power and knowledge inside, and find the opportunity to exercise power as member of Parliament. The proof of this is the language of respect in which high federal officials speak of members. Writers and students of government may speak of the Chambers as powerless and almost supernumerary, but that is not the language which federal officials use who come into contact with parliamentary committees; they may laugh, but they fear and respect. That this is likely to be the case can be seen by looking at the parliamentary career of three members:

1. National Councillor Condrau

Dr Condrau is editor of a Romansch paper circulating in the Upper Rhine Valley. He is a Catholic Conservative, and since 1953 has been President of that parliamentary party. He is mayor of the town of Disentis, has been a member of his cantonal Parliament since 1923, and was President of it in 1930. He was *Kreispräsident* of Disentis from 1933–37, and has been chairman of Grisons Oberland Electricity works since 1945, a member of the National Council since 1935, and President of it in 1957. More than one Federal Councillor owes his seat (in part) to Herr Condrau—a red-faced, busy man with a tight-clipped moustache.

He has served on ninety-three *ad hoc* committees in the National

Council since his election and been President of eleven of them (a list is given in the Appendix on page 172), and on the following standing committees:

> Validation of Mandates, 1936–39
> Gestion (Business of the Year), 1939–43
> Trade and Tariffs, 1943–44
> Committee on Emergency Powers, 1944–47
> Finance Committee, 1947–53 (Delegation, 1950–53)
> Foreign Affairs, 1954–59 (president, 1955–57)
> Trade and Tariffs, 1959–present day

2. National Councillor Bringolf (Schaffhausen)[1]
Herr Bringolf entered the National Council in 1925 as a Communist, but has long been a Social Democrat with no trace of embitteredness. His early record accounts for his late start in committees. In 1959 he was a candidate for the Federal Council, and stood a good chance of being elected—but he had the misfortune that Herr Condrau preferred Professor Tschudi of Basle (the case is discussed later). He has been President both of his parliamentary and of his political party. He is a broad man in his late 60s, with untidy black hair and penetrating, humorous eyes. He has served on the following standing committees:

> Gestion, 1939–42
> Foreign Affairs, 1941–45
> Emergency Powers, 1943–47
> Military Committee, 1946–50
> Foreign Affairs, 1947–53 (president, 1951–53)
> Military Committee, 1951–55 (president, 1953–55)
> Finance Committee, 1955–present day (president, 1957–58)
>   (Delegation, 1959–present day)

In this committee he specializes in military and foreign affairs. Herr Bringolf is a well-known broadcaster and holds the air on foreign affairs every third Friday. He is head and shoulders a greater personality than any present member of the Federal Council, except perhaps for Herr Wahlen.

3. Federal Councillor Chaudet
Officials must also remember that the day may come when one of

[1] See page 73. In 1961 he was elected Vice-President of the National Council.

the members who specializes in the work of their Department is promoted to Federal Councillor, and takes the headship of the department in which he specializes.

The career of Federal Councillor Chaudet illustrates this: Monsieur Chaudet comes from an ancient family of wine-peasants, the notables of one of the wine-villages (which have a curiously urban character) looking down on the Lake of Geneva. Fortunate constellations brought him into his cantonal executive, and other fortunate constellations brought him into the supreme magistracy.

Elected to the National Council in 1943, he served on the following standing committees:

Pardons, 1943–47
Military Committee, 1946–50
Alcohol, 1950–54
Finance, 1953–54

He was also head of the cantonal military department in Vaud. In 1954 he was elected Federal Councillor and is now head of the Federal Military Department, and, as such, in charge of very important projects for reorganization. In his career and in his person he is much less formidable than Herr Bringolf (who takes a particular interest in his department) or Herr Condrau.

BUILDINGS

No description of the Swiss Parliament is complete without an evocation of the buildings, the natural habitat of the Swiss political animal, especially as these have a very strong and unforgettable character of their own. The settings of the Swiss Diets and Assemblies of the past can also be seen today by the curious visitor, and likewise enable him to picture what they in their day were like.

The best impression of the Diet of the old régime can be had in the Ratsaal in Baden—Baden is an attractive little town at which one can change trains between Basle and Zurich. The Ratsaal is a small, dignified room of the medieval type, with the arms of the thirteen sovereign cantons in stained glass panels in the windows. The Diet met here from 1424–99 (often), and from 1515 to 1742 (regularly), and here it received ambassadors and the representatives of its allies. After the Second War of Villmergen (during which the Protestant cantons defeated the Catholic ones) in 1712 the Diet moved to Frauenfeld in Thurgau, at first for some of its business, and, after 1742, for all of it. But its meeting place and most of the town were burnt down in a fire towards the end of the eighteenth century. Catholic Diets, Protestant Diets, and Dicts of particular types, met in various places.

During the half century after 1798, the legislatures and Diets of the successive Swiss political structures had no continuous place of meeting, and after 1803 moved from one *Vorort* (capital) to another. In Berne, the place of meeting was the '*Rathaus des äusseren Standes*'. The building was originally the union society and debating club of the young patricians of Berne: it was an ambitious piece of architecture for which the bills were never fully paid. At the time of the revolution it fell, heavily mortgaged, into the hands of the town of Berne, and in 1816 it was bought by the canton. The Senate of the Helvétique sat here, the Diet of 1804, the Restoration Diet in 1815, and the Constituent Assembly which gave Berne the ancestor of its present Constitution in 1831. The Constitution of 1848 was signed here. After 1848, the Council of States sat here until 1856. It is the birthplace of modern Switzerland. The Diet which met in Berne and declared war on the Sonderbund, however, did not meet here, but in the *Heiliggeistkirche*, which was hung for the occasion with the ancient tapestries once looted from the camp of Charles the Bold (the *Heiliggeistkirche* is the church just by the railway station in Berne). The *Rathaus des äusseren Standes* has fallen into a state of neglect. Stripped of its panelling (which survives elsewhere), the debating chamber serves as a display room for camping equipment and striped umbrellas in the premises of a shop. The façade is protected as a monument (being the work of the greatest of the eighteenth century architects of Berne) but has been much mutilated.

From 1848 to 1856 the National Council met in a building which has now been destroyed, the old Casino. It then moved to the present 'Bundeshaus-West'. This is a large green-sandstone building in a style borrowed from (among others) the Strozzi Palace in Florence, and is the best of the existing federal buildings from the aesthetic point of view. Bundeshaus-West formerly housed not only the two Councils—the National Council in the west wing, and the States in the east—but the whole federal administration in the connecting block. The old name plates are on the doors of the administrative offices, and the building forms a sort of architectural history of federal administration. The meeting place of the Federal Council is also there. The old meeting places of the legislative councils have now been divided up, but an impression of what the National Council room looked like can be obtained in the bookstacks of the Central Administrative Library, which is housed in that block. This was the room which echoed (all too literally, for the acoustics were deplorable) to the rhetoric of Stämpfli and Welti.[1]

The East Block of the Bundeshaus, the *Verwaltungsgebäude*, was finished in 1892 and is an approximate copy of the west block. Between the two the modern building of the Parliament has been inserted. The first session was held in the present building in 1903, and thus the move to a new place of session coincided with a new Law on the Relations of the Councils and a revision of the Standing Orders.

This Parliament Building (*Bundespalast*) is a truly formidable edifice, linked to the west and east blocks both by a heavy covered bridge and an elegant open-arcaded bridge (which is never used: it would be a fine sight to see officials and Federal Councillors in profile crossing it). The Palace of Parliament teems with statuary. It is crowned by a statue of Helvetia (the model for which was a Portuguese dance-hostess from a night-club in Geneva).[2] The other side faces a promenade along the ramparts above the steep slope down to the Marzili quarter and the river Aar, where (upstream of the town's sewage) the shopkeepers and officials bathe during the lunch interval in summer.

From the promenade at certain times and seasons there is a magnificent view of the mountains of the Oberland. At sunset a shadow curiously like the Federal Cross can be seen on the flanks of the Jungfrau, pinkish in the evening light: it is a motif that understandably stirs all sorts of tribal romanticisms.

Symbolism has been given a free hand in the interior also, and there can be few patriotic clichés that are not somewhere evoked or expressed. But these, though not in the severest of taste, are important and should be noted. They are the things which make a nation, and William Tell and the Three *Eidgenossen* stand all over the world as symbols of political liberty. As legislative architecture the buildings are in some ways unfortunate: discussion of butter-prices is part of the proper business of an assembly, and the debates are rather an anti-climax after passing by the huge statue of the Three Confederates swearing the Federal Oath. The legislators are dwarfed by the buildings, and this at once disappoints the public and tempts members to speak at too great length and with involved sentences. But the building has its merits, the greatest of which is a superb self-confidence, and it stands up well as a public monument to rather

---

[1] Stämpfli, Federal Councillor 1854–63. Welti, Federal Councillor 1866–81 (six times President of the Confederation). Two statesmen who have become almost legendary figures. Both resigned on political grounds, and are referred to again on page 81 below.

[2] Georges Bovet, *Chemin faisant*.

severe competition from its neighbouring hotels and banks: in the circumstances that is a triumph. The building also hits off well the tastes of the unsophisticated, while imposing itself on its inmates and arousing their affection.

THE NATIONAL COUNCIL CHAMBER

The National Council room is usually seen from the public gallery,[1] beneath which, along the curved rear wall, are the forty-four seats for Councillors of States attending joint sessions of the Assembly. During the sessions of the National Council proper, however, it is quite usual for individual Councillors of States, or pairs of them, to loll informally on one of these seats in order to listen to an important debate (for example, on a matter in which he is interested as a committee member in the other Chamber) or simply to intercept National Councillors for conversation. There is a corresponding bench in the Council of States for National Councillors.

There is a small bench for officials. It is on the floor of the House, near one of the entrance doorways, so it allows informal conversation with members—who sometimes shake the officials by the hand as they enter or sit next to them to talk.

The seats of the members, with their backs to the gallery, are arranged in a spacious semi-circle, seven ranks deep, with a shallow step raising each rear rank higher than the semi-circular rank in front of it. The members have green-seated chairs with arms and a woven-cane back. Each sits at a desk in which papers and odd bits of string and pencils are kept. An earphone is available at each desk for those who wish a simultaneous translation into the other parliamentary language. Facing the members are the desks of the six tellers, and raised behind them the desk, furnished with a microphone, to which each speaker goes in order to address the House. Next to the Orator's Desk are four desks usually occupied by Rapporteurs of committees. On either side, three and three, are large ornate chairs for Federal Councillors, of which only the one on the orator's left is usually occupied. In a raised rank behind these desks sit two members of the Secretariat, the Chancellor of the Confederation (who is always busily writing) in his capacity as Clerk of the House, the President of the House himself—often reading a newspaper—and the Vice-President and two ex-Presidents.

[1] Access to the gallery is easy to obtain: during the session one simply enters one of the two doors marked *Tribüne*, walks upstairs, and pushes open the gallery door without the intervention of any official. There are also two little empty galleries for diplomats which offer no extra facilities for observation.

Behind the President's back and above his head rises a huge picture of the Rütli Meadow where the first confederate oath was sworn. The Lake of Lucerne and all the peaks are to be seen (for the view is as from a great height) and hovering in the clouds is the Spirit of Peace—or is it Liberty?—depicted as a middle-aged naked woman, seated and winged with a twig in her hand. The general effect is of a cinema-audience with the members as viewers and the Rütli Meadow on a wide screen. So accurate is the representation of the Rütli that on one occasion in 1960 Federal Councillor von Moos used it to explain how a project (to correct the course of a stream) which he was defending before the Council, would be carried out.

The journalists, in practice only the French-speaking press, are in boxes on the left and right, raised so as to permit a handshake with a member but not an informal conversation. The German-speaking journalists, more conscientious and less lively, use a subterranean press-room, listening to the debate through earphones.

They are the only listeners. A great roar of conversation floods the room, by a happy accident of acoustics inaudible to the gallery. The orator's speech is amplified by loud-speakers and it is necessary in consequence slightly to raise the voice to be heard by one's fellow-member. Members read papers, write letters, drift round collecting signatures to postulates. A new member attends with a strained face to his first week of debate, occasionally consulting a plan of the seats to identify a colleague.

This is as it should be. The formation of parliamentary opinion is better done through informal conversation than by listening to speeches—especially Swiss speeches, which scorn informality and 'debating points'. What is unsuitable is the architecture, which leads one to expect too much.

The seats are not arranged in party blocks, though there are little groups from the same party here and there, and the French-speaking members sit together. The practice is to allot a new member the vacant seat of the member he displaces (if no one else applies for it), and to treat seats once allotted as permanent, with the proviso that when a seat becomes vacant the senior applicant for it can move there if he wishes. The chairmen and tellers regain their former seats on returning to the floor after their turn of office. Because of this informal grouping it is difficult to tell, without long practice, which party or section of a party is voting for a particular measure.

THE COUNCIL OF STATES

The States occupy a room artistically less ambitious and more reassuring. Members speak from their seats, which are less crowded together. The mural painting of the *Landsgemeinde* at Stans is ingeniously brought into harmony with the room by the device of continuing the panelling and arches of the galleries into the painting itself.

The style of proceedings is different. Courtesy in a small Chamber demands some attention to the matter. Speeches are read, usually by a seated member, and the stenographer (often a middle-aged lady) seats herself in a vacant senatorial chair in order to catch the words more clearly. The word *sachlich* (factual) is usually applied to the speeches, as a term of praise. *Sachlich* they are, murderously *sachlich*, and not only full of facts but of figures too. The debates are shorter in the States than in the National Council, as befits a much smaller House.

Meanwhile the life of the Parliament flows in the corridors and the neighbouring rooms. Councillors speak to friends, to opponents, to officials and to journalists. A member shows his daughter the magnificent view from the terrace. The respresentative of a vested interest looks through the glass door of the Chamber and sends a card to a member. Herr Duttweiler holds court in the bar—which is non-alcoholic. A Federal Councillor walks rapidly from his office to the House to relieve a colleague. Letters are written, conspiracies formed, and the new member goes to the public gallery to unburden his sense of loneliness in this busy place where everyone except he seems to know everyone else.

VI
The Business of the Chambers

The business of Parliament can be classified either according to content, or according to form. This book is primarily concerned with the power of Parliament and the part which it plays in the life of the nation, and therefore it employs a classification of Parliament's business according to content. A book on procedure would, it may be presumed, follow the formal classification.

CONTENT

As regards content, the business of the Chambers may be classified as.

(*i*) *Elections* (*Chapters VII and VIII*)

Just as the foremost business of the House of Commons is to provide a government and support it, so the election of the Federal Council is one of the principal tasks of the Parliament of Switzerland. But, because Swiss government is based on a separation of powers, it is conceivable that the business of electing Federal Councillors might be taken away from the Assembly—while the relationship of the British Cabinet to Parliament is an integral part of British government.

One of the arguments of this book is that, although the Federal Council as a whole is not politically responsible to the Assembly in the way that the British Cabinet is, yet the individual Federal Councillor is half-responsible, in the sense that he can ultimately be got rid of if he loses the confidence of Parliament. The procedure of the legislative Councils only makes sense on this basis. Particular attention is therefore given here to premature 'resignations' of Federal Councillors.

(*ii*) *Legislation* (*Chapter X*)

This is the classic function of the two Councils. The role of Parliament in legislation can only be evaluated if the pre-parliamentary stages are taken into account. To do this is still rather a new venture in Switzerland, and there is very little descriptive writing about the preliminary stages. The method adopted here is to follow an actual draft from its conception to its enactment.

THE BUSINESS OF THE CHAMBERS

(*iii*) *Control* (*Chapters XI and XII*)

This is a large word, and the extent of the control of the Swiss Parliament over its executive is the whole subject of this book. In the meantime, however, the word 'control' can be used in a restricted sense to describe those procedures *ostensibly* aiming at controlling the government. Motions and postulates on the floor of the House can be included here, and so can the committees aiming at control of particular branches of administration and of the Annual Report.

(*iv*) *Co-operation* (*Chapter XIV*)

There is no hard frontier between this and control, but certain activities, in particular the interest which the Swiss Parliament takes in foreign policy, are not pursued in the spirit of control, and would be misunderstood if put under this head, rather than under that of 'co-operation'.

(*v*) *Finance* (*Chapter XIII*)

Every act of government has a financial aspect, and therefore 'financial control' describes the means of control as well as the content of it. Nevertheless, financial control is a topic which can be discussed separately.

(*vi*) *Standing Orders*

The Councils 'constitute' themselves and regulate within limits their own procedure. This is a subject of rather minor interest. It is partly considered in the remainder of this chapter, and partly in Chapter XV, which deals with the committee system.

FORM

The classification as to form is more complete and logical, since it divides the whole business into mutually exclusive categories. Using this classification, the work of Parliament can be analysed as:

(a) Leading up to a report of the Federal Council
  Motions
  Postulates
  Interpellations } All of which seek to elicit a report from the Federal Council.
  Written Questions
  'Question Hour'

(b) Leading away from a report (or Message) of the Federal Council
  Legislation and Constitutional amendment
  Financial business
  Control of the Annual Report (*Gestion*)
  Discussion of items in the *Feuille fédérale* not included under the above heads (including pardons)

  } All of which are based on a document deriving from the Federal Council

(c) Independent of the Federal Council
  Règlements (Standing Orders)
  Validation of mandates
  Elections of Federal Authorities
  Election of the Chambers' own officers
  Action on petitions

  } None of which require the co-operation of the Federal Council

For the reasons stated, the formal classification is not followed in this book.

STANDING ORDERS

Étienne Dumont, Bentham's amanuensis and disciple, was a citizen of Geneva, and in 1813 was elected to the newly constituted parliament of his native Republic. Being known as editor and translator of Bentham's celebrated Essay on Legislative Tactics, Dumont was invited to draft the Standing Orders for the elective council. This he did. The *Règlement* which he drafted continued in force until the present century, and the present Genevese *Règlement* is based upon it. At first sight it seems to owe little to Bentham's somewhat fanciful proposals, but the debt is a more generalized one: it is in the realization that the details of procedure are vitally important, and that the experience of Britain (and of France) is to be respected.

After 1830, the cantons in turn came to adopt Constitutions of the modern type, and sought inspiration from each other and abroad. They drew much from the Belgian and the French Constitutions, and also borrowed freely from Dumont's *Règlement* for Geneva, which was adapted to the Swiss conditions. By 1848 a fairly clear model of what was a suitable procedure for a Parliament working under Swiss conditions (i.e. with a collegiate executive holding office for a fixed term) had grown up in the cantons. This (and more especially the procedure of Zurich and Berne) was the basis for the *Règlements* of the Federal Chambers adopted in 1849–50. The experience of the Diet was (except in some few insignificant details) ignored. The

Règlements underwent important changes in the 1870s, and a complete revision in 1903, 1920 (Council of States, 1927), and 1946. They are now (1960) due for a further revision. Nevertheless, the basis of procedure (except as regards the method of voting on amendments and some important details of committee procedure) has changed little since 1848. In one important respect—the preliminary select committee stage—the hand of Dumont can still be traced, although on the face of it the institution might equally have been borrowed from America or France. Because the model of procedure had already been formed in the cantons before the federal Parliament came into being, the history of procedure lies outside that of the Assembly.

Procedure is regulated on three levels of law. Certain details are regulated by the Constitution itself, which limits the tenure of the chairman and prescribes certain tasks, quorums and majorities. These details, being practically unalterable, effectively limit the possibilities of procedural reform: in particular they make impossible a Speakership on the British model. The most important features, however, are laid down by statute law: only by statute can the Chambers bind the Federal Council and federal officials. The law principally concerned is the *Geschäftsverkehrsgesetz*, the Law on the Relations of the Councils (hereafter referred to as 'the law on the Councils'). The present law, undergoing revision in 1960, is the Law of 1902[1] (which repealed that of 1849). Subordinate to this are the *Règlements* of the National Council, of the Council of States, and of the Federal Assembly in Joint Session. Finally, and of a dubious status, are the *Règlements* of the more important standing committees and 'delegations', the customs of the two Chambers and the rulings and policy statements of the chairmen (and committee chairmen). The two latter are not very important as regards the procedure of the whole House (*Plenum*), but determine committee procedure.

The result of regulating procedure on three (or four) legal levels is to make experiment difficult and alteration cumbrous. The Constitution is fixed, the Law on the Councils is amended once in a half century—and when it is amended it takes the *Règlements* for granted. But the greatest barrier to experiment is that little interest is taken in procedure. Juridically, procedure is administrative law of a low grade, and therefore beneath the consideration of the learned. In consequence there is almost no intelligent speculation on procedural matters and very little has been written upon it.

---

[1] The Law of 1902 can be found, in translation, in the Author's book on *The Federal Constitution of Switzerland*.

PUBLICITY

Until the end of 1833 proceedings in the Diet were secret, though reports were sent by the delegates to their home cantons. From 1834, debates were in principle open to the public, and that, of course, is the rule today. As regards publication of debates, at the moment the situation is that all debates of both Councils are taken down in shorthand by clerks. Debates on Laws are printed *in extenso* in the *Stenographic Bulletin* (which corresponds to *Hansard*). Other debates can be so printed if the Council concerned so resolves, but if any member proposes inclusion in the *Stenographic Bulletin*, the Council in practice always does agree. Three copies of the verbatim report (typed, interleaved with the printed report where necessary) are kept, one in the Secretariat of the Assembly, one in the parliamentarians' library in the Assembly, one in the Chancellor's office. That is to say, access is only by permission or for special people.[1] The printed *Bulletin*, on the other hand, is on public sale, appearing a month or two after the end of the session. Its use is in the courts, where the debates may sometimes be cited, or at referendums to explain to an uncommonly conscientious voter the reasons for the law and the objections. As a picture of the life of the Assembly it is rather misleading because of its omissions, and it makes exceptionally dull reading.

The debates are also reported in the press, not unfairly, but rather selectively. Members sometimes hand to the press (or their own particular press) a typescript copy of a contribution which they fear might be completely lost to posterity except for the three official copies. Since speeches are not listened to in the Chamber, some market must be found for them: this market is not always obvious, but is probably always there. One of the difficulties in studying the Swiss Parliament is the lack of an accessible verbatim report.

---

[1] Permission is always given for research purposes.

VII
The Federal Council

ELECTION AND RESIGNATION

The interest of the Swiss Assembly does not lie in its procedure, which is rather elementary and undeveloped, but in the particular form a federal assembly takes in a referendum-democracy governed by a collegiate executive. All Swiss procedure (in practice) either seeks to elicit a report from the executive council, or derives from such a report. The Federal Council is the centre of the system and gives the Swiss Parliament its particular form. It is also in its own right the most interesting of all Swiss institutions, and the one which is most easily transferable to other political systems. In particular, a new state setting up its native government for the first time would be well advised to consider the Swiss Federal Council as the model for its executive.

The study of the Parliament of Switzerland is thus very largely the study of the relationship of the Parliament to the Federal Council. One aspect of this relationship is of a different kind to the rest, the fact that the Federal Council is elected by the Assembly in joint session. That the election is by the Assembly and not by the people at large is an accident—one vote in the original committee which drafted the Constitution decided it, and in the cantons popular election is the rule—but it was a fortunate accident, and a factor which raises the dignity of the Assembly and helps it to function well. Popular election, and the raising of the membership of the Federal Council to nine, have several times been proposed, but always in connexion with the claim of a particular party to a seat. The possibility of a Constitutional change started by a popular initiative is always in the background. It is one of the sanctions for the representation of all parties in the Federal Council: an unrepresented party might clamour to have the basis of representation changed.

The election of the seven members of the Federal Council is the most politically important, and the most exciting, action performed by the Assembly. The legal framework is given by Article 96 of the Constitution.

> The members of the Federal Council are chosen by the Federal Assembly for four years from among the whole number of Swiss

citizens eligible to the National Council. But not more than one member shall be chosen from the same canton.

After every general election of the National Council there shall be a general election of the Federal Council.

Vacancies occurring in the course of the period of four years are to be filled by the Federal Assembly at its next session, for the remainder of the period of office.

Article 92 of the Constitution provides that, for this election, the Chambers shall sit together in joint session, and that the 'absolute majority' of members voting must be obtained by the successful candidate. Voting is by name, and one name must receive more than half the votes cast.

A Federal Councillor who, at the end of his term of office, stands for re-election is, in practice, always re-elected. On the other hand, there are methods of getting rid of Federal Councillors, either in mid-office or at the end of the four year period. It is one of the contentions of this book that these ways of getting rid of Federal Councillors should be regarded as embodying equally important conventions of the Constitution as the practice of re-electing willing Federal Councillors. The traditional exposition of the Constitution entirely ignores the forced resignation of Federal Councillors: for this reason actual examples are mentioned in a special section of this chapter on resignations—the reader must in the circumstances forgive me for mentioning there rather too many names which may be unfamiliar. These resignations are necessary to another part of the argument of this book, which is that Swiss parliamentary procedure is in some of its aspects a mock battle in which victory is not (as it is in a true parliamentary system) the resignation of the whole Cabinet, but the resignation or non-re-election of an individual Federal Councillor. This is the ultimate sanction behind much of Swiss parliamentary procedure—in particular, behind the procedure on gestion (Chap. XII and finance (Chap. XIII). In a civilized country the ultimate sanctions are never exerted—Cabinets do not resign, prime ministers do not dissolve the Commons—but the ultimate sanctions are always there, and parliamentary procedure cannot be understood (in Britain or Switzerland) if they are ignored.

ELECTION

There is a great deal of Constitutional folk-lore concerning the manner of electing Federal Councillors, and it is not profitable to speculate about the elections in the abstract. Each vacancy presents a unique problem; nevertheless certain 'situations' do recur, and these situations can be analysed in general terms. The best method, then, is to describe first of all actual situations which are typical, and then to analyse them.

Situation 1[1]

Federal Councillor von Steiger, who represented Berne and the B.G.B. (Farmers' Party), retired, having served eleven years. The B.G.B. leaders, the Bernese B.G.B. party, and the Federal B.G.B. party agreed on their candidate. The candidate was clearly their best man and had proved himself a very able statesman as member of the Bernese cantonal government. The other parties also agreed, though with some hesitation in the case of the Catholic Conservatives. He was elected. The real election seems to have been by the Bernese B.G.B. leaders, and the Assembly simply ratified this.

Mutatis mutandis, this is what happens normally in the case of the Zurich and the Vaudois seat.

Situation 2[2]

(This is an example of Situation 1 when there is an unexpected factor)

The Federal Councillor who represented Berne (Feldmann) was found dead in the back of a taxi. Some members of the *Vorstand* of the Bernese Farmers' Party met and decided on S., the Cantonal President of Berne. The *Vorstand* itself decided likewise. A Bernese party meeting acclaimed the decision, but the federal party, remembering that it only had twenty-five out of 240 votes (in the two Chambers) refrained from taking a position. At an early stage someone said 'What about Wahlen?'—Professor Wahlen had obtained a name for himself, rather in the same way as Lord Woolton in Britain, for his work in organizing food supplies during the war. The suggestion was turned down with the quick reply that Wahlen did not want the post.

Meanwhile the other parties were approached. There is a sort of understanding that the other parties will support your candidate if you support theirs in due season. The Secretary of the Catholic Conservatives was won over to S., among other (and doubtless more politically cogent) arguments by the allegation that S. was a lukewarm evangelical whose daughter had married a Catholic. The Radical press kept very quiet and the officers of the party were won over to S. with the argument that Wahlen was in favour of a planned economy, and was suspected of being teetotal and therefore no friend of vine-

---

[1] Bundesrat Feldmann, elected 13 December 1951. For Steiger's election, see footnote on p. 79.
[2] Bundesrat Wahlen, 11 December 1958.

growers. The Socialists had their own plans. They were not represented in the Federal Council, and wanted two members or none. They were prepared to support the official Farmers' line, on the tacit understanding that gratitude would be shown later.

There seemed no reason why S. should not be elected in the same manner as his predecessor. The only hindrance was that from the national point of view Wahlen was the better candidate, and that Wahlen in fact wanted to be elected, and his old colleagues from the Food Office, a *corps d'élite*, were prepared to support him.

Then the tide turned. Evangelical circles in Basle represented that Wahlen was a Christian. The Farmers' group in Aargau preferred Wahlen. Conservative backbenchers preferred him (after receiving letters and telephone calls). The Landesring supported Wahlen. If he was after all going to be elected, it would be embarrassing for the Farmers to have supported someone else, embarrassing for the Socialists also, who would welcome a third advocate of state control of economic life in the Federal Council in the days ahead when they had two members of it. Finally it was decided that 'public opinion' was on the side of Wahlen. One by one the parties changed sides. A new, third, candidate of the Bernese Farmers (Dr Gnägi) was meanwhile proposed, because the controversy was considered to have lessened the public appeal of S. as a candidate.

In the first round of votes, none of the three got an absolute majority. Gnägi then expressed his wish to withdraw from the fray, though in words that did not quite say 'never'—he is (in 1960) the possible successor of Wahlen. In the second round, S. got the same number of votes as in the first round, but Gnägi lost eleven votes, which helped Wahlen get the absolute majority. Wahlen was fetched into the Chamber (neither Wahlen nor S. was at that moment a member of either House) to accept, and a deputation from his home village was already there to meet him. Presumably two other deputations slunk out of the side door unperceived.

Situation 3

In 1959 four Federal Councillors retired simultaneously, a rare occurrence. The three continuing members were Professor Wahlen (B.G.B., Berne), M. Chaudet (Radical, Vaud), and M. Petitpierre (Radical, Neuchâtel).

The parties, except the Radicals, decided that the Council should in future be constituted '2:2:2:1' (i.e., two Radicals, K.K.'s, and Socialists, and one B.G.B.).

The vacancies were therefore for two Conservatives (K.K.) and two Socialists. One member had to be from Zurich. The claims of

East Switzerland had to be taken into account, if possible, and also of any canton which had long been unrepresented. Preferably one member should be Italian-speaking, but that was not essential—if necessary all could be German, but preferably not, as the romance languages had had a dry spell recently.

The three continuing members were re-elected as a matter of course. The election nevertheless had some interest, since it is the custom to demonstrate dislike of a candidate by voting against him, even if the election is a foregone conclusion. In the case of Chaudet's election, for example, twenty-six blank and thirteen scattered votes were cast: for Wahlen, fifteen blank and nine scattered. Members in this way 'get their own back' for any public or private slight they may have suffered. Formerly the *order* of election was also considered a barometer of popularity, but this is no longer in any way significant.

Having filled these three seats easily, the next were the two vacancies that are by tacit agreement left to the Catholic Conservatives. Here the Catholics were left with a free hand (Situation 1). Passing over an Italian-speaking candidate from the Grisons who would have fitted the bill exactly and been a magistrate of great distinction, and a good candidate from Valais (who would not have fulfilled all the accidental requirements of place, tendency, etc.) the Catholics chose (1) a right wing candidate who had accumulated all the possible offices in a tiny canton of central Switzerland—the first time William Tell's Switzerland has held the highest federal magistracy, and (2) another right wing candidate, from Fribourg (i.e. French-speaking).

The two remaining[1] seats were claimed by the Socialists. One of them was 'the Zurich seat'. Here Situation 1 repeated itself, and a Socialist, Stadtrat (municipal executive-councillor) from Zurich, was elected.

The battle was then for the last seat. The official Socialist candidate was the Herr Bringolf whom we have already noticed: this candidature had the additional advantage of representing Schaffhausen in the Federal Council, for it is a canton which has not yet had a representative there. According to the rules of Situation 1, the seat also was a Socialist party nomination.

The Radicals, not reconciled to the formula 2:2:2:1, switched their vote to Herr Schaffner, a federal civil servant. The election of Herr Schaffner would have created a momentous precedent, for no federal official has hitherto been chosen for the supreme magistracy while in

---

[1] The elections were not actually in this order.

office.[1] The Catholics, led by Condrau, voted for a moderate Socialist from Basle, a sound administrator, Herr Tschudi. Their ostensible reason was that Tschudi is a much younger man than Bringolf. He is also a more moderate and a less colourful man, and from the Catholic point of view this was decisive: the Catholics make a point of choosing the less dominating candidate to represent their opponents.

On the first round the voting was: Schaffner 84 (Absolute
Tschudi 73 majority
Bringolf 66 116)

Tschudi loyally went to the Orator's Desk and declared that the Socialist candidate was not himself, but Bringolf. Loyalty, rather than conviction, was the keynote, and there was no absolute refusal. Yet such a declaration requires courage, and has often been the nearest a candidate has got to office.

On the next round the voting was: Tschudi 107
Schaffner 91
Bringolf 34

It was clear that even the Socialists were no longer loyally voting for Bringolf, whose powerful personality had caused enmity in his own ranks. He went to the desk, observed the disloyalty of his friends, and abdicated in favour of Tschudi. On the third round Tschudi obtained the absolute majority.

CONSTELLATIONS AND PERSONALITIES

From these descriptions of three 'situations' it can be seen that there are two sets of factors in the election of a Federal Councillor—the 'constellations' and the personalities.

1. *The Constellations*
   (i) Zurich, Berne and Vaud.

The constitution provides that no two Federal Councillors shall come from the same canton. Since cantons Zurich, Berne and Vaud have been almost continuously represented since 1848, the three seats

---

[1] That is, no federal career official in Berne. Federal Councillor Haab (1918–29) had been appointed Swiss Minister in Berlin in 1917, and was thus formally a federal official at the time of election. But he made his career as Cantonal Councillor of State and as railway director. Hammer (1875–90) was likewise Minister in Berlin at the time of appointment.

(I have left the passage as written in 1960. In June 1961, Schaffner was elected to the Federal Council in place of Petitpierre, who retired. Wahlen, who happened to be President of the Confederation that year, took over the Political Department.)

have hitherto always been considered separately—the 'Berne seat' and so on (Situation 1).

The *Zurich* cantonal seat until very recent years was traditionally held by a candidate not from the city of Zurich itself. Winterthur, a small progressive town, had had four of its citizens in the Federal Council before the capital city of the canton had obtained a single member.

The seat was a Radical fief from 1848 to 1943. But the seat is now (1960) held by a Socialist (as it was from 1943 to 1953) and there is the possibility that it will be permanently considered a 'Socialist seat'. This would be a blow to the Radicals, for Zurich is their spiritual capital. It would also be a misfortune for the Confederation, because it would exclude the best source of recruitment for a good Radical statesman: the Zurich Radical councillors have been statesmen of the highest quality, since it is not possible to attain the highest post in the Radical politics of the most lively canton in Switzerland without exceptional ability. Of the three Socialist Federal Councillors hitherto chosen from Zurich, only Professor Weber (1951-53) came up to the quality of his Radical predecessors.

It is the formal, hereditary, cantonal citizenship which counts. Nobs (1943-51, Socialist) was Bernese by origin, but obtained Zurich citizenship by naturalization, an easy thing to do, for a cantonal statesman. Weber was Zuricois by origin, but lived and lives in Berne: when he was elected the bunch of flowers sent by the canton was tied with ribbons of the federal colours, red and white, instead of the cantonal colours, blue and white, as a mute protest.

Berne was a Radical seat until 1929, but in that year a Farmer was elected. It has since become 'the Farmers' seat', with back effects both on that party and on Bernese politics. From the standpoint of the ambitious young man, the avenue leading to a seat in the Federal Council from Berne is the B.G.B. (Farmers') Party. But too cosy calculations can always be upset, as in the Wahlen election. The system sometimes provides magistrates[1] of moderate or low quality, though Feldmann (1951-58, a double citizen of Glarus and Berne) was a distinguished statesman. Wahlen, as we have seen, breaks the rule in any case.

Vaud is still a Radical fief. There have been two gaps in the past

[1] Federal Councillors are often described as 'magistrates' in Switzerland employing the term in its seventeenth century sense of 'lawful rulers'. The doctrinal overtone of the word is difficult to convey to the English reader.

in the representation of Vaud (when Ruchonnet turned down his election in 1875, and from 1944 to 1947) and its moral claim to a permanent seat in the Council is rather weak. One result of this claim has been to make it difficult or impossible for a better candidate from Geneva to be elected. The Vaudois members have occasionally been brilliant, sometimes unstable, and seldom long in office—they are said only to rent their flat in Berne, while other Councillors purchase theirs.

Within Vaud (as with Berne and Zurich) there are also 'political constellations', and it has happened that a Vaudois Cantonal Councillor is elected to his cantonal executive in order to balance the council by a member from a particular part and a particular tendency, and has then been elected a Federal Councillor to satisfy federal constellations.

(ii) When these three seats have been filled, the other four seats are not enough to satisfy the demands of the other desirable 'constellations'. These concern language, party and religion, and regions and cantons.

(b) Language

Representation of Vaud brings a French-speaker into the Council. There must always be one, because justice and the balance of power require it; and there should be two, and sometimes are three, non-German speakers.

Italian is not always represented, but after a turn of not being represented obtains a very strong claim to one seat: this means normally Ticino, but the day may come when the Italian valleys of the Grisons send a member—there was a strong candidate (Tenchio) in 1959. Occasionally a Rhaeto-Romansch speaker, whose normal language of communication will be German, can be reckoned a representation of the romance languages (Calonder 1913–20)—but this again means Grisons.

In combination with the religious and party requirements, a Catholic from Fribourg may enter the Council. The Italian-speaking member is almost certainly also a Catholic and a Conservative, but it is not inconceivable that the constellations will one day call a Radical Ticinese to the Council, though it is difficult to see how.

(c) Party

The party history of the Federal Council is as follows:
From 1848 *until* 1891, when Zemp was elected, the Federal Council was exclusively Radical. This gives an impression of greater harmony

than was the case. The Council was the scene of bitter party disputes and close divisions. The Radicals, the *Freisinnige* and the Liberals were at each other's throats, but until 1891 didn't admit their Sonderbund enemies to their counsels, and then only a very moderate Catholic.

From 1891 *to* 1919 it contained six Radicals and one Catholic Conservative.

From 1919 *to* 1929. With the election of Musy in 1919 a second Catholic Conservative entered the Council—Ador, his predecessor, had been a Liberal of decided Conservative tendencies. This can be seen as a logical consequence of proportionality in the National Council. But there were still five Radicals, and after 1919 the Radicals had sunk to little more than one quarter of the National Council.

From 1929 *to* 1943. In 1929, a Farmer, Minger (a real peasant, in his own right) was elected to the Berne seat. The balance was now four Radicals, two K.K.s, one Farmer.

From 1943 to 1953. In 1943, as a reward for wartime loyalty, a Socialist was elected, Ernst Nobs, Mayor of Zurich. He was the successor in Zurich of Emil Klöti, also a Socialist, who would have made an excellent Federal Councillor. Nobs was succeeded in 1951 by Weber, who resigned in 1953 as a result of the rejection of the Finance Reform in a referendum. The seat passed out of Socialist hands, at first into the hands of a Radical from Zurich (Streuli) who was recognized as the best man in the country for the finance problem. The balance was thus temporarily again 4:2:0:1.

From 1954 *to* 1959. In the next year there were three retirements, of which two could be foreseen. The Socialists allied with the Catholics, an irresistible combination, to elect three Catholics, so the proportion stood at 3:3:0:1. The Socialists reckoned that the Radicals would be more prepared to sacrifice one seat to them if the Catholics did so also, and now aimed at two seats. It was not worth while sacrificing the advantages of opposition for a single seat.

In 1959[1] their opportunity came, and the proportion 2:2:2:1 was at last established.

(d) Religion

This is now taken care of automatically by the party constellations. The Catholic Conservatives naturally choose a Catholic, the Radicals and the Farmers a Protestant, and the Socialists a personality whose confessional loyalty is not too pronounced. If the Catholic Conservatives ever aspire to the Adenauer solution, the situation may

[1] Elections to the Federal Council are usually in December, and councillors then enter office some time in the following January: the dates given are those of formal election. The subsequent year could equally be given.

suddenly change. For the moment there are two Catholics and the remainder are lapsed or active Protestants, and this is the natural state of affairs. The confessional issue on the federal level has for long taken third place to social and economic problems. The relations of Church and State are, in any case, primarily a cantonal matter: on the federal level it is personnel-policy which is the only interesting 'religious' issue. The sleeping dog may, however, suddenly wake.

(e) Regionalism and Cantons

East Switzerland has a claim of a certain sort to a seat. There is also a claim, much more difficult to satisfy, for Geneva and Basle to have an occasional chance of office. Within eastern Switzerland all whole cantons have now had a turn, some of them had several turns.

Double-citizenship sometimes enables two cantonal birds to be killed with one stone, thus Feldmann had the citizenships of Berne and of Glarus, and Glarus felt honoured when he was elected to the 'Berne seat'.

(f) Experience[1]

The Assembly prefers candidates whom it knows, particularly those it knows but does not know too well. There is an informal *cursus honorum*—service in important standing committees and a quick rise to teller and to President of the Council. Experience on the cantonal level is some sort of substitute for membership of the Assembly, but it is best to combine the two, either simultaneously or by moving from the cantonal (or communal) level to the federal one. Occasionally a pressure group has brought members from quite outside the inner parliamentary circle (e.g. Kobelt in 1940), but without ever being conspicuously justified by the result. The overwhelming majority of past Federal Councillors, and the greatest, have served in one House of the Assembly or the other. There is no preference for the National Council over the Council of States in this respect.

The really important thing is that the magistrate should have, and retain, the support of his own party, and his own pressure group. Service as teller and President are the best evidence of this. A Federal Councillor who cannot persuade his own party (not in every case, but over the years) is no use to Parliament or to his colleagues.

2. *Personalities*

At any given time the constellations, especially as regards the four seats not appropriated to a particular canton, indicate more than one person. The choice of a magistrate then is determined by the

[1] Note Chaudet's career on page 57. Bringolf and Condrau might equally, at one time, have become Federal Councillors.

personality of the candidate. This does not mean that the 'best' candidate is chosen. There are two contradictory tendencies.

(a) Preference for the weaker candidate

There is a tendency for the less able man to be preferred to the abler: election, after all, is by the political opponents of the candidate. National Councillor Walther of Lucerne, 'the King-maker', achieved a certain bad eminence in choosing colourless candidates to represent other parties (e.g. Chuard instead of Maillefer in 1919). Needless to say this is a statement which can be proved by no one example, for there are always many factors involved, including the unpopularity of great men with their own party.

Such a choice may even serve the national interest—for there are democratic advantages in not making the Federal Council an aristocracy of merit, and in not packing one room with seven forceful personalities belonging to different parties. It is also in the interest of the Confederation that there should be greater men outside the executive than within it, and that some of these should sit in the Assembly.

In 1934 Herr Baumann, a lawyer-peasant from Appenzell, was chosen against Dr Ludwig of Basle (who did not properly satisfy the constellations). In the result, Baumann at the Ministry of Justice was faced with the greatest moral dilemma of the half-century—the admission of Jewish and political refugees from Nazi Germany—and by the greatest thugs of Europe. He made an unimpressive showing. In 1940 he was succeeded by Dr von Steiger,[1] a Bernese aristocrat.

---

[1] Concerning the election of von Steiger, there is an anecdote related by the Secretary of the agricultural lobby, Dr Laur, which opens up a further field of inquiry, namely the extent to which Federal Councillors are elected by, and depend on, their own pressure groups.

'We owe special gratitude to the Appenzeller Federal Councillor Baumann. Under him as head of the Department of Justice the new land law and the Law on the Removal of Indebtedness of Farming Homes were passed. His successor was the trusted agent (Vertrauensmann) of agriculture, Eduard von Steiger. In the decisive days of his election I was in hospital in Basle. Although I had hardly come round from the narcotics I had been given, I demanded access to the telephone. I succeeded thereby in persuading my friends that in the circumstances von Steiger was the right candidate. The election came off brilliantly, and our subsequent experience justified my action.'

(*Erinnerungen eines schweizerischen Bauernführers*. E. Laur, 1942.) Dr Laur's evidential value is not very great, and this story should be taken as evidence of what it is possible for the secretary of a lobby to say about himself, rather than as what actually happened. Steiger would probably have been elected in any case. The circumstances of besieged Switzerland, and not lobby pressure, were what helped agriculture.

By a neat vengeance of fate, the final word on the way in which these two acted as trustees for the honour of Swiss liberty was spoken by the same Professor Ludwig in the moving Report published in 1957. In the circumstances, the election of Baumann was a tragedy. It is curious to note that the war-time Federal Council, which was given far greater powers than any of its predecessors, was manned by a personnel unusually weak.

(b) *Opposite tendency: the best man can make his own rules*

The other possibility is that shown by Professor Wahlen's election, for the best candidate to make his own rules. The average capacity of Federal Councillors is certainly high, and the Council has often included one or more of the great men of Switzerland.

It is from the standpoint of the candidate that (of course) there is most often disappointment. Looking at the careers of parliamentarians, one repeatedly sees statesmen of great merit, who work through all the offices which usually are required for successful candidates—cantonal executive office, presidency of one of the legislative councils, membership of the three most important standing committees, and office in the party. Then the constellations shift, and they are left as mayors of a small town or as editors of a newspaper, while people of less merit hold the places for which they spent their lives preparing themselves. The corps of disappointed candidates is always more illustrious still than that of active and retired Federal Councillors.

RETIREMENT

It is well known that statesmen are not dismissed but 'retire', but when analysing institutions it is necessary to leave aside the circumlocutions of good taste. 'Federal Councillors are always re-elected so long as they choose to stand,' it is said, but one must add that if they are not going to be re-elected, they sensibly do not choose to stand. The admirable use made of the power, which election by the Assembly gives to party-leaders and fellow Federal Councillors, to 'take their colleague by the arm' and call to his mind the pleasures of retirement is a chief justification for parliamentary (rather than popular) election.

In the early days of the Confederation, no one pretended that an existing Councillor had a right to office. Two failed to be re-elected (Ochsenbein and Challet-Venel) and one committed suicide (Anderwert, 1880) in office. Existing tenants (Munzinger, Näff) had to fight hard to retain their position. Näff only secured election on the third round in 1866 because his opponent refused office. But he stayed at his post nevertheless from 1848 to 1875.

In recent years things have been arranged more smoothly. Hoffmann resigned in 1917 'of his own free will', that is to say, at the request of his colleagues[1] and in face of the anger of French Switzerland and France—he had apparently supported a separate peace between Russia and Germany. Forrer resigned 'of his own free will' also, less precipitately, when the defeat of the central powers seemed certain and an office had been found for him to retire into. Decoppet resigned in a similar manner two years later, having lost (unjustly) the confidence of French Switzerland during the war.

Musy resigned in 1934 for reasons which are variously given as his plans to tax *schnapps*, the political affiliation of his son, and private difficulties; after retirement he was elected for one legislature into the National Council, but on the next occasion failed to be elected. Loose from the moorings of office, he drifted into strange company. Pilet-Golaz enjoyed some of the sympathy of the National-Socialists, and dropped a hint on the wireless that he himself might be considered for the highest office if Switzerland adopted a more contemporary form of government—to express clearly the worst suspicions the case will bear. He resigned in November 1944.

Baumann did not face re-election in 1940. It is difficult to believe that his colleagues would not have 'taken him by the arm'—it was high time—if he had not retired, and it is possible that they did. Kobelt was chosen by a mysterious process that is still not quite explicable, in wartime, and was given the military department. He seems to have been on permanently bad terms with the General,[2] an interesting case of difficult civil-military relations. He only retired in 1954, but would surely have been willing to serve longer had his country called him. Celio retired to the Embassy at Rome in 1950: perhaps hints were dropped in his case also.

In 1953 Weber resigned as a result of the rejection of his department's proposal in a referendum. This was felt to be unusual. Two of his greatest predecessors, Stämpfli and Welti, had done so, and there are five apparent cases of premature retirement induced by disappointments at defeats in the Assembly or the country in the whole history of the Confederation—not always immediately after the defeat, or giving that as the reason.

---

[1] Motta was sent round to Hoffmann's house, where he found the family in tears, to ask for the letter of resignation. Hoffmann had it ready and handed it to Motta, his friend. It was Hoffmann's 60th birthday. See Aymon de Mestral, *Le Président Motta*, Lausanne, 1941 (p. 51).

[2] i.e. the Commander-in-Chief in time of war. See page 91.

Häberlin (1920–34) resigned as a result of a rebuff in 1934. On the other hand he had already in 1922 and 1927 accepted startling humiliations.

A matter which used to affect resignations more than at present was the availability of cosy international posts, for example, the directorship of the International Postal Bureau. But retired Federal Councillors now have a pension after five years and a diplomatic passport for life. Moreover, they are now usually provided for (especially if they are Radicals) by private enterprise, a comfortable directorship of heavy industry, for example. It remains to be seen what will be the occupation of retired Socialist Federal Councillors —perhaps a cantonal railway or bank directorship.

Professor Weber, after his resignation, sought election as a candidate for the National Council, and was 10,000 votes ahead of his next competitor and at the head of his party list. In a second election he was still ahead, but by a lesser margin. To rejoin the National Council also was felt to be unusual, and Musy's disappointment in a second election has been recalled. He has three other predecessors, however, as retired Federal Councillor in the National Council (Knüsel, Challet-Venel, Hammer), and a very successful predecessor in the Council of States (Lachenal, who made a reputation there). Weber was suggested as a candidate for re-election to the Federal Council in 1959, but this was vaguely felt to be un-Swiss.

The whole question of resignation from the Federal Council deserves a further study, based on a squadron of theses discovering the facts in particular cases.

In face of these examples it is not possible to talk as if Federal Councillors 'were always re-elected so long as they chose to stand' without qualification. The statement is false on more than one level. What remains true, however, is the stability of the Federal Council as a whole, and a certain relative stability of the individual Federal Councillor.

In form he is elected for four years, in practice he is morally entitled to about six (i.e. to have his turn as President, and a little more). But even within this period he must keep a life-line to the place which is the basis of his power, and keep at least a part of the public on his side. The atmosphere is not like the English judicial office—'public opinion be damned'. It is a truly political atmosphere, though with a strong tinge of the administrative.

This stability is not an institution 'on its own'. It corresponds to the form of parliamentary debates (as will be seen) where there is no procedure for expressing lack of confidence in the government as a whole. And it corresponds (historically,[1] as well as logically) to the institution of the referendum: the referendum makes a too-stable government tolerable for the citizen. Furthermore, it is a part of the whole pattern of Swiss social life—cantonal government everywhere has the same broad sort of executive-legislature-people relationship, for example, and so have many thousands of other public, semi-public, and private institutions.

---

[1] For example, the effect of introducing the referendum in the 1860s in Zurich was that an exciting political period suddenly passed into a calm one. Proportionality had the same effect. For a very intelligent discussion of the Swiss system as a whole, see Erwin Akeret, *Regierung und Regierungsform der Schweizerischen Eidgenossenschaft*. Zurich, 1940. It is a dissertation, but its author comes from a family with a political tradition. He is now in the National Council, and when asked in 1959 if he found anything to alter in the book, he replied that (so far as he remembered) he did not. In support of the general theme of the later part of this chapter, p. 113 should be noted, where Herr Akeret refers to the system of suggesting to the representative [of the parliamentary party] in the Federal Council very quietly ['in aller Stille'] that he should retire'. Although everyone who reflects must realize this is so, it is a statement which very rarely appears in print.

VIII
Other Elections by the Assembly

Election of the Federal Council is the most important of the recurring acts of the Assembly. The Assembly also undertakes a number of politically less important elections of high officers of state. To explain what these offices are takes longer than their importance warrants, but in explaining them some light is shed on the place of the Assembly in the Constitution.

These high officers of state elected by the Assembly are: the President of the Confederation and Vice-President of the Federal Council, the Chancellor of the Confederation, the Judges of the Supreme Court, and the General of the Federal Army. The Assembly also elects the President, Vice-President and Deputy Judges of the Supreme Court (Federal Tribunal), the Judges of the Federal Insurance Tribunal, and the Extraordinary Public Prosecutor and the Extraordinary Military Tribunal. The two latter have never in fact been appointed.

THE PRESIDENT OF THE CONFEDERATION

The President and the Vice-President are elected by the Assembly from among the members of the Federal Council. The convention has grown up that the offices shall rotate by seniority among members of the Federal Council, the Vice-President being regularly elected President. The Constitution only provides that the offices are to be held for one year, and that the retiring President cannot be President or Vice-President for the ensuing year, nor can the vice-presidency be held two years in succession. In the early years of the Confederation the wording of the Constitution was followed literally, and Furrer (1848–61), for example, was elected President in every third year, whereas Näff (1848–75) was elected President once in 1853, and never again.

In modern times, however, the Constitution has been supplemented by a rigid convention. The convention is: (1) when the President retires, he goes to the bottom of the list of existing members; (2) the Vice-President for the preceding year is now elected President; and (3) the new Vice-President is the member who is now at the top of the list. In determining who is at the top are counted (4) seniority as a member of the Federal Council, and (5) as between members elected on the same day, the order of election. (6) The newly elected member ranks below the retiring President of the year of his election.

It is generally felt to be fair that a Federal Councillor can continue in office, even if he is not very competent, until he has been President once. Ador, elected as a stop-gap after Hoffmann's resignation, was a very old man, and was allowed to jump the queue and be President in his third year of office, only eighteen months after his election. He was in a position to make his own conditions, and had stipulated for the Political Department vacated by Hoffmann (against the lively opposition of Schulthess, who wanted that post). It is possible that he informally stipulated for the presidency also,[1] intending to retire at the end of his year as President.

Apart from this exception, the presidency has in recent years rotated regularly, including a Socialist President, Bundesrat Nobs. If the Assembly were at loggerheads with a member of the Federal Council, it presumably could still pass over his name when his turn as President came, and perhaps thus force his resignation. But matters now never reach this stage.

The presidency has not always been a merely titular office. In 1848 it was envisaged as a very powerful post—an approach to the office of Landamman of Switzerland during the Napoleonic period—so powerful indeed that the office must not be left too long in the same hands. The President had 'the political functions' and a special presidential office, the 'Political Department'. The way things worked out, however, was that the President's powers to restore order in the interior were not needed, and in practice were exercised by the appropriate specialized department and by the Council as a whole. The Political Department became then little more than a Foreign Affairs department. Neutrality, and a certain torpor (which lost Switzerland the opportunity to acquire two new provinces, Chablais and Faucigny at the time when Napoleon III acquired Savoy) made a rotating foreign office possible.

In 1887, however, Numa Droz was President and, as such, foreign minister. He enjoyed his functions, and the next in the line for the presidency dreaded them, for he could not speak French at all well.

[1] Müller, whose turn it was for the presidency, resigned, it is said, in a huff. He had three times been President, but it is natural to wish to hold that office a last time before retiring. 'I do not think the slight pressure exerted to retain his renunciation of the presidency for 1919, in favour of Ador, had much influence on his decision' to resign, wrote the General Secretary of the Radical Party from 1919–46, 'but I admit others may be justified in thinking otherwise'. Dr Ernst Steinmann, *Aus Zeit und Streit* (incomplete autobiography). Berne, 1953.

So the experiment (which required legislation) was made of dissociating the presidency from Foreign Affairs. The Political Department continued with Numa Droz, and the presidency to rotate. At the same time the interior political functions of the Political Department were divided among the other departments, who in their turn lost some of their functions in the negotiation of treaties in their own sphere. It is thus that the Swiss foreign office acquired its peculiar name.

When Droz retired in 1892, the old system was restored in that the presidency was linked with the Political Department again. The old system had its advantages because it forced a certain rotation of department among the Federal Councillors—each member became familiar with three departments at the least (as a rule), though it was sometimes the practice to victimize a new member by electing him each year to the department the President of the year had vacated. Schobinger (1908–11), for example, having spent thirty-four years in a single cantonal ministry—the department of Public Works in Lucerne—during little more than three years in the Federal Council occupied four different departments, and died in office. Then, as now, election to a particular department was in the hands of the Federal Council, which in practice respected the claims of seniority.

The old system was said to have enabled the Council to act as a college in a more real sense: under the modern revival of the Droz system a member may only know a single department, and is unlikely to know more than two, and this implies he has no means of controlling the assertions of his colleagues. The whole field is open to dispute: the problem of collegiality is discussed below.

In 1914 Hoffmann was President, and in charge of external affairs in that fateful year. It was natural to continue him in office at such a time, and he seems to have acquired a certain pre-eminence even among the exceptionally able Cabinet of that time. In 1917 came the disaster, with Hoffmann's incursion into high politics and his swift retirement at the request of his colleagues. Instead of going to Schulthess, then President, the Political Department went to Ador, Hoffmann's replacement.

Ador was a little old for the task. 'I live in a dream,' he wrote pathetically. 'My life is like a cinema, people flashing before me, hour by hour, each talking of a different matter. It is enough to break my head.'[1] Elected President for 1918, he took the Department of the Interior while Calonder took over foreign affairs. Ador however did not settle down to the day by day routine of a head

---

[1] See Frédéric Barbey. *Un homme d'état suisse. Gustave Ador.* Geneva. 1945.

clerk,[1] but regarded himself as primarily a statesman, with his chief interest still in international matters. Motta succeeded Calonder, and took over the Political Department with the presidency, but retained that department when his year was up. He continued in the Political Department until his death in office in 1940, when Pilet-Golaz (who happened to be President that year) took over his department. Pilet was the Hoffmann of 1939–45, and retired prematurely in 1944. His place was taken by Petitpierre, who was elected as his replacement in the Federal Council. Petitpierre is still there in 1960. [He retired in 1961, and was succeeded by Wahlen, then President, in the Political Department.]

Apart from Droz himself, Petitpierre is the first real success in that role. Hoffmann seriously endangered neutrality, the essential theme of Swiss policy at that time. Motta as an Italian Swiss felt Italy to be his second spiritual home, and studied at a German university and acquired a great respect for that country. This scale of preferences was more suited to the 1920s than to the 1930s, and Motta outstayed his greatness. Starting as the idealist who led Switzerland into the League of Nations, he ended up as the darling of the right wing who led Switzerland out of it. His reputation would be easier to assess had he gone to another department after ten years. Pilet-Golaz, again, was not the ideal statesman for the foreign affairs of a neutral country, though not ill suited to the situation of Switzerland as an island of liberty in a sea of slavery, a situation requiring a certain flexibility in contact with Nazis. But Petitpierre, a solicitor from Neuchâtel, has increased his reputation by a long and uncontroversial tenure of high office. Nevertheless, after fifteen years it would not be felt a national disaster were he to stay in the Cabinet in another capacity and use his experience to advise his successor. [These remarks were written in 1960.] The 'Droz system' is still not beyond the reach of controversy.

Under the new system, the presidency is an empty title, apart from the following attributions:

(i) 'Representation of the Confederation at home and abroad'—though there is not much difference between his representative capacity and that of any other Federal Councillor: it is usual for two councillors, of whom one may or may not be the President, to perform these functions—inspecting troops in the rain and shaking hands with the King of Siam or the Prince of Monaco.

---

[1] Steinmann (cited p. 85). The Hoffmann case has been described several times, notably in George Soloveytchik's entertaining book *Switzerland in Perspective*, Oxford, 1954. I should like to express my agreement with the general description of Swiss foreign policy expressed there.

(ii) He has a special relationship with the Federal Chancery, and a responsibility for the business of the Federal Council—that the right documents are there, and the agenda are in order.

(iii) Certain emergency and delegated powers (Law of 1914 on the Organization of Federal Administration, article 16). These might some day prove important.

(iv) The chairmanship of the Federal Council itself, and the casting vote in it. Votes are, however, now seldom taken. In early years the casting vote was important.[1]

THE CHANCELLOR OF THE CONFEDERATION

The Diet of 1814 inherited from its predecessors the office of Federal Chancellor, and inherited also the person who occupied that post under the Napoleonic régime, Chancellor Mousson. This remarkable man had first held office under the Helvétique, and then under every subsequent régime until his retirement in 1830. The Federal Pact of 1815 duly provided for the office of Chancellor,[2] and also for that of Clerk of State (*Staatsschreiber*). As the Chancellor was a French-speaking Protestant, the Clerk was a German-speaking Roman Catholic. The two officials were each (after 1816) elected for two years, one each year in order to preserve continuity. In practice, the two officers were regularly re-elected. From an entry in the Decisions of the Diet for 1840, it is clear that the Chancellor took part in the discussions in an advisory capacity, but had no vote—he had claimed a casting vote unsuccessfully.

Mousson resigned in 1830, having obtained the election of his son as Clerk, and the previous clerk (Amrhyn, a Catholic) moved up to Chancellor. The son did not stay the course, and in 1833 August von Gonzenbach took his place as Clerk. Meanwhile the Chancery expanded quietly, there is mention of assistant clerks, of a Registrar, of an Archivist.

Gonzenbach, though a Protestant, was a high Tory, and came into conflict with the Diet. A certain Ulrich Schiess was elected in his

---

[1] In the 1860s when the President was absent it was necessary to cast lots in order to come to a decision. See Hermann Böschenstein, *Bundesrat Carl Schenk, 1823–1895*. Berne, 1946.

[2] Though there were no purely federal offices apart from the Chancery (unless a special commissioner or a General were appointed in an emergency), the civil service of the canton which was for the time the capital-city (*Vorort*) provided an executive for the Diet. Special arrangements were made by the cantons when their turn as *Vorort* came to obviate the confusion of authorities. Had the Sonderbund War been a little delayed, Lucerne would have been the *Vorort*. Then the fat would have been in the fire.

place. Then, in 1847, the Diet resolved on war with Lucerne and the Sonderbund. Amrhyn, a Lucerne patrician, could not bring himself to countersign the attack on his fatherland, so resigned. Schiess moved up into *his* place, and a Catholic was elected as Clerk until the new Constitution should come into force.

When the new Constitution, however, was drafted, there was no Constitutional provision for a Clerk of State. Schiess ruled the roost alone, and continued in office until the end of 1881, so that he countersigned both Federal Constitutions. His successor was expected to live a few years only, but in fact survived many of those who elected him.

In all there have been eight Chancellors since 1848. Election is by the two Chambers in joint session, and takes place immediately after election of the Federal Council and of the President and Vice-President—the retiring Chancellor being regularly re-elected until he reaches the time of retirement. In practice one of the Vice-Chancellors is understood to be the successor designate. The only time the election has been of importance was the occasion of Chancellor Leimgruber's election in 1943. Herr Leimgruber was a Catholic, and until then all Chancellors since 1848 had been Protestants. The election was important because it was the occasion of a shift of alliances between the parties in the Assembly: the Socialists supported the Catholic Conservatives, and the anti-Socialist *bourgeois* block broke. Since then there has been a regular understanding between the Social Democrats and the left, or social, wing of the Conservatives (the 'Christian Socialists').

The curious thing about the chancellorship is that it has neither proved the germ, nor the head of the federal Civil Service, but just a dead branch. The Chancellor is secretary of the Federal Council, he (and a Vice-Chancellor) is secretary of both Chambers and of the Chambers in joint session. He has the duty 'of preparing laws and decrees on the organization of federal administration', 'of securing economy in the Federal Administration', and of 'giving information to the Press' and he has a special position as regards the Assembly by which he is elected and with whose members he comes into contact. Of all this successive Chancellors have made nothing. Federal Councillors take advice in their departments, and not from the Chancellor, who does not speak in the Federal Council. The holder of what might have been the most illustrious office in the Confederation, an office which for almost two generations *was* the Confederation, writes *procès-verbaux* in longhand during the sessions of the Federal and National Councils, and that is almost his sole political activity.

The reason why nothing has been made of this little kingdom, while empires have risen under newer dynasties, is partly, no doubt, the personal character of the early holders of the office. But more important is that the Chancery never managed to get a stranglehold on business, in the way the British Treasury has: it had no sanction to back its demands. The intention, no doubt, was that it should be backed by the power of the President. But the presidency proved a broken reed. The person who could influence the President, moreover, was the President's adviser in foreign affairs and not the Chancellor. In each department the staff of the personal secretary of the departmental chief silently proliferated, so that by the end of the nineteenth century there were seven flourishing administrative staffs sprung from the assistants of the seven secretaries to the Federal Councillors, while the Chancery (intended as the seedling of the future Civil Service) remained a dead twig. Even among the services that have sprung up in connexion with the Federal Assembly the Chancellor cuts no great figure. The Secretary of the Assembly, the Secretary of the Joint Finance Delegation, the head of the Organization and Administration Section of the Finance Department, all hold offices of growing political importance. But the chancellorship is merely dignified—a pleasant and highly honourable office to hold, and very little more.

JUDGES OF THE FEDERAL TRIBUNAL

The Judges of the Federal Tribunal (Supreme Court) are elected by the Assembly in joint session, for a term of six years. Willing candidates are regularly re-elected. The actual procedure is for the 'Committee of Presidents' (of parliamentary parties) to agree on new candidates,[1] so that the party balance on the bench is preserved. It must be repeated that in Switzerland party affiliation is as much a matter of status—religion, place of residence, etc.—as of opinion, so there is no need to be a partisan in order to be elected on a party ticket: the important thing is to satisfy the 'constellations'. The political election, on the federal level, does not lead to any difficulties or lower the standard of the bench. On the whole, it guarantees a high standard by making it possible and usual for academic lawyers to be chosen. But the judicial career, and the legal profession generally, are so different from the English that comparison is not very fruitful.

There is no supervision by the Courts, of federal legislation.

---

[1] See the illustration on page 190.

OTHER ELECTIONS BY THE ASSEMBLY
THE GENERAL

In times when war threatens, a General is elected by the Assembly, on the proposal of the Federal Council. Generals have been elected in 1849 and 1856 (Dufour), 1870 (Herzog), 1914 (Wille), and 1939 (Guisan). In 1914, there was a disputed election, but the Federal Council's candidate was successful over the opposition's (Colonel von Sprecher). General Wille was unpopular, a Prussian trained officer, more efficient than diplomatic. Guisan (1939–45), however, was universally admired, and became a sort of father-figure to the nation —a cult with rather curious manifestations. Above all, Guisan rallied the country in a decisive moment to defend itself and not to fall silently under Hitler's influence. History has applauded his courage. At that time only the General could have done this, and Guisan, a *chevalier sans peur et sans reproche*, did it better than anyone else could have done.

The institution seems to break every rule of civil-military relations, and even of military efficiency, but has, in a sense, justified itself by this one action of Guisan's.

Other elections. None of these calls for any comment. The Insurance Tribunal, at Lucerne, is concerned with the state social insurances.

IX

The Federal Council at Work

The work of Federal Councillors can be classified under three heads—ceremonial, political and administrative.

CEREMONIAL ACTIVITIES

1. *Representing the State*

There are few countries so under-developed as not to have an ambassador, and all the incidentals, at Berne. The formalities of diplomacy—the reception of letters of credence, the polite phrase, the posing for a photograph of hands being shaken or cocktails being sipped, and attendance on national days at obscure and illustrious embassies—are entrusted to one or to two Federal Councillors for the occasion. These duties are shared on a rota: they are not exclusively a burden on the President of the Confederation.

The tradition is that the President of the Confederation does not travel abroad to make state-visits, and Ador was criticized on the grounds that he had done this in 1918—the incident was due to a misunderstanding. Individual Federal Councillors do sometimes travel, to conferences or meetings, and more especially since there is no League of Nations today in Geneva. In recent years they have sometimes been criticized for doing this too much.

2. *Attendance at domestic ceremonies*

To every important shooting competition or singing feast or 350th anniversary a Federal Councillor is invited. The more significant occasions see two or even three Councillors, and on rare great festivities the whole executive college attends. An individual Councillor may have two or three half-days a week devoted to such duties, and for this purpose the week includes Sundays. Officials never cease to be surprised at this readiness to attend trivial celebrations, and deplore it as a waste of time. But Federal Councillors evidently feel such public appearances to be vital, and even those go who evidently do not much enjoy these things. Perhaps pity is out of place: these may be the rewards of office rather than the burden. Certainly the influence of the Federal Council in the country as a whole is increased by the personal attendances of Federal Councillors, and, irritating though they may find it, they would presumably be more annoyed if they were not invited. One wonders whether there is not a little competitiveness between Councillors, and between the parties and interests which they represent.

POLITICAL ACTIVITIES

1. *Attendances before the Chambers*

This is an activity which undoubtedly takes up much time. During the sessions of the Chambers there is always one Federal Councillor sitting in each House listening to the debate, and the Assembly sits for about fourteen weeks in the year. The offices of five of the Federal Councillors are close to the Chambers, with communication under cover and on the same level, and each has a small loud-speaker in his room so that he can follow the debate, if he cares, from his office. As the subject of debate changes, one Federal Councillor relieves the other in the Chamber.

It used to be the practice for two Federal Councillors to attend each House. They then, of course, sometimes disagreed, and this was a great moment for the spectator.[1] It is now only when the Assembly is in joint session, or at the sessional 'Question Hour' in the National Council, that more than one Federal Councillor is present.

2. *Activity as member of a political party*

When a statesman is elected to the Federal Council he does not break the connexion with his own political party. On the contrary, if it was loose in the past, he makes it closer now. The support of the party is essential to his own personal position, and it is, as it were, the dowry he brings into the family circle of the Cabinet—he would be no use to his colleagues if he could not, over the years, carry his parliamentary party with him. The system would break down if the link between party and the executive were snapped.

The parliamentary parties hold regular meetings during the session, with members of the two houses sitting together without distinction. They admit only their own journalists (as a rule), but the meetings are discreetly reported nevertheless in the Press. At these meetings the same procedure is followed as in the Assembly, though with less formality. For example, bills pass through the three stages of debate

---

[1] Sir Francis Adams and C. D. Cunningham, *The Swiss Confederation*. London, 1889. This is a valuable work for the history of the Confederation, being based on fresh observation and written with the collaboration of experts of the greatest distinction—including, for example, both Bryce and Dicey. It gives a lively impression of Switzerland in the 1880s.

which they do in the whole House. At these miniature debates, also, Federal Councillors play the same part as they do in the whole House. The difference is that only Federal Councillors *of the party* attend, so that one or two Federal Councillors must reply to questions concerning all departments, and represent to their party the collective views of the Federal Council as a whole. Occasionally they lead their party to understand that they themselves were voted down in the Cabinet Chamber. Sometimes they may use their party to give weight to their voice in Cabinet as against their colleagues, at other times they may put themselves at the service of their colleagues in the Cabinet to 'talk their party round'. 'A loyal indiscretion' is the classic statement of the attitude of Federal Councillors, torn between the collegiate principle of the executive and their allegiance to a particular section of the Assembly, or to a pressure group outside it.[1]

During the period 1953–1960, when the Socialists had no Federal Councillor, they occasionally requested a Councillor not of their party to attend, and explain the Government's proposals. These invitations were accepted.

At such meetings, the members of the party who sit in a committee will also act as if the meeting were a miniature committee-stage of the bill. They, too, will have a conflict of loyalties between their own private views and the views of their colleagues on the committee, to which they have subscribed at the committee table.

[1] A curious example of the relations between a Federal Councillor and the pressure group which he represents is the incident in 1936 related by the Secretary of the Farmers' *Verband* in Brugg, Dr Laur:

> We (the *Bauernsekretariat*) represented the point of view that, although the consequences of devaluation of the Swiss franc could not be accurately foreseen, it was probable that the disadvantages would outweigh the advantages—for agriculture at least. A confidential [!] memorandum from ex-Federal Councillor Schulthess, on the other hand, recommended the Federal Council to devalue. I had a talk with Bundesrat Minger, and got the impression the Federal Council were going to change their minds. I laid before Minger the reasons against devaluation, and explained that agriculture in particular did not stand to gain from it. But it was too late. Bundesrat Obrecht had already won a majority of his colleagues for devaluation. . . . On the 25 Sept 1936 it was still being said that the Federal Council would reject it. On the next day I suddenly had a feeling that all was not going well in Berne. I tried to get Minger on the 'phone. The reply was that he was in an Extraordinary Session of the Federal Council. When at last I got through he told me that the decision had just been taken to devalue, against the advice of the Head of the Finance Department (Bundesrat Meyer) and the Chairman of Directors of the Swiss National Bank (*Erinnerungen*, 1st ed., p. 219).

Dr Laur held no official position at all. Federal Councillor Meyer, whose objection to devaluation was widely known, did not resign until two years later. Minger was the Farmers' Party representative in the Federal Council.

Federal Councillors maintain a connexion of a more reserved sort with their mass parties and, of course, with the canton which they represent. Needless to say, they give up all other employment and directorships during their tenure of office. A Councillor does not need to be popular in the whole country, but it is essential for him to retain the confidence of the interests which originally backed him; this is his *'Hausmacht'*.

ADMINISTRATIVE ACTIVITIES

1. *As members of the Council*

The Federal Council usually meets twice a week. Occasionally a drive to reduce work gets the number of annual meetings below 100, and occasionally pressure or bad management drives it higher, but twice a week, in the morning, is usual. Meetings usually leave a trace in the *Feuille Fédérale*, which records the business performed. Occasionally annual figures are published of meetings and decisions (e.g. 2,000 items of business a year—the average load is a little heavier than this), but it is difficult to attach precise meaning to such figures.

The meetings are held in the grotesquely ornate room set aside for the purpose in Bundeshaus West. They are usually at 9 a.m. and last until some time between 11 and 12.30 a.m. Gathering first in an ante-room, the seven Federal Councillors, the Chancellor and a Vice-Chancellor then seat themselves on as many thrones set in front of desks upon which are the relevant documents and lists. The outer door of the ante-room is left open, as a sign that the supreme council is in session. No officials attend, though occasionally a high civil servant, e.g. from the Political Department, or, in time of war, the General or a high officer from the Food Office, has been present. Proceedings are strictly secret. All that is published officially, and notified at once to waiting journalists by the Chancellor, is the list of decisions taken.

As regards the proceedings in the Cabinet Chamber, the following description is derived from the Federal Chancellor. 'If a department wants to bring a proposal (*Antrag*) before the Federal Council, it normally does so in writing. The *Antrag* is handed to the Federal Chancellor. If it is an important matter, the six other heads of department have a copy sent to them direct. If it seems to the Chancellor that there are other departments which should be consulted, he sends them the *Antrag* for an Additional Report (*Mitbericht*). This especially often happens in the case of the Finance Department—and always when the proposition involves an outlay.

'On the basis of this *Antrag*, and of any Supplementary Reports, the Chancellor makes out the agenda. He hands the President of the Confederation the complete file of all the items.

'At the opening of the session of the Federal Council the Head of the Political Department reports (if the circumstances call for such a report) on the general situation. If necessary this report is discussed. After this the President of the Confederation presents the *Vorlagen*, one after the other—they are *not* therefore presented by the Head of the Department [as I had thought. C.J.H.]. It depends on the personality, and on the burden of work, of the President whether he has himself minuted all the problems, or whether he has left this task to a departmental official or, on occasion, to the Federal Chancellor.

'Most of the *Anträge*, of course, are not discussed at all. To take an imaginary example: the President will say "Proposition of the Political Department to concede *agrément* to the new Ruritanian Ambassador. The man is all right. No suspicions or reservations". A look round the circle: no one asks to speak. "Accepted". In this manner one item after the other is settled, though, of course, there may be a longer or shorter discussion about some things. At the end come the general remarks (*allgemeine Aussprache*). In exceptional cases, and when it is really urgent, the Federal Council discusses concrete items even without written reports.'

Not only substantial business, but also appointments in the Civil Service are made by the Federal Council.[1] There is also some judicial business—the administrative justice of the Federal Council—on which the report of the Department of Justice is considered, and usually followed. The Law provides that a majority decision shall be taken, voting by raised hands, but although there is evidence of this being done in the past, it seems that now this method is rarely used. Until 1945 only final decisions were recorded. It was impossible, for example, when compiling the Ludwig Report[2] on the treatment of refugees to find how frequently or for how long the Council had discussed the question. There was no record.

The complaint is often made that the Federal Council can find no time to discuss policy in general, apart from individual items of business. This complaint would seem to be based on a misunder-

[1] The Swiss Civil Service differs radically from the German in that appointment is for four years at a time only. There is no legal claim to be re-elected, but the decision must not be 'arbitrary'. Dismissals (i.e. refusal to re-elect) are not unknown, especially of Communists and suspected Communists. The Federal Service is not divided into an 'administrative' and an 'executive', &c. class—though graduates can expect a higher initial appointment.

[2] Ludwig Report (cited, p. 36), p. 362, French edition.

standing: there is no such thing as policy in the abstract. The business of the Federal Council in plenary session is to take decisions for the Chancellor and Secretary to record.[1]

In addition to the main Cabinet council, there are several committees, of three or four members. These are of greater or lesser formality, sometimes having formal power to make reports to the whole council, sometimes being more in the nature of an *ad hoc* conspiracy. Permanent 'delegations' composed of Federal Councillors are provided for by the Law of 1914 on Organization which gives the Council power to set up other *ad hoc* delegations. Using this as a basis, the Federal Council in 1919 set up a Delegation for Foreign Affairs, evidently as part of the decision to go back to 'the Droz system'. The number of sessions of this delegation is recorded for some years in the *Rapport de Gestion*: it is clear that it met once or twice a year only. There is said to be a Delegation for Military Affairs at the present day which actually meets.

One reason why these committees of council are not much used is because as institutions they are superfluous, even though they may sometimes solve a difficult personal equation. The rooms of three of the Councillors are practically adjoining in Bundeshaus West, and the others are very close. The Councillors meet often, and the college may sometimes continue for half a dozen years without much change in composition. Lonely in high office, Federal Councillors get to know each other, officially, well. Several, but not all, Councillors address each other as 'Du' (information conflicts on this simple point). They can, at all events, easily drop in on one another for a cup of luke-warm coffee served in the office, and frequently do so. It should be added that there will be personal contacts amongst many of their senior subordinates, members of the same student corporations, comrades in shooting practices and so on, as well as in more formal committees on that level. Official life is on a much smaller scale than in Whitehall.

[1] E.g. Report on Gestion for 1937, 'In recent years, the pressure of work has increased to such an extent that the Federal Council has often had no time in its ordinary sessions to discuss important problems of general policy that needed consideration. Extra sessions had therefore to be held, which interfered with the departmental business of Councillors. The Council tried to get over this by delegating powers to the President and, by doing this, managed to cut down the time spent on current business. The result was that, whereas in 1936 it needed 114 sessions to deal with 2182 items of business, in 1937 it only needed 92 sessions to deal with 2183 items. In this way,' the Report adds naïvely, 'it won time to deal with questions of general policy.' The figures quoted, however, show that it merely met less often, and Councillors spent the time in the departments.

2. As Head of a Department

A Federal Councillor is more of a civil servant, and rather less of a politician, than his British ministerial counterpart, and spends a long time as head of a department doing ordinary administrative work—being, in fact, his own permanent secretary. This activity is regarded as extremely important, and a councillor who neglected it would lose the respect of his subordinates. Perhaps it amounts in all to half his activity, all others combined taking roughly the same time as his departmental duties.

Towards the end of the last century, Federal Councillor Ruchonnet exclaimed: 'There is no Federal Council—there are only Federal Councillors,' and his words have often been repeated since. The danger of the Swiss system, however, would not seem to be lack of co-ordination between departments, each pursuing its own policy, but too great a predominance of the 'executive frame of mind'. *Sachlichkeit*, the virtue of the good civil servant, is accorded too great a prestige. There is a sort of policy in having no policy, but it means in practice the unconscious adoption of values which seem unquestionable only because they are accepted by one's middle class elder contemporaries. The weakness of the practice of *Sachlichkeit* is that it assumes as best something which is in fact only second best, namely uncontroversial administration.

The trouble with Swiss public life is not that the Federal Council never finds time to discuss the great issues of public policy, but that no one discusses them. There is too cosy an acceptance of urban Protestant middle-class values. The other factors in society, the Church, the Land, Labour, regard themselves as pressure groups—with a bad conscience because they are out for their own hand—and do not try to win Switzerland to their own values, but rather try to ensure that they each get their share of the winnings. This is the strength of Switzerland, and also the *malaise*: the point is that it is not concentrated upon the Federal Council, but is endemic in Swiss society.

Furthermore, the Swiss constitutional system *assumes* that the Federal Council will have no policy as a college. There are sanctions which can be brought against an individual Federal Councillor. Life can be made intolerable for him, and he can be forced to resign.[1] But the Federal Council as a whole cannot be forced to resign: it is not a parliamentary Cabinet. It follows that the Federal Council can formulate no policy, for policy implies anti-policy. Put in another way, there is no procedure for indicting the Federal Council. It can

[1] This is the argument of Chapter XII. On the cantonal level, the resignation of Tettamenti in the Ticino in 1960 can be cited.

do no wrong in the sense that the British king can do no wrong; therefore it can do nothing (in a democracy) that implies a policy. So it does not waste its time in discussing policy in the abstract.

DO FEDERAL COUNCILLORS OVERWORK?

Bundesrat Munzinger (1848–55) worked himself to death in the endeavour to get the accounts of the Confederation to balance, and in the meanwhile checked the books of the Confederation, and presumably the cash balance, himself, monthly. The first federal Cabinet spent three months deciding on the design for the one-franc piece—Munzinger having to refurbish his school Latin in order to decide on the inscription[1]—and there were debates on whether the bosom of the young lady representing Helvetia was not a little too prominent. The point is, that it is always possible to overwork oneself, even if there is nothing to do. It depends on the character of the minister, and on the climate of opinion. Switzerland still clings to the habits of a very small country, the good as well as the bad. A Federal Councillor turns up at the office, perhaps travelling by public transport, at 8 a.m. 'The Herr Bundesrat himself, I must admit, always sets the best example' a high official told the writer. It is a luxury which could be given up if Councillors died too fast. At the moment, while some kill themselves in office in five years, others are willing to soldier on after three or four legislative periods. Kobelt and Etter appeared to be reluctant to retire after fifteen and fourteen years respectively, and others have spent as long or still longer in office: for example Motta (1911–40), Schulthess (1911–35), Musy (1919–34), Häberlin (1920–34), Pilet-Golaz (1928–44), and Petitpierre (1944–61).

A continual source of dismay to officials is the time Federal Councillors spend cultivating public opinion. It is significant of the nature of the office that no Councillor forgoes these activities, though some (often the more able) perform them with bad grace. Attendance at debates in the Assembly, similarly, is regarded by officials as a waste of the time of their head of Department.

Federal Councillors themselves sometimes take this attitude.[2] A

[1] The eventual inscription was simply 'Helvetia', so much scholarship was in vain. See the biography of Munzinger by Dr Hans Häfliger. *Bundesrat Josef Munzinger*, Solothurn 1953.

[2] In 1947, for example, Federal Councillor Stampfli, on the verge of retirement exclaimed in the National Council, 'Once more I have had to ask myself what I have done wrong that I should be condemned to the tortures of Tantalus by virtue of my office, and be made to sit through such an endless and useless debate.' (*Sten. Bull.* N.R. 1947. 489.q. in Eichenberger, p. 182.) Parliamentary processes,

new rank of civil servant has therefore been unofficially proposed, the 'Secretary of State'. This is not, as the Englishman would expect, to relieve the Federal Councillor of his office-boy work, but to relieve him of his political activity attending debates:[1] nothing could be more typical of the Swiss worship of *Sachlichkeit* than to regard the signing of papers prepared by officials as the real work of a statesman, while educating public opinion can be left to a subordinate.

---

[1] During both world wars, senior civil servants have in fact, by permission, appeared before the Chambers to defend their policies—in particular Herr Käppeli of the Food Office during the last war.

---

it appears, are a waste of time for such an important person as a Federal Councillor. Stampfli (1940-47) had been a Cantonal and a National Councillor but his habit of mind was formed in heavy industry. 'The matter has been settled behind the scenes, so why discuss it in public?' seems to be his reasoning.

X
Legislation

The word 'Law' is a technical term in the federal Parliament. 'Laws' are subject to the referendum-challenge (the petition of 30,000) and cannot be withdrawn from it. There is, however, an alternative form of statute, the Federal arrêté. Federal arrêtés which are declared to be '*de portée générale*' are subject to the referendum like laws. But until 1949 federal arrêtés which were *not* declared *de portée générale*, or which were declared 'urgent', were *not* subject to the referendum-challenge: in fact, these forms were used as a device to withdraw legislation from it.[1]

Before 1875 laws were distinguished from arrêtés by their greater importance, though in practice often no good reason can be found for the one or the other form being used. After 1875 the question of the referendum has been the most important consideration, though in general the practice is to amend Laws by Laws, and arrêtés by arrêtés. Apart from the procedure for resolving urgency or 'universal applicability' there is no procedural difference between the two. Both can be discussed under the heading 'legislation'.

Legislative procedure in the whole House is regulated by the Standing Orders (and by the Law on the Councils, with some details fixed by the Constitution). But the remainder of the stages that lie between drafting and enactment are not regulated by any written instrument at all. However, a procedure has grown up which governs the pre-parliamentary stages and is now almost fixed. In its outlines it is older than the present century, and it is even alluded to in a recent amendment of the Constitution.[2]

[1] By a recent revision of Article 89 *bis* of the Constitution (11 Sept 1949) a majority of the total number of members in each Council—this is a rather difficult requirement to fulfil sometimes—can resolve 'urgency', and arrêtés go immediately into force instead of waiting for three months to give an opportunity for them to be challenged. But a referendum can still be demanded, in which case the arrêté goes out of force within one year unless confirmed by a popular vote at a referendum within that time. The 'urgency' loophole is therefore now stopped, and the Constitution has lost some of its elasticity thereby. However, the climate of opinion has also changed, and is now against withdrawing statutes from the referendum. The device was much used in war-time and during the depression of the 1930s.

[2] Article 32 of the Constitution, which affects the 'Economic Articles' of 1947, provides that:
  The Cantons shall be consulted in the drafting of the Laws carrying out these

STAGES OF LEGISLATIVE PROCEDURE

The stages a law passes through are the following:
(a) The pre-parliamentary stages;
   1. The initiative
   2. The departmental draft, and submission to the responsible Federal Councillor
   3. (i) Consultation with interests and cantons
      (ii) The Committee of Experts
      (iii) The Conference of Directors
   4. Preparation of the final draft, and submission to the Federal Council
   5. The official Draft Bill and Message
(b) The parliamentary stages;
   6. The committee of the First Chamber
   7. Consideration by the parliamentary parties
   8. Consideration on the floor of the First Chamber
   9. Committee of Second Chamber
   10. Floor of the Second Chamber
   (11. Divergences between the Chambers, if any)
   12. Committee of Redaction
(c) The post-parliamentary stages;
   (13. The referendum, if challenged)
   14. Interpretation in legal literature and the courts
   15. Delegated and consequential legislation; Credits.

The stages are best described by reference to an actual example. This will be the first time that the genesis of a particular law has been publicly described in this manner, after unrestricted access to all the relevant documents that it seemed necessary to consult. To protect anonymity the officials concerned have been given invented names.

The example chosen is the Law on the Contract of Agency (*Agenturvertragsgesetz*) of 4 Feb 1949.[1] It was chosen as an example

---

[1] Even when the Federal Code of Obligations of 1883 (which codifies the law of contract) was revised in 1911 there was still no mention of a special contract of agency. The profession of agent had not yet forced itself on public attention, and the courts had dealt with the practical problems satisfactorily. At first they did so by wholesale borrowings from German statute law (the *Handelsgesetzbuch*), 'presuming' that the parties had intended to incorporate German law in their

---

Articles. As a general rule they shall be entrusted with the execution of the federal provisions.

The economic groups concerned shall be consulted during the drafting of the laws carrying out these Articles and may be called upon to help apply the regulations.

of a bill of reasonable length, which required consultation of interests, of which the story could be told without embarrassing any living person, and where investigation did not infringe the rules of official secrecy. It is untypical only in that no consultation of the cantons was required.

(*a*) *The Pre-Parliamentary Stages*
1. The Initiative (*Die Anregung*)

Most laws start with a postulate or motion in the Assembly, formulated in general terms. There is no reason why a Member of Parliament should not formulate the motion as an actual draft but this is in practice never done.

In the case of the Law of Agency, the initiator was an interest-group—the *Verband der kaufmännischen Agenten der Schweiz*, the Agents' Union. This union had been founded in 1909 and had long sought statutory regulation of the contract of agency. In the 1930s it formed an 'Action Committee to Fix the Rights and Duties of Independent Representatives and Agents' of which Herr Mathys was the chairman. The initiative came from this committee.

The committee did not (as it might have done) contact a friendly deputy but went straight to the Federal Bureau for Industry Trade (*Gewerbe*), and Labour (*Arbeit*), which is colloquially known as B.I.G.A. This was in January 1938. The Union thought in terms of a model contract of agency and of a special protection as regards bankruptcy. In April 1941 B.I.G.A. came to the conclusion, familiar to those who have Civil Service experience, that the matter was not one for them but for the Department of Justice.

2. The Departmental Draft (*Der Departementsentwurf*)

In December 1941, accordingly, there was a conference between the two departments 'and the representatives of certain interests'. The conference requested the Department of Justice to submit a draft. On 10 April 1942 the first departmental draft was prepared by 'Dr Fisch',[1] of the Department of Justice. Dr Fisch and his immediate subordinate, 'Dr Berger',[1] remained in charge of the bill

---

[1] A pseudonym, to protect his anonymity.

---

contract and then, when a body of case-law had been built up by the Swiss federal courts, they relied upon this case-law. By the 1940s this method had led to difficulties, especially as the German statute law, in any case, was under revision. The *Agenturvertragsgesetz* solves these.

The definition of agent in section 1 of the Law can already be found in the case of Eisenhut *v.* Rohner of 1903 (B.G.E. 29, ii, No. 15).

throughout its career. Speaking from memory, Dr Fisch says that he drafted[1] it at home, brought it to his office (a room in Bundeshaus West overlooking the whole range of snow peaks of the Bernese Oberland), and consulted his immediate superior.

The question arises how far back into the drafting process does the influence of Parliament and the long shadow of the referendum reach. I questioned several officials in different departments, independently, about this and they all assured me (once they had understood a question which was new to them) that at this stage there was no calculation of political constellations at all, and no thought of the referendum. Doubtless when the administration decides to grasp a well-rooted nettle the answer is different, but all the evidence is that, at this stage, the administration decide what they consider to be best in the circumstances, as objectively as their upper-middle class, law-trained, background permits them. This is an important assertion; it means that there is an independent role of the executive. At this point the 'conspiracy theory' (that, for example, the whole country is run by the '*Vorort*') breaks down: the conspiracy is not, at any rate, a conscious conspiracy.

The 'First Draft' was circulated to the B.I.G.A. and amended as a result of its comments. The Second Draft was dated 24 June 1943. This was circulated within the Department of Justice and discussed inside the department. Comments and suggestions were made and on the basis of this the Third Draft was made. This draft was translated into French (for the first time) and was the draft which went before the First Committee of Experts.

The Third Draft was also submitted to the head of the department, i.e. the Federal Councillor concerned. If the matter had required a financial outlay, at this stage there might have been (before submission to the Councillor) 'an informal consultation', '*unverbindlich*' and 'over a cup of coffee', with an official of the same rank in the Finance Department. As will be apparent later, the Finance Department is not the Swiss equivalent of the British Treasury.

---

[1] Dr Fisch is himself a trained jurist of academic distinction who lectures at the University of Berne on occasion. Apart from his own thoughts, his sources of inspiration were the case-law of the Swiss Federal Tribunal, and the German statute law by which it had for a short period been decisively influenced, and Austrian Law. Reference was made to French law at one stage and also, extremely superficially, to English law. Two dissertations on the general subject had recently been published, and are cited in the proceedings.

The draft remained in all its stages an uneasy mixture between an attempt to codify Swiss case-law on the one hand and an adventure into social legislation (protecting the weaker party to a contract) on the other. It was the latter aspect that interested the *Verbände*.

The principle is that the political head, the Federal Councillor responsible, is to be consulted before the draft gets outside the Civil Service. The political head might, in some circumstances, informally consult his colleague at the head of the other departments concerned (in this case, the Department of Public Economy). A further reason why the head of the department has to be informed is because he might wish to preside over the Committee of Experts. The Federal Council *as a college*, however, is never consulted at this stage. It would be wrong to do so, for the college must take its stand when the draft has been through the phase of 'consultation' and 'experts'. Nor do party-political considerations (normally) come in at this stage, there might be a quick calculation of 'Is it worth going further?' and 'Is it right?' in the mind of the Federal Councillor, but that is all. As for the referendum calculation, at this stage it would be merely 'Will people stand for this sort of thing?' not a totting up of interests and figures: this is left till later.

3. (i) Consultation (*die Vernehmlassung*) with Interests and Cantons

There is no fixed order for these stages—consultation of the *Verbände* (interests) affected, consultation of cantons, committee of experts, conference of cantonal ministers—and the Stenographic Bulletin gives examples of experts and cantons being consulted both before and after the *Verbände*. It depends on the nature of the proposal. If it hits the cantons in the first instance then they will be consulted first.

The usual procedure would be for the official in charge to consult the card-index which has the names of the *Verbände*, indexed under subjects, and take out a maximum range. These *Verbände* would all have the draft sent to them, with a request for comment. At the same time the cantonal ministries would be written to, enclosing a draft. Then, out of the answers and out of the lists, a smaller selection would be made of those it was worth while calling together to join the committee of experts.

The committee of experts is composed of (i) *Verband* representatives,[1] (ii) often an independent expert or experts, perhaps from universities, (iii) the official delegation, and (iv) very often a National Councillor and a Councillor of States. It is said that the latter just happen to be there, as experts in their own right; no doubt this is generally true of the National Councillor, but the Council of States is too small to contain experts on very many subjects. The best formulation is probably that the parliamentarians are not there as

[1] Sometimes individuals are invited by name, and sometimes the *Verband* is merely asked to send 'a representative'.

party-members, but as Assembly-members and (if possible) experts. The Councils have no right to a member, and there is no need to put a member on the committee, but the impression is that a member of each house does almost, if not quite, always 'happen' to be on.

The *Verband* representatives are as far as possible balanced as between French and German, as between regions (Basle and Zurich, for example), as between capital and labour, and as between the conflicting interests—without, of course, a precise proportion.

In the instance under consideration there was no need to consult the cantons, though they were probably informed as a matter of courtesy. The written consultation was said to have been very little wider than the actual representation of interests in the committee, but this would be different in the case of a very important bill. There was no conference of 'directors' (cantonal ministers).

(ii) The Committee of Experts

The First Committee of Experts was called on 9 March 1944, in the administrative buildings in Berne. The Third Draft, of 28 January 1944, was under consideration. The committee had fourteen members and a chairman, who was our friend Dr Fisch. Dr Berger and another civil servant were the Secretariat.

> The members were: Two representatives of the Agents' Union, from Zurich.
> One member each of three other agents' unions (from Basle, and Geneva).
> Two representatives of *Verbände* of firms who commission agents.
> A representative each of the *Vorort*, the Importers' *Verband*, and the *Gewerbeverband*.
> A Professor, as legal expert.
> A National Councillor, who was also an expert, and Herr Iten, a 'lay' member of the Council of States, who was in private practice as a lawyer.

When opening the first session, the chairman charged the committee in the following words:

> The draft before you is intended merely as a basis of discussion, and will not in any way prejudice the further discussion of our department with B.I.G.A. What we hope to get out of this committee is, first and foremost, to clarify our minds about whether there is a need for legislation or not. Then we want to

make progress about the individual problems. On the basis of these talks we will make a draft for the Federal Council, and it will then decide whether the matter will be pursued farther. If it decides to go on with it, then a Message will be submitted to the legislative councils, and the ordinary legislative process will follow.

About today's discussions, I want to make the following proposition: first of all we shall discuss *'eintreten'* (entering upon the matter). Afterwards we shall go on to the individual proposals in the draft. We will vote on the result. But these votes will only be for guidance. Anything we decide will not be binding either for the Department or for the Federal Council. Nevertheless they will be important as guiding principles for later work.

The reason why we are discussing *eintreten* is only to clear up the *question of need*. Should there be special legislative provision for the contract of agency, or shall we leave the law in its present state? Even if you decide against *eintreten*, that doesn't dispose of the matter for your committee. We must still discuss the individual proposals. This is partly so as not to have to call upon the committee again if the Federal Council should decide to go on with it notwithstanding. And it is partly because discussion of the particular propositions sometimes makes the question of need clear for the first time. A question we shall have to decide in connexion with 'need' is whether to include insurance agents or not.

It is clear from the Protokoll that the employers' representatives were against *eintreten*, and the agents for it. At this stage the Councillor of States said that he was sure that insurance agents should be included, and his personal authority seems to have been such that the committee chairman decided thenceforth to include them. It appears that they had already been consulted by letter, and were not invited because, on the basis of their reply, it had seemed that both sides wanted to be left out. There was a suggestion that the wrong *Verbände* had been consulted, and the chairman asked for advice as to who should be asked.

Having decided by a vote in the morning for *eintreten*, in the afternoon the committee considered the title and the first article (which was an important one). They were then adjourned, the chairman saying that to the next session representatives of the insurance companies would be invited. Members requested more documentation, and that the committee should not sit in Berne on the next occasion.

Only once was there any hint of a referendum threat—a member said that 'the People' do not like this sort of provision: the remark was made by one of the employers' representatives. But it was the sort of law that is unlikely to be worth challenging to a popular vote.

The Second Expert Committee, with the insurance representatives, was held in the Bear Hotel at Langenthal, an industrial village of little charm on the main-line from Berne to Olten, on 15 and 16 November 1944. The committee was larger, with twenty-two members, and the chairman a more senior official—the head of the Division. The previous chairman and draftsman, Fisch, was a member of the committee. Berger and an official from the Federal Insurance Office (Department of Justice) formed the secretariat. The basis of discussion was now the Fifth Draft, couched in the form of additional articles to be posted into the Code of Obligations (Contracts).

Insurance representatives on this second committee stated unanimously that they did not wish to be included. This was an interesting case for it turned out that this was not, in the case of the insurance agents, the view of the members of the *Verband*. Having made their standpoint clear, the insurance representatives took a normal part in the discussion.

In the two committees it was the Professor, the *Vorort* representative, and the Councillor of States who spoke most. The Councillor of States said frankly: 'I am not speaking as member of an economic group, but as a parliamentarian. I have an open mind. I haven't read Padel's dissertation yet, but I should like to say a word from my experience in practice as a lawyer.' He seems to have been the member whose opinion carried the most authority. In many respects he formed a contrast to his colleague from the National Council. In the first committee the National Councillor was the only member to be absent—with apologies. In the second committee the National Councillor (a different one, the absentee having resigned) spoke little, and then as representative of his *Verband* rather than of his Chamber. Neither of the National Councillors on the Committee of Experts was in the subsequent legislative committee.

The record of the committee (and of the subsequent committees) was not an agreed 'recommendation', but a summary account of what each speaker had said. It is thus in the form of a reported conversation. Swiss committees do not call experts in front of them, like British select or departmental committees, but are themselves composed of experts. They thus (like Swiss courts) intermingle the functions of judge and witness.

4. The Final Draft (*Die Bereinigung*)

Until the second committee of experts, the successive drafts had borne some resemblance to the first draft—with a big change after the first committee. The drafts now took on almost their final form. After the committee, a sixth draft was dated 12 Jan 1945, and a seventh draft on 15 May of the same year. This latter was the one submitted to the Federal Council, which found time to approve it on 27 Nov 1947—the delay is easy to explain. The draft now became the official bill (*Entwurf*) which was the basis of all subsequent discussions. Henceforth only minor changes (though these are very numerous) were made. The *Entwurf* is in wording quite unrecognizable from the first draft. The Act is very like the *Entwurf*.

5. The Official Draft (*Entwurf*) and the Message

The bill was accompanied by a Message. The Message gives (1) the history of the project in outline, (2) the names of the experts in the two committees. (3) It discusses the question of need, and (4) the question of whether to include insurance agents, and (5) whether the law shall be a special law, or in the Code of Obligations. Then (6) it comes to the details, which it considers one by one. Now comes (7) the bill itself. The *Entwurf* and Message were published in the *Feuille fédérale*, and a copy sent to each member of Parliament. They can be found in the *Feuille fédérale* for 1947 (B. Bl, 1947, iii, 661).

(b) The Parliamentary Stages
6. The committee of the National Council

The National Council had 'priority' in the example under consideration. The official draft was therefore referred to an *ad hoc* preliminary committee of that Council. The method of selecting members for such a committee is described on page 157 below.

The committee was of fifteen members, of whom one was absent and sent apologies. The composition, as always, was proportionate to party strength. Two of the members were prominent local government administrators, one, the Liberal, was (as manufacturer, and as representative in the Council of the employers' organization in the watch industry) professionally interested in the matter under discussion. The remainder were lawyers: it is difficult to say which, if any, of these were directly interested—one further member, at least, may be suspected of being concerned with the employers' side. Herr Condrau, who has already been noticed in these pages, was chairman: it was the first important committee of the Council that he had presided.[1]

[1] See Appendix Two on page 172.

The statement has been made, and repeated, that in committee only the chairman really masters the subject, and the other members just follow his lead and that of the officials and Federal Councillor. It is implied at the same time that the chairman, being briefed and in close contact with the officials, really represents the officials' point of view in any case, and therefore (as the Federal Councillor is similarly briefed and no one else takes part) the committee stage is only a 'rubber stamp'. It must then be emphasized here that in neither the National Council nor the Council of States was this so. In the National Council committee the chairman, though clearly master of the subject (and with legal training) presided as impartial arbitrator— occasionally giving the business a shrewd prod in order to get it moving, but not pushing his own views and, indeed, hardly expressing them. In the Council of States committee, on the contrary, there was a masterful chairman who dominated the proceedings. But, when required, he dominated the officials also. In general, one does not get the impression, in conversations with deputies or officials, that the *official-minded* dominating chairman is a common type. Indeed, the idea does not quite make sense, either from the point of view of the chairman or of the officials.

The Federal Council's Draft and Message were published on 27 Nov 1947. The committee of the first Council did not start work until 23 January of the following year. The delay is unusual. The first committee is usually held before the fractions (parliamentary parties) have had an opportunity of meeting, and it is important that this should be so. The explanation in this case is that a general election had intervened, and therefore the committee had not been constituted before the December session.

The Committee met in the Casino at Schaffhausen, no doubt on the invitation of the Mayor, Herr Bringolf. In addition to the members, Federal Councillor von Steiger (Department of Justice) and Dr Fisch, his 'adjunct', attended. Berger and another official (a French-Swiss) composed the secretariat. Steiger and Fisch spoke frequently, defending their draft without bigotry. They do not give the impression of wishing to push through their draft to satisfy their *amour propre*, but of being equally concerned with the committee to find the best solution. The situation was different in the committee of the Second Chamber.

During the first morning the question of *eintreten* was debated— the question whether there should be a law on the subject at all. It sometimes (though seldom) happens that the majority of a committee vote against *eintreten*. In such an event the project nevertheless goes to the whole House, and the Rapporteurs of the majority seek to persuade the House not to 'enter' but to refer the draft back again to the Federal Council. If the House does not agree, and votes *eintreten*, the project goes back once more to the committee to consider the details.

The committee voted for *eintreten* by a large majority. It then 'passed to the discussion of the articles'.

On the first clause members brought forward cogent criticism, so that von Steiger proposed to send back that clause to his department for redrafting. He accepted two verbal alterations willingly, stating that he himself preferred them. On the second clause, likewise, he at once accepted an amendment from the committee—which got involved in a rather intricate series of voting upon proposed amendments. The acceptance, however, was qualified by the reservation 'provided the department does not advise otherwise'.

In this manner the draft was worked through clause by clause. Each member spoke his native language, French or German. Von Steiger, as a Bernese aristocrat, spoke both with equal fluency. The character of the discussion was all along one of give and take between members of the committee speaking as individuals, not as party members, and in contradiction to each other on occasion. The Federal Councillor and the chairman helped business along, and Fisch provided explanations for his chief when required. It must be emphasized that on all the occasions where the committee disagreed with the Federal Council's draft and went on record with a counter-proposition (and very few articles were unamended), von Steiger had accepted the amendment. The ultimate order-paper of the committee therefore, which showed the committee as continually rejecting the Federal Council's draft, is in this respect misleading.

The whole bill was dealt with in one long day, with a fair number of questions left over for decision in the future. The date of the next meeting to settle these was fixed for Friday, 5 March, in Berne. The chairman, Condrau, a Romansch-speaking Catholic Conservative from Grisons—whose second language is German—was appointed German Rapporteur, and Monsieur Péclard, a Radical from Vaud, was appointed French Rapporteur.

Clause *s* and the *Verbände*

The most important of the matters left over was clause *s*. This concerned the inclusion of insurance agents, and the insurance companies are among the most powerful interest groups in Switzerland. Their parliamentary power does not simply rest on their wealth and influence in the business world generally, but on the consideration that insurance is one of Switzerland's great export industries:

the interest of the insurance companies is the interest of Switzerland.

It will be remembered that the insurances were left out of the first draft, but that insurance representatives were brought in for consultation on the recommendation of the first committee of experts. Both sides of the industry opposed inclusion during the second committee of experts, though the agents' side afterwards repudiated this standpoint. The powerful party, however, was the employers' side, and this side continued to oppose inclusion. It is this which makes the present incident interesting as a test case of the power of a *Verband*.

The draft approved by the Federal Council still excluded insurances (section *s*). When the National Council committee came to this clause, Fisch told them how contested it was—though the members seem to have known this already. Two members proposed that the clause be omitted. They then left the room (and it is not clear why; one of them, at least, as a cantonal minister, could not have been an interested party). Members of the committee gave their view in turn, only one, and the chairman, remaining silent. Each of the arguments turned on the point of what was fair from the standpoint of social justice, and all (except for the one member who had personal knowledge and interest) were in favour of including the insurances. The Federal Councillor spoke last: he was also (against the Federal Council's official draft) in favour of including insurances. The chairman intervened to reserve a report of the department on one matter, and the committee decided, without opposition, to include insurances.

Between the committee session of 23 January and the second session fixed for Friday, 5 March, the Department of Justice tried to bring the two sides of the insurance industry together. But the employers refused to be talked round, and wrote to Herr Condrau enclosing documents, and stated that they considered the whole draft should be jettisoned or, at least, the insurances should be excluded from it. Nevertheless they agreed to meet the employees' (agents') side in a conference to which von Steiger had invited them. This was held in the President of the Council's Room, an ornate room opening off the long, curved lobby of the National Council. It was a dramatic meeting.

The room is dominated by a long table, and round this the representatives, four from each side, must have sat. Five of the eight representatives had already served together on the committee of experts. Steiger was in the Chair, at the head of the table—an aristocratic solicitor bearing some facial resemblance to Mr Harold

Macmillan. Fisch represented the Department of Justice. There was a civil servant from the Federal Insurances Bureau, and Berger was the secretary. Steiger opened by stating that the National Council committee had resolved on *eintreten* and would not now change its mind. But he had promised it to sound the interested parties once more. He had the impression from the documents he had received that they were not yet fully agreed.

An ill-tempered and impassioned discussion broke out.

Then von Steiger intervened. Their positions were now clear. The companies refused to agree that the provision concerning compensation on dismissal could not be contracted out of. The agents take the opposite view, and wish the measure of compensation left to the courts. He added: 'I shall report in these terms to the committee, and explain the standpoint of the two groups in the National Council. The National Council's committee has made an honest endeavour to find a solution to which you could both agree. It is not my place to go on discussing the matter with you here. It was simply that I regarded it as my duty to try and obtain an understanding.'

No doubt he gathered his papers together as he spoke. The discussion took on a note of urgency, the two officials and then the Federal Councillor breaking in from time to time—'I think in that case we can find a form of words to lay before the committee tomorrow', and eventually Fisch read out a draft which met the needs of both parties. The two parties named representatives with whom Fisch could get in touch to agree on the final draft, in German and French. The representatives later agreed on the telephone without reservations.

It is clear: (i) that the agreement would not have been secured except under the pressure that the bill would go forward regardless of the *Verbände*, and (ii) that the agreement having been secured, the hands of the Councils were to a certain extent bound. This did not mean that the hasty draft scribbled during the discussion in the President's Room had passed into the Code of Obligations as such. Though it has left its mark on the Code of Obligations (section 418 *u* in its final form), the clause was in fact turned inside out syntactically, and even altered slightly as to its content, during the later proceedings.

The National Council Committee met briefly on the Friday, as planned. The last-minute agreement came as a surprise to them. Steiger insisted that the wording agreed upon should not be altered in any way, or the parties would recover their freedom.

7. Consideration by the parliamentary parties[1]

On the afternoon of the first day of the session the parliamentary parties ('fractions') hold their sittings—and hold further meetings on Tuesdays during the weeks that Parliament sits.

The members of the two councils sit together in all 'fractions'—this gives a twist to bicameralism which is difficult to assess since no party is proportionately represented in the Council of States. Apart from the members of the two Councils, the Federal Councillors representing the party attend, and some journalists of that party are often present to report the meetings. Reports in the press are brief and rather uninformative.

The procedure is like that of the full House, but less formal and often shorter. On a typical bill the discussion would open (as in the House) by a report by one, or two, of the party members who had sat in the committee on the bill, describing what the points of issue were, and recommending *eintreten* or not-*eintreten*. The discussion would then be thrown open, and possibly the Federal Councillor would speak at the end, usually representing the views of the college as a whole (it is said). Then a decision would be taken, which might well be that in the Chamber there should be a free vote: fraction discipline, on matters indifferent, is not often, or even usually, required.

It has already been noted that the fraction sitting almost always comes *after* the committee of the First Council has come to its conclusions. It means that the committee members are not bound in advance to represent a party standpoint in the committee mechanically.

In very important political matters, on the other hand, it is likely that the fraction and perhaps the whole party has come to a conclusion beforehand. The party members in the committee are then more or less delegates, not independent minds. In the Law on Army Reform (for example), which is being discussed in 1960, the parties had already formed their opinions before the committee met.

The question has also been raised whether federal officials or army officials can appear before these sessions (of 'their own' party) in opposition to the views of their hierarchical head of department, and the matter has sometimes been debated before the whole House. Needless to say, the Federal Council does not encourage officers and officials to appear.

On some occasions there may be an informal party-committee

[1] The author has not sought access to the protocols of the fraction sittings on this bill. Several members of parliament have described, however, the normal course of proceedings to him.

(in addition to the real committee, and overlapping it in membership) to discuss an important project from a party or electoral standpoint.

8. Debate in the 'First' Chamber
   (a) *Eintreten*
   The debate, in this case in the National Council, opened with 'The Proposition of the Committee', which was '*eintreten*'.
   There are three parts of the *eintreten* debate (which corresponds to the Second Reading Debate in the House of Commons).

   (i) *The Reports* (Berichterstattung): The committee names two Rapporteurs, one of whom speaks German and the other French. One of the two is usually (as in this case) the chairman of the committee. It sometimes happens that the chairman in fact opposes the committee's decision, but even in that case it often happens that he nevertheless acts as one of the Rapporteurs, speaking not for himself, but for the majority. These reports are the best public work of the Swiss Parliament, clear and fair. The German and the French reports are independent of one another, and it is worth listening to both though they cover the same ground. If there were a minority, proposing 'not *eintreten*', then it would name its Rapporteur or Rapporteurs. On insignificant questions only one Rapporteur speaks.

   (ii) *The General Discussion:* The matter is now thrown open to debate. Sometimes other members of the committee speak, especially if their committee vote does not tally with the standpoint of their party. This is called a *Votum*, an explanation of the vote, as in the old Diet. Usually a member from each party speaks, explaining the party's position. There is strictly speaking no debate, only a series of *vota*, not replying to one another or arranged in any order. After half a dozen *vota* the interest of the observer begins to flag, unless he is also concerned with the background to each member's crisis of conscience. The same arguments are mercilessly repeated.

   (iii) At the end of the General Discussion, *the Rapporteurs* have the right to reply, and it is usually then that *the Federal Councillor* exercises his 'right to be heard at any time'.
   The moment when the Federal Councillor speaks has been described, sarcastically but not untruly, in the following words: 'Now comes the solemn moment. Hush, children, pay attention. The debate is closed and there steps forward a Herr Bundesrat, weighing his judgements well and patting the good people on the head, and telling the naughty ones where they were wrong.' There is in fact a marked change of atmosphere. On the floor of the House during speeches there is a subdued roar from the conversations,

dominated by the crackling voice of the loudspeaker into which the orator is talking. But this noise dies, and members and journalists alike attend as the Federal Councillor speaks. The contrast is so sharp as to be unpleasant.

In the present case *eintreten* was not disputed. It is quite clear that some members doubted the necessity for the law—but they had done their political sums and did not want to make themselves needlessly unpopular if they were to lose anyway. Federal Councillor von Steiger must have been present (and perhaps Dr Fisch and Dr Berger were on the little bench near the entry to the Chamber which is used by officials) but, seeing that victory was assured, Steiger did not choose to engage himself and perhaps raise difficulties by a superfluous speech.

The Council then adjourned, and continued the debate the next day. There was only one speaker from the floor (the committee Rapporteurs have a seat near the desk from which speeches are made), a Socialist from Aargau, who had been on the (parliamentary) committee. He had spoken in committee; as Dr Eichenberger says, it is a legend that members who are silent in the House have been active in committee—the silent are always silent and the active everywhere active. An old and well known figure, he just stated that 'we' are in favour, without indicating whom he meant by 'we'. The German Rapporteur was a Conservative, and the French a Radical, so it was in place for a Socialist to state his own fraction's standpoint. No one else spoke, and *eintreten* was decided without any other proposal being before the House.

(b) Discussion of the Articles

The decision to 'enter' automatically involves 'passing to the discussion of the articles'—corresponding to the committee stage in the House of Commons. The discussion of articles was, in this case, held immediately after the *eintreten* debate. All the clauses were rapidly taken, accepting the committee's decision wherever it varied from the Federal Council's draft until section *s* was reached. Here trouble was expected. The last minute agreement was on a cyclostyled paper on each member's desk.

Condrau and the French Rapporteur briefly spoke, explaining that the provision had been agreed between the interests. Then National Councillor Speiser spoke, moving the amendment he had tabled. Speiser was a member of the board of Brown-Boveri, and the spokesman of the employers' side of the exporting industries as well as being a prominent Basle industrialist in his own right. His proposal was that insurances should be allowed to contract out of the law's provisions. Two committee members and the two Rapporteurs spoke in favour of the committee's draft, and succeeded in allaying some of Speiser's suspicions. The Rapporteurs emphasized the agreement of both sides in Thursday's conference. The amendment was not pressed and the insurances were therefore included.

(c) Vote on the Whole

There was then a vote on the whole, at which there must be a majority of a quorum of the House. The quorum (which is not always observed) is one half the total membership. In this case there were 119 votes in favour and none against. The appearance of unanimity had been obtained.

9. Committee of the second Chamber

The draft was then passed to the *ad hoc* committee of the Council of States. This committee was of a different type from that of the National Council. The chairman did not merely preside, but expressed opinions and summed up and, indeed, played more part in the proceedings than any other single member. Fisch, attending as an official, also played a very large part. On one occasion Fisch even proposed an amendment: he had, on reflection, regretted an alteration made by the National Council in his original draft. A member took up his proposal, which is referred to in the minutes (by an oversight) as 'the Fisch proposal'. At this stage also Dr Fisch did not appear to welcome alterations: he had by now formed his opinion, and fought for it—a contrast to his attitude before the committee of the First Chamber.

The committee met on 5 April in the Hôtel du Lac at Vevey. It had nine members, and appointed its chairman Rapporteur. Herr Iten, who had been on the Committee of Experts, was a member, and spoke much. The other members were curiously diffident about making their suggestions in the form of definite amendments, and perhaps were less well prepared than the National Council's committee: this is unexpected, as the Council of States has a reputation for administrative expertise. The committee was attended by von Steiger, Berger and the same French-Swiss official as attended the National Council's committee, as well as by Dr Fisch.

There was no mention in the committee of a specifically *cantonal* point of view at any stage. One of the amendments was stated as being to give effect to opinions expressed in the National Council. Section *s* was amended, in spite of von Steiger's plea 'I lay more weight on keeping the words we have obtained agreement on, than on improving them.'

10. Consideration on the floor of the Second Chamber

On 8 July 1948 the bill came before the Council of States itself. The President of the Chamber was Ständerat Iten. This accident was later decisive, for it was the casting vote of the President which determined the final vote on the bill in the Council.

The Rapporteur proposed *eintreten*, which this time was contested. Herr Speiser had been promoted to the Council of States in the interval between the readings, and therefore he had the unusual chance to oppose the bill in both Houses. The voting was 16:3 in favour of *eintreten*. The House passed to the Discussion of Articles, but the title and preamble were also contested (by Herr Schoch, a non-member of the committee) on the floor. Schoch proposed that the bill should not be an addition to the code, but a special law. Bundesrat von Steiger replied to this: 'The Department and the Federal Council have also, of course, concerned themselves with this question.' He proposed, however, referring it back to the committee. Schoch agreed, but made other objections. As the draft was going back to the committee in any event, these were also referred to it. Then came section *s*. This was Herr Speiser's opportunity. The matter also was referred back.

The committee met again in the middle of the holiday season, in a *Kurhaus* on the Lake of Zug. Two members and (for the first time) Dr Fisch were absent. It was a good tempered committee. Like all its predecessors it was helped by a special report of the department concerning the alterations it had to deal with. But in determining the decisive words of section *s* it did not follow this report. These words were due to Ständerat Iten, the individual who (next to Fisch) had the most influence on the actual text.

On 21 September the bill again appeared before the Council of States. There were no speeches in opposition to the Rapporteur, but on the final vote on what form the law should take there was a division 14:14, decided, as has been said, by President Iten's casting vote.

11. Divergences

The Council of States had altered the bill in several small, but not unimportant respects. It now came back (16 Oct 1948) to the National Council committee, which met in the Hôtel Central at Lausanne. Bundesrat von Steiger, Fisch, Berger and Nationalrat Condrau were all there. The committee went through the States' sixteen alterations carefully, and agreed to all of them. On the final vote, however, two were against acceptance, and these two (without developing their standpoint in the committee) said they would move a 'minority resolution' in the Chamber.

In the National Council, however, only Herr Condrau spoke. The minority did not in fact move a resolution. 'The reference to a minority proposal is a mistake' the Rapporteur remarked. The proposals (to agree with the other Chamber all along the line) were accepted without vote or opposition.

12. The Committee of Redaction

The bill then went to the Committee of Redaction, composed of the Rapporteurs of the two committees, the second Vice-Chancellor, and the interpreters of the two Councils. No doubt Fisch attended, or sent a memorandum, as well. All the Committee did was to re-number the clauses consecutively. As a result, clause *s* became clause *u* in the final text.

13. The Final Vote

This was then taken formally. There was unanimity in the Council of States (thirty-one votes), and on the same day, 4 Feb 1949, the bill was transmitted to the National Council, where again it was accepted unanimously (118 votes). The National Council transmitted it to the Federal Council for promulgation. It was not actually published until 14 April 1949, and (the date of application having been delegated to the Federal Council) came into effect on 1 Jan 1950. A referendum against the law could have been launched and would have had to collect its signatures within three months of publication. Needless to say, none was launched.

POSTSCRIPT

The postscript is a sad one. Alas for human endeavour, the leading Swiss Law Review started its criticism of the act with the words 'The *Agenturvertragsgesetz* is, of course, no flawless pearl of legislative art'! And it must be confessed that the final result is clumsy, and a blot on the Code of Obligations. The thanklessness of the officials' task is well illustrated by this comment.

XI
Motions, Postulates, Interpellations and Questions

There are four ways in which members of parliament can elicit a reply, or a formal report, from the Federal Council. These are called motions, postulates, interpellations, and questions. It must again be emphasized, for the benefit of the British reader, that in Switzerland there are no Government parties and Opposition parties, and there is no real conception of 'debates'. These procedures are thus not closely paralleled by any British ones,[1] and they do not dominate the life of the Swiss Parliament or give it its *raison d'être*. The uses to which these procedures are put are very varied, and the reader is invited to suspend his judgement upon them until the end of this chapter.

Until the Law on the Councils of 1902 came into force there was no consistent distinction between the terms 'motion' and 'postulate'.[2] The Law and the *Règlements* of the Councils now make it clear, however, that a motion is a resolution in identical terms of the *two*

---

[1] The nearest equivalent to the first three procedures mentioned would be Private Members' motions on a Friday—for example, the House of Commons debate on Friday, 24 June 1960, on the Wider Ownership of Industrial Shares.

[2] An illustration of a postulate—the reproduction of the original document as handed in to the Secretariat—is given on p. 191. The number and the date have been added by the Secretariat, and the words which give the postulate its short title have been underlined, and a French translation suggested for the title. The postulate reads:

The Federal Council is invited to lay before the Federal Chambers a project for an increase in the tax on beer to the rate at which it used to be, i.e. 12 francs a hectolitre. The additional yield of this tax should be used to improve the health of the people, especially with an eye to popularizing milk to drink and products of milk. (Signed) R. SUTER. (Supporting signatures) Gitermann. Arnold. Revaclier. Vontobel. Bächtold. Duttweiler. König. Brochon. Jaunin. Pidoux. Dürrenmatt. Arni. Zeller. Bonvin. Schwendener. Dellberg. Eggenberger. Schwendinger. (18).

National Councillor Suter is one of the Landesring of Independents. So are four of the signatories. There are also five Socialists, five Radicals, one Liberal, one Farmer, and two Catholics. The same document could equally well have been termed a motion, in which case, if passed, the Second Chamber would have it placed on their agenda.

Councils and is 'obligatory'. It should therefore be couched in *mandatory* terms. A postulate, on the other hand, is a resolution of *one* Council only. Appropriately it *invites* the Federal Council to take some action.

The action which a motion demands and a postulate requests is very often 'that the Federal Council should submit a Report and a draft Bill'. Thus motions and postulates are often the parents of laws, and set in motion the procedure of drafting legislation which has been sketched in the previous chapter. But motions and postulates may, and not infrequently do, request the Federal Council to take certain *executive* action.

An interpellation differs from a postulate in that it is in the form of a question.[1] As the question frequently runs 'Is the Federal Council prepared to submit a report and a draft?' the distinction is not in practice very great. A formal distinction is that an interpellation requires ten signatures (in the National Council: three in the Council of States). Also, no vote is taken on an interpellation. It is 'developed' by the interpellant, the Federal Councillor replies in the name of the whole Federal Council, and the interpellant declares himself satisfied or dissatisfied. Whatever the reply, and whether satisfied or not, the interpellation is thereby 'liquidated', except in the unlikely event of the Council resolving on further discussion.

Motions, postulates and interpellations are all usually 'motivated'. That is to say, as well as requesting action they state a fact, and often a consequence of this fact which is considered harmful. The form often is that of a political syllogism: 'Agriculture is finding difficulty in obtaining workers and numerous young peasants are leaving agriculture to follow other trades. This is often because there is a housing shortage in the country. The Federal Council is invited to submit a report and project to remedy this.' Brevity, however, is not usually a characteristic of motions and postulates: they often spread over three or four paragraphs. A variation of this form is to

[1] The following is an example of an interpellation. The interpellant is National Councillor Max Weber, a former Socialist Federal Councillor:

The International Monetary Fund and the International Bank for Reconstruction and Development have, since they were set up in 1944, aimed at stabilizing currencies, expanding commerce, and assisting under-developed countries.

Does the Federal Council not think that Switzerland should support these tasks by taking an active part in these institutions? Is it inclined to submit to the legislative chambers a project whereby our country can adhere to the IMF and the IBRD?

The request for interpellation is supported by: [thirty-three signatories—all members of the Social Democrat fraction].

start with the words 'The Federal Council is requested . . . because . . .'

A written question is a miniature version of an interpellation. It requires no supporting signatures beyond that of the questioner. The text is circulated in typescript to members and the press, and a Federal Councillor gives a written reply to it, which is published in the report of proceedings. There is no possibility of asking supplementary questions.

There is also a sessional *question hour*, an hour, or half an hour, at the end of the three-week session. This is almost the only occasion on which more than one Federal Councillor is present in the House, and now and then there is an approach to spontaneity in the answers. The questions, written, are handed in during the session, at least three days before Question Hour comes on. The Federal Councillor's reply can give rise to no parliamentary comment or supplementary question. As an imitation of British procedure it is totally misconceived, but has some advantages in its own right. Both the written question (*Kleine Anfrage*) and the Question Hour exist only in the National Council. The Question Hour was introduced in 1946.

Though in form these procedures are very different, being carefully graded from the most weighty, the motion, through the postulate, interpellation, written question and oral question, in their practical use they work out very much the same. The reason why these procedures work out so much the same is that there is no sanction to enforce the demand of the Chambers. This flaw runs through all the procedures whereby the Swiss Parliament attempts to control the executive.

Motions indeed are described as 'obligatory': this is a brave word. The *Règlements* of the Chambers go on to provide, however, that motions to which no effect or reply has been given four years after they have been adopted are to be struck off the list, unless action is taken to keep them on. This is realism. In 1959, fifty-three postulates and six motions were adopted. In the same year twenty-five superannuated postulates and one motion were quietly struck off, while forty-three postulates and seven motions, not replied to or given effect to, were preserved on the list because the administration had not yet had the opportunity of getting around to them in the four years. A few of them dated from the 1940s. The Federal Council, in fact, treats motions and postulates as mere suggestions. It replies to them in the same form as it replies to interpellations, saying whether it is prepared to give effect to them or not. The language of obligatory motions is one derived from a régime of 'Cabinet and Parliament'. When it comes to Swiss conditions (where the executive is irremovable), commands, requests and questions are treated alike, as suggestions for future action.

PROCEDURE

The procedure of initiating a postulate or a motion can be seen from the illustrations on page 191. At home, or in the writing room, a member types out the text, labelling it 'postulate' or 'motion' as seems best to him. He then brings it with him to a session of the House, and drifts round his political friends during the debate (or at his hotel, or in the corridors or restaurant of the Parliament Building) collecting their signatures. The extra signatures are not a formal requirement, but they add weight, and indicate which parties or interests support the motion. He then hands the paper in to the Secretariat of the Assembly, which gives the postulate a number and puts it on the *white* pre-sessional order paper. If the Federal Councillor intends to reply, or if it can be woven into an existing debate, it goes on to the *green* pre-sessional paper of the objects which will *actually* be discussed. When the day comes, the member usually (and superfluously) reads out the text to his Council and speaks 'briefly' (not more than twenty minutes) in support of the motion. Other members may choose to speak, limiting themselves to ten minutes, but seldom do so. The speech is directed very definitely to the Federal Councillor, even by the express title 'Herr Bundesrat', though it should logically be directed to the Chamber or the chairman. The Federal Councillor then sometimes replies on the spot. In the case of an interpellation the member thereupon declares himself satisfied or dissatisfied. In the case of a postulate or motion, however, the Chamber 'votes'. This vote is usually a mere formality: because postulates are not administratively effective the Chambers are 'good natured' about adopting them. In his reply to a motion the Federal Councillor often says (not wishing to have the debate twice) that he will accept the motion 'in the form of a postulate'. The member usually graciously agrees. In either event, whether accepted or rejected, there is no automatic follow-up: the Federal Councillor may accept it and still do nothing about it.

Committees, both *ad hoc* and (more often) standing, frequently themselves initiate postulates. Committee postulates are among the most effective pressures, because by the nature of things the committee usually has it in its power to be awkward. Moreover, whereas a decision of one or both Councils is taken lightheartedly on the floor without much consideration (there being no effective *debating* techniques), the decision of a committee is always entitled to a certain respect. The two great standing committees, Finance and Gestion, not infrequently couch their suggestions in the form of postulates, which are debated with the Estimates or with the Report on Business as the case may be.

POLITICAL ROLE OF POSTULATES AND MOTIONS

The political functions served by these procedures can be illustrated by six 'typical' situations. (These are imagined situations, compounded of real incidents.)

Situation 1

A *Verband* wishing to attain some object, its deputy in the National Council undertakes a desultory correspondence with the Department concerned. Failing to make progress, he puts down a postulate. This at once gives the member a basis to bargain from, justifies him with his *Verband*, and serves to advertise its aims. Under this pressure the officials make certain concessions. The matter never actually comes up to be debated and the postulate is erased after four years. But it has attained its end and has, as it were, regularized the contact of the member of the National Council with the federal official. The actual demands of the *Verband* expressed in the official conversations are not in fact quite those formulated in the postulate, so there is no occasion formally to write the postulate off. On the surface it has failed. In reality it has succeeded.

Situation 2

A spending Department wishes to undertake a certain venture but foresees that there will be opposition in the Federal Council from the Finance Department. The spending Department has a friend in the National Council, the veteran of a score of committees affecting it and the *jass*-partner and dinner-neighbour therefore of one of the department's officials. The official explains his dilemma. 'Could you put down a motion?' he asks. The motion is duly put down, and the head of the spending Department accepts it, in qualified terms, on condition it is changed into a postulate. The official gives the member a grateful glance. The Finance Department withdraws its opposition. The motion has succeeded, but this is not a victory of Parliament over the executive, but of one department over another.

Situation 3

As a result of arguments brought forward by the *Vorort* the Federal Council resolve on a certain course of action. An official does some research in the files, and discovers that a dozen years ago some members handed in a postulate advocating a similar course of action. In drafting the Message (or before the Committee of Experts) the impression is given that the project is a belated reply to this long buried postulate. This lightens the parliamentary task, and gives an impression of due subservience to the representatives of the people.

Situation 4
A member, in touch with some current of public opinion, perceives a grievance and the best method of rectifying it. His postulate forces the Federal Councillor to study the matter, and is backed up by a personal approach. The Federal Council accept the postulate, which becomes in due time the basis of a Message and project. The member is placed on the *ad hoc* committee, and eventually the project becomes law. This is the 'straight' situation with the happy ending, the only one referred to in the textbooks. It does regularly happen.

Situation 5
To his chagrin a member sees that he will not be included in the committee to consider a burning issue in the next ensuing session. It is quite likely, also, that he will not obtain a place in the debate. He puts down a motion. This will automatically bring his point of view to the notice of the committee when it considers the bill. In the debate, the Rapporteurs of the committee do in fact refer to the motion, and take up a position regarding it. The member obtains a good position in the discussion, because it is decided to call the motion as part of the debate on the bill. The Federal Councillor also refers expressly to it, but asks for it to be withdrawn, which the member does, being 'satisfied with the explanation'.

Situation 6
Switzerland proposes to join the European Free Trade Area ('the Seven'). The instrument whereby this is done is not subject to the referendum. A member thinks it should be, but the Federal Councillor explains that as the Constitution stands, such a course would be 'unconstitutional'. But, adds the Federal Councillor, if the member will put down a proposal for Constitutional amendment (the 'Assembly initiative') the Federal Council 'will be very ready to examine the proposal'. The member then quickly formulates a postulate, and asks the Chamber to consider that day's debate as having been the debate upon it. The postulate, as it were, becomes the procedural peg on which (in due time) the Federal Council will hang a Message. Drafting the Message will be a nice little job for

one of the young gentlemen in the Political Department to try his hand on, and there is no hurry whatever about it.

CONCLUSION

On the basis of these 'situations', which could be multiplied, some sort of general statement can be made about what a motion (or postulate, etc.) is. From the standpoint of political sociology it is a *threat*. It is a threat on the part of a member to use the power of Parliament to further the interests of a group which he represents. The threat is directed to the Federal Council, and takes the procedural form of a demand, or a request for action or for information. What lies behind this threat is another matter: this may be as varied as human motivation, and is limited only by the power of the Federal Council on the one hand (for it is no use trying to get it to do something which it is not able to do) and by the sanction available to the member on the other hand. This sanction is the power of Parliament, that is to say, the whole power of Parliament throughout the whole session. To estimate this power is the principal task of this book, and it cannot be characterized at a shorter length, including as it does a Constitutional, a legislative, a moral, a social and a political power. Postulates and motions, interpellations and questions, are not the power itself, they are the procedural forms whereby this power is often exercised.

APPENDIX

The part played by an Interpellation in the story of a project

The following timetable is taken from the Speech of M. Georges Borel (Socialist, Geneva) to the National Council on 9 March 1960.

1. 31 Jan 1958. Federal Arrêté encouraging Welfare Housing (*logements à caractère social*), based on Article 35 quinquies of the Constitution.

2. Cantonal governments and the *Union Suisse pour l'amélioration des logements* (U.S.A.L.) approach the Federal Bureau for Housing, which was charged with execution of the arrêté.

3. Meanwhile Herr Bommeli, the federal official concerned in charge of the Bureau, gets in contact himself with U.S.A.L.

4. 17 May 1958. The French-Swiss section of U.S.A.L. hold a conference at Neuchâtel.

5. 31 May 1958. The National Congress of U.S.A.L. adopt the

MOTIONS, POSTULATES, INTERPELLATIONS AND QUESTIONS

French Swiss motion, unanimously, immediately following an address by Herr Bommeli.

6. June 1958. The President of the Confederation receives a deputation 'in the presence of Herr Bommeli', from U.S.A.L.

7. 24 Sept 1958. Being only partially satisfied with the result, Borel hands in an interpellation, with twenty-four Socialist signatures.

8. 2 Oct 1958. National Councillor Steinmann, Chairman of U.S.A.L., hands in a further interpellation, much more detailed, and with thirty-three signatures, including that of Borel.

9. March 1959, Bommeli visits Borel and asks him not to develop the interpellation during the course of that session.

10. U.S.A.L. agrees 'on condition that the Federal Council modified the subordinate legislation' in a certain sense.

11. There were various speeches made on different occasions in the National Council, and a written question was asked.

12. During the debate on the Abolition of Price Control on 8 March 1960 the two interpellations were made a part of the debate. They were replied to, as a part of his answer to the whole debate, by Bundesrat Wahlen on 16 March.

Both Borel and Steinmann were on the *ad hoc* committee concerned.

The whole debate is of great interest, from the list of lobbies concerned to the declaration by Wahlen of his duty as Federal Councillor. There are very full explanations in the Official Report (*Bulletin Sténographique*) of what happened in committee and who were consulted. It is an easily accessible corroboration of the generalizations made in this book, and a demonstration that the incidents selected are in fact typical.

XII

Gestion

Article 85 (11) of the Constitution gives to the Assembly 'the high supervision of federal administration and justice', while Article 102 (16) imposes on the Federal Council the duty of 'laying before the Assembly, at its ordinary session, a report on its conduct of business (gestion), and a report upon the state of the Confederation at home and abroad, and draws its attention to the measures it considers will further the common welfare. It also', the Article adds, 'submits special reports when the Assembly or one chamber requires it'.

The last sentence is taken to refer to motions and postulates. The ordinary session referred to is the once-yearly session which the Constitution foresees. The 'report on the state of the Nation', however, is a little mysterious, and seems to show that the founding fathers had no clear picture in their minds of the political creature they were siring.

That there can be no overall Federal Council policy in set terms, and therefore no President's Speech from the Throne to explain it, is a logical consequence of the whole Swiss system. For if there were a formulated policy, there would be criticism of the policy, and criticism implies power to give effect to the criticism. And this could only mean the power on the part of the Assembly to dismiss the whole Federal Council and set up a new one. It is basic to the system that there is no power to hold *the whole* Federal Council responsible: the Federal Council is not a parliamentary executive, and cannot be removed. Its position is, in this respect, like that of a Constitutional monarch and it follows the same logic. The King can do no wrong, *ergo* he can do nothing. The Federal Council as a whole cannot be removed, therefore it cannot *formulate* and submit a policy. The executive college, being irremovable, is uncriticizable. In terms of parliamentary procedure, there is no way of criticizing federal policy *as a whole*.

What can be, and what is, criticized is the action of the departments. All such action has been approved by the Federal Council, but it is the head of the department who must defend the action, even if it was not really 'his' action, but the decision of his colleagues. It follows that the annual report of business is the report of the activities of the seven departments—all of which have been sanctioned by the Federal Council as a whole. What it is not, and cannot be, is the report of the Federal Council as a whole concerning *its* past policy. In this somewhat over-refined distinction lies the chief originality of the Swiss Constitution. In plain terms, the wording of the Constitutional document is here ignored, and what is submitted to the Assembly is a report 'of the Federal Council' concerning the activities of the seven departments (and of the federal judiciary and Chancery) during the last year.

The *Rapport de Gestion* (Report on the Conduct of Business) is set down regularly as the chief business of the June session. The Report itself is a bulky document (in 1960 it was 578 pages in its German edition).

In 1960 the Report dealt with the calendar-year 1959, and was published as a separate document (not included in the *Feuille fédérale*) in March 1960. It comprised, as it regularly does, the following:

(a) '*General Administration.*' This is a report from the Federal Chancery. It contains a short but very interesting section on the administrative aspects of the Federal Council (to which the Chancellor is secretary), and a long and perhaps unnecessary list of motions and postulates handed in by the two Chambers (for the Secretariat of which the Chancellor is also responsible) noting those which have been dealt with, etc. This list is of some interest to the student of government, and no doubt it is a convenience to those responsible for arranging the business of the session. As it occupies nearly 150 pages of print its inclusion in full seems excessive.

The report from the Chancery is a little anomalous since the Chancellor, of course, does not defend it in the Chamber himself. The President of the Confederation does so.

(b) *The Departments*, in order of seniority, report on the past year. The Political Department alone allows itself some general reflexions, even mentioning in 1960 the Lunik. The report of the Department fills some sixty pages, giving the impression of being collated from reports of various offices without much regard to the purpose of the report—the control of administration. Some embassies report an unpleasant experience of a Swiss visitor, others that a treaty has been abrogated by mutual agreement, but each reports a single incident. The general effect is curiously idyllic, like Mr Parker's reports on Nepenthe.

The other departments start by a report on the motions and postulates addressed to them, and then say something about each section in turn and about each obvious subject—thus the Justice Division of the Justice and Police Department reports, *inter alia*, that '63 written replies were given to inquiries concerning the permissibility of divorces between foreign spouses in Switzerland or Swiss spouses abroad. In 1958 the figure was 62.'

It can be imagined that several hundred pages of this sort of reading do not interest a wide public. The Report serves some purpose, no doubt, within the department, but being provided by the department itself with the aim of not affording a basis for criticism, it falls short in its main purpose, which is precisely to facilitate parliamentary criticism.

(c) *The Federal Tribunal.* As 'an appendix' to the Report, the Federal Tribunal and Federal Insurance Tribunal send a report on their activity. This (in the case of the Federal Tribunal) only occupies some ten pages, merely giving figures of the number of cases: it is, incidentally, the best introduction for the student to the very complex jurisdiction of the Tribunal. As in the case of the Chancery, this report is in a way anomalous, since those who submit the report do not come before the Assembly to defend it—the head of the Department of Justice and Police does this—but it has a justification, since the Assembly is responsible for servicing the courts and determining their establishment. In 1960, a member (not on the Gestion Committee) brought up a question on the trend of decisions of the Tribunal. This was unusual, and in a sense improper: the Federal Councillor refrained from going into the matter in his reply, since judicial decisions do not depend on him. He 'is not responsible' would be the British phrase, but a phrase not quite applicable to Swiss conditions.

It is with 'B', the reports of Gestion of the Departments, with which we are here concerned.

RESPONSIBILITY OF MINISTERS

There is some ambiguity as to whether the Report, or what the departments have actually done, is the subject of the Assembly's sanction. But there is a bigger ambiguity than this, namely what would happen (it is said never to have occurred on the federal level) if the Report of any particular department were not sanctioned. What would *not* happen is quite clear, there would be no threat on the part of the *whole* Federal Council to resign. But would the Federal Councillor who was head of the Department resign? Otherwise, what is the point of the procedure?

This ambiguity is a basic weakness of the federal parliamentary system which one has to accept—a very similar difficulty occurs in the case of the Budget and Accounts. To answer the actual question 'What happens?', there are two lines of approach. On the one hand, on the cantonal level it has happened that a minister has been forced to resign because his gestion was not sanctioned by the cantonal Parliament. As a matter of fact, it happened in 1960 in Ticino. On the other hand, there is a Law on the Responsibility of Authorities[1] which provides a sort of impeachment procedure: one can speculate as to whether there is not some link-up between the sanction of gestion and a minister's liability to this law, namely, that the sanction exculpates him as regards his official acts. But this is not the stuff of ordinary politics. What really would happen if one House were to refuse sanction would be precisely nothing: the sky would not fall down, the Councillor would not resign, the Chamber would simply turn to the next item. There are, it has been hinted, ways in plenty of getting rid of individual Federal Councillors in time, and it is conceivable that the day may come when a refusal by both Chambers to sanction gestion is the decisive nail in a minister's political coffin—but this would only be the case if he were impossible on other grounds and had lost the support of his own political friends. In the ordinary debate on gestion (as on the Budget and the Accounts) the Assembly is a toothless watchdog. At the decisive point procedure is weak and muddled because it has no precise action at which it can aim. This weakness strikes very deep indeed, and is the most obvious point of criticism in the Swiss 'system'. There is *some* concept of ministerial responsibility, and ministers do resign, but the procedure is not openly directed to this point and this is one reason why the proceedings of Parliament do not hold the attention.

THE COMMITTEES ON GESTION

In principle neither Chamber handles any business without having to hand a report from one of its committees. The Report on the Conduct of Business is therefore sent in the first instance to the Committee on Gestion in each Chamber.

Until 1920 this Committee was not a 'standing committee' in either Chamber, but was re-elected each year. Since then, however, the National Council has set up the committee after each general election for the whole legislature period: this is now four years. In the Council of States it is still not a standing committee: this is reasonable in such a small Chamber. The committee is a large one; in the National Council it has seventeen members and in the Council of States it has nine.

The 'priority' in the handling of Gestion, that is to say, which Council deals with it first, alternates from year to year. Each Council's

[1] Law of 14 March 1958 on the Responsibility of the Confederation, repealing the Law of 1850.

committee meets to consider the Report as soon as it becomes available (without waiting for the other Council), but the 'first' Council considers its own committee's verdict on the Report before the matter is handed on to the 'second' Council of that year: the committees work simultaneously, but the Councils themselves debate Gestion successively. One would expect there to be close co-ordination between the Councils and their committees, but I am informed by both members and officials that there is in fact no co-ordination between the two sets of investigations: this almost staggers belief.

Early in the year (in 1960 it was in February) the full committee is called together by its President.[1] The business of this first meeting is to divide the committee into 'sections' (sub-committees), and to charge the sections with any item of business which the full committee requires to be investigated. The sections are mostly composed of five or six members, one section for each department and one (of two members only) for the Federal Chancery. It follows from these figures that each member will sit in two sections. Each section has a different president, the president of the whole committee (in 1960) taking the presidency of the section investigating the Chancery, and being an ordinary member of one of the other sections. Allocation is made taking the specialized interests of the members into consideration, and an approximate balance of parties. The full committee, on the suggestions of its members, charges each section with seven or eight (or more) definite questions, such as 'What is the present situation of the plans for improving navigation of the upper Rhine?' (to the Department of Posts and Railways' section). Some of these may already have taken the form of postulates.

It is now the turn of each of the Presidents of the sections to summon his section together. This is done in a set form by the Secretariat of the Assembly, with a copy to the President of the whole committee, and a copy to the Federal Councillor concerned—with a request that he attend—and to the heads of the divisions of the department, with a request that they hold themselves in readiness to be sent for. At the same time the special questions with which the section is charged are on the paper, with a request to the department for a written answer.

The sections then, at their meetings (in Berne in the first instance) further sub-divide the business among their members, for by this time the Report on Gestion is in their hands and they can see what they have to do. Having discussed their tactics they call the Federal

---

[1] The description is henceforward of the National Council, and the procedure as in 1960. See illustrations, pages 192–4.

Councillor before them (sitting round a table in one of the smaller rooms in the Parliament building), and then each divisional chief in turn as required—the Federal Councillor being still present. They have the power also to take evidence from independent experts. The business consists in chasing further the written questions, and in members' further questions arising out of the replies. To obtain further information the Rapporteurs of the informal sub-sections may find occasion to ring up and call upon the official in charge of the business under investigation.

By May the sections have satisfied themselves and prepared their reports, and the whole committee is summoned by the president once more, usually to meet in a quiet resort on the periphery of the country (Rorschach, in 1960). The meeting is a long one—two days—during which the committee decide on their agenda for the great debate on Gestion. In 1960, under an exceptionally vigorous President, an attempt was also made to check that the previous year's recommendations had been enforced by the executive, and it is evident from his subsequent speech to the National Council that in this year, at any rate, there was a full and critical debate in committee and a real will to assert 'the prerogatives of the legislature'. The discussions seem to have borne fruit also in other debates, other than that on *gestion* itself. No fewer than eighty verbal reports by members of the committee to the Chamber were on the final agenda for the gestion debate proper.

DEBATE IN THE WHOLE HOUSE

On 13 June the great debate was opened by a speech from M. Grandjean, the committee's President for that year—the presidency is for a single year. It was a fighting speech, delivered in a loud nasal patois: the former characteristic, at least, marked it as a rather unusual event in the Assembly. It is in this speech, if anywhere, that a report on the State of the Nation is to be found. As none of the debates on the Report were printed in the *Stenographic Bulletin*, the speech is more or less lost for posterity. To ensure an accurate report in the newspapers, a cyclostyled copy was later circulated and delivered to journalists.

The procedural peg on which the opening speech is hung is the resolution (perhaps not necessary) 'to pass to the discussion of the Report'. This, of course, is accepted, and the discussion passes to each department's report. In each case the Rapporteur of the section opens, couching the opinion of the committee in the form of requests and suggestions. He is followed by the subordinate Rapporteurs for the informal sub-sections. Meanwhile, of course, it is open for non-members of the committee to intervene: when they do so it is not usually 'to debate', but to express the view of some organization, a *Verband*, a party (the very small parties being unsatisfactorily represented in committees), or of another parliamentary committee. The only element of debate is when the Federal Councillor replies.

The Federal Councillor in charge of the department whose report is being discussed is present the whole time, and his presence is the nub of the discussion. All remarks are directed to him. He accepts, evades or rejects, the committee's suggestions, and passes them on (it is hoped) to his department. It was one of the salutary features of the 1960 committee that some attempt was made to check that the requests accepted had been actually enforced.

The 'debate' forms the main business of the National Council for only three (or four if need be) days, and in the Council of States for a single, or for two days. As with Swiss parliamentary life in general, the part which takes place in public is rather unimpressive, and an anticlimax when considered as the goal of so much careful preparation. One would have expected some twenty parliamentary days of impassioned debate, and one discovers five days of desultory, ineffective, and largely unreported, formal lectures. It will be argued in this book that the conclusion is not to be drawn that the Swiss Parliament is especially weak and ineffective, but there is no evading it that, at first view, it does appear to be so. The real climax, in fact, is not the public debate, it is in the acceptance of a point of view by the executive at one of the preliminary stages. The British tendency is to see the main value of parliamentarianism in the process itself: the Swiss might reply that a process is merely a means, and the real value is in the influence which 'the people', the non-bureaucrats, have on the bureaucracy.

In a notable contrast to British ways of thought, the redress of individual administrative grievances (which is the basic technique of Parliament in controlling the methods of the executive in Britain) plays no part in the Swiss procedure. None of the eighty-odd 'special questions' in 1960 concerned individual grievances. The procedure for dealing with these grievances is not political at all; it is by means of 'an appeal in administrative law'. For Parliament to interfere (except by means of revision of the sentence on appeal, or by pardon or amnesty) would be an infringement of the separation of powers. The element of discretion is built into the legal system, a much less 'strict law' than in Britain, and is not provided by the political system.

The reader is perhaps beginning to see how fundamentally different the constitutional techniques of Britain and Switzerland are, yet how each is nevertheless striving for the same result. It is for this reason that a step-by-step comparison (e.g. with British 'estimates procedure') is not attempted. The result can be compared, but not the procedure by which it is attained.

XIII
Finance

In Britain Parliament has a stranglehold over finance, and the Government can neither raise money by taxation, transfer money from the Exchequer account into the Treasury ('appropriation'), nor spend money without annual legislation by Parliament. Administratively, the whole finance of Government is controlled by a special department, the Treasury, which thus has a sort of supremacy over other departments. Financial policy is in the hands of the Chancellor of the Exchequer, and his plans for taxation are unfolded annually in what is popularly called 'the Budget'. The most effective of all parliamentary controls, however, is that exercised by the Comptroller- and Auditor-General, who reports to the Public Accounts Committee of the House of Commons: this control is effective at the stage of 'appropriation' as well as of audit. Only the House of Commons has any authority (in the long run) in financial matters. But by the most famous and ancient of its standing orders, the House has abdicated its right of initiating projects of expenditure into the hands of Her Majesty's Ministers, and it makes no grant of public money 'except on the recommendation of the Crown'.

None of these statements applies to Switzerland.[1]

The power of the Swiss Assembly to debate finance at all is derived from the Constitution, whereby the estimates of expenditure for the ensuing year (called in Switzerland 'the Budget', by a mistaken analogy) and the accounts for the previous year are approved by the two Chambers. The legal effects of this approval are difficult to determine, and are discussed below, but certainly there is no stranglehold. While control of finance is the root of popular government in Britain, in Switzerland it is merely one of the flowers, one, among many, of the 'more especial matters within the competence of the two Councils' listed in Article 85 of the Constitution. The Estimates are not much used as a general administrative control, for discussion is in fact confined to the financial aspects. Appropriation is only an administrative process, not under parliamentary control at all (so far as the Constitution is concerned), and the Accounts are treated as being of almost no parliamentary interest whatsoever. There is no

[1] A friend in the Swiss Political Department considers that this chapter underestimates the strength of control by the Finance Department. For the *Mitbericht* of the Finance Department, see p. 95.

FINANCE

Treasury: there is a department of finance, but it has no supremacy over other departments (even though, under its present head, it seems to be acquiring one). Taxation is not annual, but by virtue of permanent legislation. Both Houses have equal rights in the matter of finance. Proposals for the expenditure of public money are frequently made on the floor of both Houses and, indeed, such expenditure is the burden of most speeches and its stimulation the most important activity of most deputies.

And yet, the necessities of the case being the same, the lineaments of the British system keep on appearing in a different form. One has the impression that in fifty years' time the British system of 1960 will be firmly established in Switzerland—an impression which is flattering, but disconcerting when one is aware how fundamentally ineffective the whole excellent British financial machinery is, and how much better things seem to be run in Switzerland with a machinery that is at every point deficient.

THE LEGAL EFFECT OF THE BUDGET

Just as with the approval of the Report on the Conduct of Business, when one asks what precisely is the legal effect of the Budget and the approval of Accounts, one gets a vague and unsatisfactory answer. When one goes on, with British constitutional logic, to ask what happens if one or other is not sanctioned, the ultimate answer (probably) is 'nothing at all'. For this reason, it never comes to that. The toothless watchdog barks, and then wags his tail. But this does not mean that the bark is ineffective, nor (to drop the metaphor) that Parliament has no effective financial role to play. It only means that the control of finance has never been made a logical part of the Swiss system, and cannot be fully integrated into it. Intellectually, the Swiss is an unsatisfactory system, but it works after a fashion, and even this is a sort of praise of an institution of government.

The Swiss Budget is not necessary either for taxation or (strictly speaking) for expenditure. Taxation is imposed under permanent legislation. Traditionally the only considerable source of federal revenue is from customs duties, for the Constitution allots direct taxation (by implication) to the cantons, and all cantons have an income tax. The income from customs rises and falls according to the volume of trade, and the government can do rather little about it, so in the old days the government could not really have a financial policy at all. But since 1916 a federal income tax has been levied under one form or another, and for the greater part of the time unconstitutionally. In recent years temporary Constitutional amendments have been made from time to time to grant the central government its income tax. Administratively this has made things difficult for the government, but politically it has kept a healthy discussion going: in this way, by the back door, one of the aims of parliamentary control (i.e. animated discussion) has been attained. By one means or another, by bank rates and currency controls and influence, the Federal Council has in modern times even acquired the means whereby a true financial policy is made possible. Indeed, it is not always easy to discuss what actually happens in Swiss public finance in terms of the myths encouraged by the wording of the Constitution.

Like taxation, expenditure is legalized by permanent statutes. In Switzerland (unlike Britain) it can be asserted that if the object of expenditure is legal, the expenditure also is lawful: for example, if the Federal Government is entitled to maintain an army, it is *ipso facto* entitled to pay for it. The Budget merely authorizes again what was already lawful in itself, and in this sense it is (from the strict standpoint of the constitutional lawyer) superfluous.

What does sometimes happen is that expenditure which was not previously lawful is legalized for the first time by the Budget. Between 1875 and 1900, indeed, the federal civil service expanded largely *via* the Budget, without any other legal authorization. This practice is frowned on by constitutional lawyers: the Budget is not a law.

The chief use of the Budget may be called its internal-legal use, as giving the green light to the Civil Service to spend, and as co-ordinating expenditure and checking it. The Budget is the internal expedient (one could almost say) which the Civil Service adopts to conduct its own affairs. The Assembly has cognizance of the document, and gives its comments upon it. It has a further use in checking the accounts of government, for the Estimates for one year virtually *are* the accounts at the end of that year. They are kept in the same form, and there should be no divergence.

ADMINISTRATIVE EFFECT OF THE BUDGET

Most of the beneficial results which flow in Britain from the legal importance of the financial work of Parliament are obtained in Switzerland by administrative processes. This is why it is necessary here to explore the administrative side more thoroughly. Administrative procedure is the back-door whereby Swiss financial control reaches the same goal as the British control. This procedure has three aims, to secure (i) legality, (ii) probity, and (iii) that expenditure is in accordance with estimates.

The method by which this is done is best explained by an example.

FINANCE

Suppose a department (e.g. the Military Department) wishes to spend money on an object authorized by law (e.g. to buy sports shoes for headquarters military personnel). The Department sends an indent, with the requisite number of copies, to the *Contrôle des Finances*. The *Contrôle* checks the legality of the payment, and sends copies, stamped with its *visum*, to the Cashier's and Accounts Office—another independent sub-office of the Finance Department. Here the indent is fed into a machine, which debits the appropriate account. If the credit voted by the Assembly under that head is exhausted, the penny, as it were, simply fails to drop, and no payment can be made until a credit is available. One copy of the indent then comes back to the Military Department, while the other acts as a post-cheque to debit the Confederation's consolidated account (*Trésorerie*: in English we would say Exchequer) at the National Bank. The whole procedure takes three days.

THE *CONTROLE DES FINANCES*

The *Contrôle des Finances* is the point at which the Swiss Parliament has chosen to exercise the sort of control which the Public Accounts Committee exercises through the Comptroller- and Auditor-General. It therefore has a particular importance for this study.

The present legal basis of the *Contrôle* is the 'regulative' of 2 April 1927. 'Regulative' is not an accepted term of art in Swiss law, and the legal status of the one establishing the position of the *Contrôle* is unique. It is a decree of the Federal Council 'approved by both Chambers': the reason why this peculiar solution was adopted is unclear, and departmental tradition sheds no light on the problem. Until the 1880s the Federal Councillor in charge of the department was himself supposed to make all the necessary checks, including the books and the cash balance, 'at least once a month'—the provision had lived on from the earliest days of the new Confederation, when this had really been done in person. The Assembly, however, was suspicious, and wished either to control the accounts itself, or have them supervised by a neutral body. To disarm the proposal to set up a *cour des comptes* (Court of Audit) the Federal Council itself introduced a Control Bureau in 1882, which a few years later received its modern name, and in 1902-3 in essentials its modern form. The *cour des comptes* solution (which works well in Western Germany, for example) always remains a possibility should the present system break down.

The 'regulative' lays down that 'the *Contrôle des Finances* is autonomous and independent as regards its relations with the various divisions of the federal administration . . . It takes its decisions quite independently of its departmental superiors'. Thus, while a part of the administration, it has performed the feat, almost impossible under the Swiss Constitution, of disengaging itself from the authority of its Federal Councillor. Having acquired a sort of quasi-judicial freedom from its departmental superiors, it has sought a protector in the Federal Assembly.

The actual duties of the *Contrôle* are enumerated in the regulative, they are, briefly, concerned with the three issues mentioned—legality, probity, and compliance with the estimates or supplementary estimates of the Assembly (or the supplementary credits granted on the provisional authority of the Federal Council). The role of the Assembly in this process is to be the power which shall enforce these principles when they are threatened by the departments. The Constitution sets up two centres of gravity, two fields of attraction, and this makes it possible to set a body, such as the *Contrôle*, as it were equidistant from the two, free to act out of its own conscience.

The connexion with the executive is clear. The members of the *Contrôle* are federal officials, appointed for four years by the Federal Council, and in their service relationships and promotion under the Head of the Department of Finance in the ordinary way. It is only within this scheme that its officials have their independence of conscience.

The connexion with the Assembly is more complex, and the office seems not quite to have reached the end of the journey on which it is evidently embarked. The connexion is through one of the subdivisions of the *Contrôle* which has a very special relationship with the Chambers. This is the Secretariat of the Joint Finance Delegation. To explain what this is, it is necessary to start from the other gravitational pole, the Assembly.

THE FINANCE COMMITTEE OF THE TWO CHAMBERS

The Finance Committee (*commission des finances*) is in each Chamber considered to be, on the whole, the most important of all the standing committees. It is regarded, in consequence, as forming a part of the *cursus honorum*—the model career—of a parliamentarian aspiring to the highest offices that are available to him in the existing political constellations. To mark out its somewhat special dignity, it is provided for by Law, the Law on the Councils, and this has the advantage that it clearly subordinates the executive (Federal Councillors and civil servants) to the legal obligation to give facilities to the committee (without, however, providing a sanction if these are not afforded). Under the Law the Councils have given themselves a joint *Règlement* for their respective finance committees, and one for their Joint Finance Delegation. The committees are elected for six years (with obligatory retirement at the end of that period) 'by the whole Council'. The practice of agreeing between the parties on the names to be included is, in actuality, no different from the ordinary one in the case of committees selected by the *bureaux*, but the greater importance of the Finance Committee is marked out by the more elaborate procedure of election by the Council as a whole, and the greater authority with which the committee is thereby clothed. The two committees nominate their own chairmen. In the Council of States there are eleven members (one quarter of the whole Council); in the National Council there are fifteen.

Both committees divide themselves into sections, like the Committee on Gestion, to each of which is allotted a definite portion of the estimates and of the accounts. It is on the estimates that interest is concentrated. The sections (instructed by the whole committee) then go through their portion of the estimates, item by item, trying to pare them down. As with the Gestion Committee, the Federal Councillor concerned, and his officials as necessary, defend the departmental projects. It is a type of financial control (item by item) which experience in Britain of the Estimates Committee, in the form it took from 1920–38, has shown to be quite ineffective to secure economy. Swiss experience only confirms this generalization. In a modern state the source of waste is not that this official or this purchase exacts too high a price, it is that whole services are ill-planned or partially unnecessary. The item-by-item approach only duplicates, from the standpoint of ignorance, work that has already been done from the standpoint of knowledge. Small reductions, which have later to be restored at a greater total expense, are the result of this 'penny note book' attempt at economy.

The committee, however, is immensely valuable. It forces officials to explain their mental processes, and this helps to ensure that these are rational, and it gives the members of the committees an insight into, almost a co-operation with, the administration. The threat to reduce the estimates is, it could be said, the sanction which the committee exerts in order to secure executive co-operation with the Assembly. It must be remembered (once more) that the members of Parliament are not innocents prowling around the administrative palace in naïve wonderment. Some of them will be cantonal ministers, others familiar with business or trades unions—with sources of information other than official channels. In a small country no member of the political establishment has his ear far from the ground.

Conviction that the system is valuable does not come from talks with members (who may sometimes be cynical or depressed) but from officials. They do not laugh at the system, and would be brave men if they did, and they find contact with members valuable: in the matters where officials are amateurs, parliamentarians are experts. No doubt attendance before the committees is irksome to officials, and inquiries may be embarrassing or even unfair, but the value of the institution is recognized in the same way as a soldier acknowledges the value of discipline: it is a nuisance, but it makes him what he is. The silence of the committee is the nearest most officials can ever expect to come to being appreciated by the public they serve.

From the standpoint of members (who yearn to *do* things, in the same way that officials yearn to be popular) the committee has a further interest. It is the avenue to service on the Finance Delegation, and service on the Delegation is the nearest to being a minister that a Swiss parliamentarian can get on the federal level, while retaining his seat in the Chamber.

THE FINANCE DELEGATION

The Finance Delegation (*délégation des finances*) is a joint committee of the two Chambers. The Finance Committee of each Chamber elects, for 'a legislative period' of four years, three members from among its own numbers. The six members of the Joint Delegation elect two chairmen for the whole four years—the presidency being held by the Council which has priority in the Budget for that year, and the vice-presidency by a member of the other Council. The delegation is required by its *Règlement* to meet every two months, but its investigations are in a sense continuous. For it also splits into 'sections', of two members each, one from one Council and one from the other. Hunting in pairs, the members have remarkable powers, for they are each armed with a pass which entitles them at any time to appear in any federal office and demand to see the papers they require (with almost no restriction).

Such full powers are sparingly used. The members of the Delegation are formidable enough in themselves. In 1960 Herr Bringolf, for example, was a member, and was in the section specializing in the affairs of the Military and the Political Departments. A member of the Council since 1925, he has served (it will be remembered from the list on page 57) on the Committee of Gestion, the committee on Foreign Affairs, the committee on Full Powers, the Military Com-

FINANCE

mittee, Foreign Affairs again (which he presided for four years) and now on the Finance Committee. He was currently serving also on the *ad hoc* committee concerned with the revision of the structure of the Federal Army and in 1960 he had narrowly failed to be elected a Federal Councillor. Armed with his Delegation pass, he must exercise briefly, and in the name of the legislature, an authority which is not to be despised.

The Secretariat of the Delegation is provided by the *Contrôle des Finances*.

THE SECRETARY OF THE JOINT FINANCE DELEGATION

In this secretary's hands, therefore, all the threads come together: he is at the hub of the whole system:

(i) he is secretary of the Delegation,

(ii) he is secretary of the Finance Committees of the National Council and the Council of States, and

(iii) he is a member of the *Contrôle*, the autonomous sub-department without whose *visum* no payment can be made,[1] and which audits the Accounts. (It is not, however, *his own visum* which is required, and thus he is in a weaker position than the British Comptroller- and Auditor-General.)

It must not be concluded from this that the secretary himself is a power in the land: in his own right he is not. It is not in general a Swiss solution (as it is a British solution) to concentrate power in the hands of an office-bearer and then to isolate him from pressures and give him a semi-judicial position: even judges in Switzerland do not have such a status. It is that he stands at the point where executive and legislature meet and are indistinguishable from each other, and is the instrument whereby the legislature can exert a pressure on the jugular vein of power. An English observer would regard his position

[1] The following diagram may be of use to the reader who is bemused by names and designations:

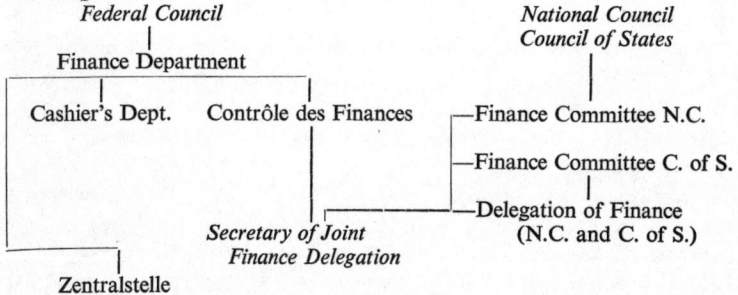

```
       Federal Council                          National Council
            |                                   Council of States
       Finance Department                              |
   _____|_____                                  |
   |       |        |                                  |
Cashier's  Contrôle des Finances  ——Finance Committee N.C.
 Dept.              |
                    |             ——Finance Committee C. of S.
                    |                             |
                    |             ——Delegation of Finance
                    Secretary of Joint            (N.C. and C. of S.)
                    Finance Delegation
   |
Zentralstelle
```

143

in the departmental hierarchy as far too modest in view of his Constitutional significance: the same criticism would be made of the secretaryship of the Federal Assembly.

The Delegation is consulted by the appointing authority, when a new Secretary is required to be appointed.

THE BUDGET AND THE ACCOUNTS BEFORE THE ASSEMBLY

Just as the Report on the Conduct of Business (*gestion*) is the chief routine business of the June session, the Budget is the chief routine business of the December session. The Accounts of the previous year (e.g. of 1959, in 1960) are considered in the June session.

The debate on the Budget follows very much the pattern of the debate on gestion. There are Rapporteurs for each department. First comes the debate on *eintreten* for the whole Budget—the procedural peg for a general review—and then the departments in turn are debated. The figures are usually knocked down a little during the debates, and these reductions (if carried in both Chambers) have to be accepted by the Federal Council. But usually the attitude of the Federal Councillor concerned is decisive, and the executive 'gets its way'. Reductions made can later be nullified by supplementary credits if necessary, but are usually accepted in good faith, even if they are not, in fact, genuine economies: the Finance Committees are always there to maintain the prestige of the legislature and to see its will is not cynically flouted.

There is no reason why further expenditure should not be voted during these debates, but in practice this is not the occasion for doing so. Demands for subsidy are made continuously, in and out of Parliament: a Federal Councillor in 1960 said, after six months in office, that not a single day had passed without some new demand. But in the debate on the Budget the cry is for economy—the subsidies, but not the consequence of the subsidies are what are demanded: more money distributed but less expenditure. This is not just a natural weakness of assemblies, it is a logical and sensible aim to pursue. Only very recently is there any sign that the process is getting out of hand in Switzerland: it remains to be seen how the political system would now stand up to the demands of an economic crisis.

As with the debate on gestion, the visitor's impression is, on the one hand, of unreal economies of small sums and real expenditure of vast sums due to political weakness on the part of the legislature, and, on the other hand, an impression that the executive always seems to get its way. This is true of the open debates, but it is not so true of the whole system. In general, the balance between the demands

FINANCE

of the pressure groups (which the Chambers are not always able to withstand) and the needs of the country is not unsatisfactory. The administration itself is very economical—a rather higher pay to federal civil servants might be an economy in the long run—and is very uncorrupt. Even the fundamental Constitutional weakness of the Assembly and the confusion of thought that seems to lie at the basis of the Constitution, can be defended. Only a weak legislature can afford to be strong: a strong legislature like that of Great Britain becomes a slave to its own strength, the executive being potentially so much under its control that the executive is forced to dominate it. The doctrine of responsibility is the glory of the British system, but in its extreme form it is the downfall of popular government. It is the merit of the Swiss system that it does not have the extreme system of responsibility (whereby the Prime Minister is held responsible, for example, if he fails to have the law amended). There is a curious, and accidental, logic about its illogicality, as with the institutions of all those peoples that can claim a genius for politics.

A feature of the Swiss Assembly is its lack of interest in the Accounts, the activity in which the British Public Accounts Committee is most effective. The interest of the House of Commons is perhaps due to the reflexion that if a Civil Service can be caught out in an already committed extravagance or mistake, it is compromised indeed. But because there is ultimately no applicable sanction under the Swiss system, and therefore no real point in catching a minister red-handed, there is no political interest in the Accounts. Members want to influence the future, not nag about the past.

THE *ZENTRALSTELLE FUR ORGANISATIONSFRAGEN*

The absence of an active presidency, or of a Finance Department with a stranglehold on other departments, gives rise to various administrative difficulties. One of these is the expert examination of Organization and Methods in the administration as a whole. The attempt has been made, in the past, to make the Federal Chancery into a controlling office, but any such attempt is in vain so long as there is no effective President. The Chancellor has no power: he cannot hold a refractory department to ransom.

The problem of Organization and Methods became urgent after 1945. From 1913 to 1938 the Federal Civil Service (excluding the Posts and Railways) had doubled, and by mid-1944 it had almost doubled again. By massive dismissals the Federal Council forced the numbers down after the war. The dismissals reduced the morale of the Service at a time when expansion had reduced its prestige, and the existence of a swollen Federal Service was continually brought to the electorate's notice by the repeated post-war Constitutional crises over federal finance. The Federal Council tried, somewhat helplessly, to deal with the problem by the usual expedients—outside committees of experts (the surest way of destroying a service's morale), circulars, an 'office for co-ordinating economy and rationalization proposals', and so on.

The Federal Council was spurred by the Finance Delegation, who launched a postulate in the National Council, and by a non-parliamentary committee of critics, who started to launch a referendum for a Constitutional amendment. Faced with a Constitutional Initiative (which gathered the requisite number of signatures in a very brief space) the Federal Council acted daringly. Refusing to submit a counter-project of *Constitutional* amendment, they proposed to the Assembly a federal law which would take the wind out of the sails of the initiants, and the law was passed by the two Chambers in October 1954 (and made subject to the 'facultative referendum'—the legislative challenge). The initiating committee withdrew their project and the law came into force in March 1955.

The Initiative proposal was for a Control Committee of three experts chosen from outside the service. The counter-proposal contained in the law was for a semi-independent office within the administration. It was this latter which was accordingly set up, being fortunate to find for its head an expert, from private industry, of remarkable drive, knowledge and personality. The new office was given the colourless name of *Zentralstelle* ('Centre' is the nearest English equivalent).

The *Zentralstelle* went to work on the model of the United States administration—the British Civil Service now commands no particular veneration on the Continent—though the methods may well, in origin, be as much British as American. Instead of 'controlling', it set itself the task of gaining the confidence of the administration, and of training within each office a group of 'collaborators' (*Organisationsmitarbeiter*, called, significantly, 'O.M.s'). It also set about integrating itself into the federal system.

This was done by contacts with (i) the Federal Personnel Office; (ii) the Federal Supply Office (*Drucksachen- und Materialzentrale*); (iii) the Cashiers' Office in the Finance Department; and (iv) the Finance Control. It is the last of these which is the most significant, because through the Finance Control the *Zentralstelle* has access to the Delegation and the Finance Committees, and thereby to the Assembly. It also keeps contact with the Gestion Committees. The Assembly does its part by supporting the *Zentralstelle* wherever possible.

FINANCE

The local habitation and the formal place of the *Zentralstelle* is in the Finance Department: its offices are not, like the Secretary to the Delegation's, in the Parliament House proper. Ultimately, its power rests on the vigilance of the Assembly in supporting it, but its methods are strictly those of advice and co-operation. It considers it can only do its task if the heads of the sixty-odd divisions (*Abteilungen*) are on its side, and retain full responsibility for their divisions.

The setting up of this *Zentrale*, and the new spirit animating the Secretariat of the Finance Delegations, and perhaps one could add also the Secretariat of the Assembly, are perhaps the main victories of the spirit of democracy in federal affairs since the end of the war: even in a referendum democracy 'freedom is a plant that grows in the interstices of procedure', and that is the importance of these highly technical innovations.

XIV
Co-operation

In 1960, now that the formula of proportionality in the Federal Council seems to have been accepted, it is apparent to all the world that a 'parliamentary' relationship between the legislature and the executive is out of the question. They are too closely connected, and in both there is a perpetual coalition. This new relationship started in the 1930s when it became apparent to Social Democrats that their real enemy was not liberalism and the church, but was Fascism and Germany. Since 1945 the unity has been strengthened rather than weakened, and economic prosperity has created a contented working class. Rightly or wrongly, the working man feels very conscious of the privilege of being Swiss, and not at all conscious of the disadvantages of being an unprivileged Swiss.

Furthermore, there is no historical tradition of victories of legislatures over executives: the tradition is one of democracy (the referendum and so on) being victorious over aristocracy. In consequence, the conviction that parliamentary *control* is necessary is rather weak: the tradition of co-operation is rather strong, for it is normal on the communal and cantonal level. The effects of a lack of a parliamentary opposition are felt in parliamentary procedure. Since the 1930s the procedure of an opposition has been giving way to the procedure of co-operation, or, if one wishes to stress the dubious aspect, of complicity. Two of the permanent committees, in particular, have so strongly the character of committees of co-operation that it would now be wrong to discuss them under the heading of 'control'.

These are the Foreign Affairs Committee and the Military Committee, of each House. The best example of co-operation, however, was the Full Powers Committee (*Vollmachtenkommission*) of 1939–52, set up to supervise actions taken under Emergency Powers. The committee, having secured the dismantlement of these powers, perished with its own success. The Military and the Foreign Committees have taken up its torch.

THE FOREIGN AFFAIRS COMMITTEE

The first attempt to set up this committee was in 1916. The Federal

Council and the Army leadership had been accused, with abundant justification, of being pro-German, and a 'cleft' between German- and French-speakers, and between executive and people, was becoming apparent. The proposition was therefore made (by the Social Democrats) that there should be a standing committee for foreign affairs in the National Council. The Federal Council rejected the proposal, and a majority of the National Council rejected it also.

The grounds for resisting the Committee on the part of the executive have always been that foreign relations are an executive matter *par excellence*: the legislature therefore had no right to set up such a committee; it would be unconstitutional. The Constitution can perhaps by an unnatural interpretation be construed as tending this way, but on an unprejudiced view seems to give the Assembly equal competences with the executive in a manner to which it is difficult to find a parallel elsewhere. The proposal for such a committee was pressed in a desultory fashion, and, when Switzerland joined the League of Nations, an annual Committee for League of Nations Affairs was in fact set up by the National Council to consider the Annual Report to the League. It served some of the purposes of a Foreign Affairs Committee. Meanwhile the possibility of challenging treaties to a referendum had been added to the Swiss citizens' Constitutional armoury: treaties, of course, needed Assembly sanction in any event, and therefore each Council set up an *ad hoc* committee whenever a treaty came under consideration. The inactivity of Swiss foreign policy[1] makes for unimportant and occasional treaties: a trickle of minor agreements with neighbours rather than a torrent of matters on which public feeling is aroused and which determine the national destiny.

From 1926 to 1936 the project slept. But Motta's growing uncertainty of touch, and his steady drift towards the right wing, created a real need for such a committee under the Swiss system of permanent departmental heads. In the meanwhile, moreover, the Socialists had become a national party, and had a genuine claim to representation in executive matters, but they had no representative in the Federal Council itself. The Socialists were not merely 'loyal' in 1936, they had become essential and enthusiastic partners in the fight against Nazism. In that year, therefore, it was logical to accept the motion of the old revolutionary, National Councillor Grimm, for a Foreign Affairs Committee. The committee was set up, but its terms of reference seem to have been unsatisfactory. It was to consider the drafts of treaties, and Reports to the League and, 'not

[1] See Appendix One on p. 167: 'Swiss Foreign Policy'.

regularly', to receive reports from the Federal Council on its diplomatic activity. Lacking any effective sanction, apart from refusing to recommend the sanctioning of treaties, and lacking active good will on the part of the foreign minister, it led an indecisive existence until 1939, and thereafter a miserable one.

In 1939, the Emergency Powers Arrêté[1] passed on the outbreak of war in Europe (besides conferring full powers on the executive in unqualified terms, and, indeed, virtually suspending the normal Constitution) contained a provision for a Full Powers Committee in both Councils. This provision was added to the arrêté in the Assembly —the proposal was not contained in the original draft—on the insistence of the Socialists. The Committee rapidly became the most important of all, and set up a sub-committee for foreign affairs. It seems that only three projects fell within the purview of the Foreign Affairs Committee during the years of war.[2]

By 1945 the government had a change of heart. The science of Public Relations had been born. The relations between Parliament and executive were cordial in respect of the big issues of national policy. The committee, when the National Council demanded its reactivation, was seen to be a help to government, to be, one might say, an instrument to obtain public support or to smother criticism as the case might be. It received as such the full co-operation of government.

The result would not disappoint a diplomat of the old school.

The committee is regarded as one of the most important ones. A councillor ambitious of being considered eligible to the executive considers that service on the committee is an important stage on his *cursus honorum*. This alone shows that it has power: members themselves would not be deceived on a matter like this. As regards the government, the committee has something to offer, namely the co-operation of the parliamentary parties (through the fractions' own informal foreign affairs committees). In return for this, the government (to be more precise, the head of the Political Department) is prepared to give the committee 'inside' or 'semi-inside' information, and to allow the committee to comment and suggest and argue. There can be no doubt that the exercise is valuable for both parties. The government rationalizes its decisions, and has a forecast of public reactions to them, and neutralizes criticism. The Assembly

---

[1] Printed in Hughes *The Federal Constitution of Switzerland: Text and Commentary*. Oxford, 1954.

[2] My source is the Debate in the National Council in 1946. I suspect that if checked this figure would not be accurate, but the fact of a miserable existence is abundantly established.

has much more information (seeping out to confidential sessions of the fractions) and some of its members have the chance of putting questions to Federal Councillors and officials.

THE MILITARY COMMITTEE

Like the Foreign Affairs Committee, the Military Committee concerns a subject peculiarly the prerogative of the executive power: in its present form it is (again, like the Foreign Affairs Committee) a sign that the full logic of the all-party Federal Council has been accepted. It was set up as a standing committee for the first time in both Chambers in 1946; the Council of States had for a long time had a Military Committee—but had dropped it in 1928.

The new committee was welcomed by the Federal Council, and attracted from the start the leading figures in the Chambers—especially those interested in foreign affairs, for military policy has implications for foreign policy.[1] As will be seen from Herr Bringolf's committee career on page 57, a National Councillor who specializes in foreign affairs can alternate these two committees, and also cover the same ground (from a more critical point of view) in the appropriate Sections of the Finance, or of the Gestion, Committees.

The success of these two committees shows clearly in which direction the Swiss constitution is, at the moment, developing.

---

[1] For example, the cruel dilemma whether Switzerland should have an army that would play a useful role by the side of the N.A.T.O. forces, or whether the doctrine of neutrality means that one must not guess against whom precisely one is likely to have to defend oneself.

XV
The Committee System in General

Many of the most important committees and forms of committee have already been mentioned. It is time to describe the whole system of parliamentary committees, and to explain how they are appointed and what are their duties.[1]

The first distinction is between standing and *ad hoc* committees. Standing committees are committees elected for a period of time, either four years or six. *Ad hoc* are those elected for a particular task; for example, to consider the draft of a bill.

THE STANDING COMMITTEES OF THE NATIONAL COUNCIL

1. The Committee of Verification of Mandate (*Vérification des pouvoirs*)

The National Council checks the credentials of its own members, but at the beginning of the session immediately following a general election there is a sort of deadlock. No one knows who is elected until the Council has decided, and the Council cannot decide until it knows who its members are. The Council has no President, and can appoint no committee, until it 'constitutes itself'.

The way the Council gets out of this logical impasse is laid down in its *Règlement*. Before the date of meeting the *doyen d'âge* (the oldest member or presumed member) nominates a 'provisional bureau' of six, over which he presides. The provisional bureau nominates a committee to verify the mandates of members. In the first session of the Council the *doyen d'âge* presides, and the provisional committee report on the uncontested elections. As soon as half the seats are validated the Council can act, and members take the oath.

The committee is in one sense the very oldest of all the committees, for the first National Council elected in 1848 was faced with a large number of hotly contested elections, which it wished to determine on party-political considerations. But it was not made a standing committee until 1876. Under the system of proportional representation

[1] In this chapter I owe a special debt to Dr Claus Burkhard's brilliant study, *Die parlamentarischen Kommissionen der schweizerischen Bundesversammlung*. Zurich, 1952.

it is not really necessary for the committee to exist once the election petitions have been adjudicated, but it does sometimes have a case to consider during the session, and its decisions on Constitutional questions may be very important. As the members of the Council of States are elected by the cantons, under cantonal law, there is no equivalent committee in that Council: the cantons themselves decide who is elected.

2. The Finance Committee

The early practice of the Councils varied until 1876, and as a standing committee this dates from then: it has already been discussed.

3. Committee on Gestion

This also has already been discussed, in Chapter XII. In the early years after 1848, the Annual Report was sometimes referred to the Committee on the Budget or to that on the Accounts, or, sometimes, to an *ad hoc* committee. In 1876 the committee received its present name, but continued an annual committee down to 1920 in the National Council, and to the present day in the Council of States. The arguments against making it a standing committee were (i) the fear of erecting a too powerful committee, a 'second government', and thereby eroding the responsibility of the Federal Council, and (ii) the desire to rotate the membership as much as possible, so that all members could, in time, acquire an insight into the working of the administration. The argument in favour of making it a standing committee was to give it more effective supervision and to see that its demands were realized—more especially the informal demands and suggestions made in the course of committee meetings and only recorded in the transcript of the committee's deliberations.

Like the Finance Committee, it is elected for six years, with a prohibition of two consecutive terms.

4. The Alcohol Committee

This has been set up in both Councils since 1890 to control the nationalized distilling industry (a federal monopoly since 1885). From 1894 there has been a Joint Alcohol Delegation.

The Alcohol Committee, the two Railway Committees, and the Posts Committee are committees of direct supervision, and thus form a class of their own. If Socialism came to Switzerland this is a type of committee which would, no doubt, proliferate.

5. The Committee on Petitions

The Federal Diet had a committee for petitions, and this committee was set up as a standing committee in the two Federal Chambers from the start. For a generation it was the only standing committee.

The Chambers now receive half a dozen petitions or so every quarterly session. They are treated 'bicamerally', that is to say they are dealt with by each Chamber in turn.

The petitions vary in nature. Very many are irreceivable, being concerned with matters which the Constitution does not place within the competence of the Assembly. A few of them are of a legal nature—requesting the Chambers to give the authorization necessary for certain types of proceedings against federal authorities, for example. Some treat large political matters, and these are sometimes referred to other committees (e.g. the Foreign Affairs Committee). There is the usual faint air of lunacy and pathetic despair about some of the cases revealed, and the usual action is to declare them irreceivable. A few attain the stage of being rejected. A very few are adopted in the form of a postulate requesting the Federal Council to take action.

Unlike the House of Commons, the Swiss Chambers consider petitions seriously, both as to form and content.

6. The Committee on Pardons

Pardons (as opposed to amnesties) are the work of the Assembly in Joint Session. This committee is therefore really a committee of the Assembly, and is now composed of nine National Councillors and four Councillors of States, sitting as a single committee. This business is referred to in the 1902 Law on the Councils in a memorably unhappy phrase: 'The Joint Bureaux of the two Councils are authorized to nominate committees for urgent affairs, or for those of less importance, notably for pardons, which affect the Assembly.'

Nevertheless, pardons are taken seriously, both in committee and in the whole Assembly, which almost always alters some of its committee's decisions. The pardons referred to are for certain specified offences against federal law. Federal law deals with some very important matters, such as high treason, but also with many trivial matters (in connexion with posts, railways, federal monopolies, and customs duties, for example). As things are now arranged, the Federal Assembly spends its time on offences which are rather too insignificant for such an august body, especially smuggling offences—while the cantonal parliaments and executives deal with major crimes against the criminal code, robbery, murder, and the like. Except for the high political offences in wartime, there is now no death penalty in Switzerland: the wording of the Constitution is misleading in this respect. Death penalties in wartime are very carefully considered by the Assembly.

There is something rather touching in the humility of the Assembly in submitting to its peace-time task of pardoning and reducing sentences for smuggling a cheese or falsely declaring the value of a typewriter. There is some suggestion, also, that the time and the emotions spent could be better directed.

7. The Committee on Railway Concessions

Railways are a federal monopoly, but in many cases and areas (including the greater part of the Grisons) railways are run, not by the Confederation itself, but by private companies under federal 'concessions'. These concessions have to be renewed periodically. The cantons nominate directors to most of these railways, and these directorships are among the sweeteners of political life on the cantonal level. In the network of intrigues and gratifications which joins federal, cantonal and communal political life into a living system, the Concessions Committee plays its part. A living political system harnesses all sorts of motives to its chariot, and only those versed in the affairs of Appenzell Outer Rhodes and the communes of the Valais can estimate the precise political value of serving on such a committee.

8. The Committee on Federal Railways

While private (or semi-private) companies run branch lines, the serious railways (as the traveller knows) are for the most part run directly by the Confederation. The political impulse to serve on this committee appears to be similar to that for serving on the Concessions Committee—scores to be settled and favours to be granted. To many communities the question whether, and when, a train stops at its station may be more important than almost anything else. For the first half century of the modern Confederation's history, railway politics were the essence of federal political life. That is the historical reason why the Assembly exercises this particular power. Its interest in it is as much political as it is administrative, and its influence on personnel policy may be locally important.

9. Committee on Customs Duties

Customs duties mean for a trading and industrial community what communications mean for a village. It is significant of the desire to serve on this committee that it has twenty-nine members in the

National Council, and fifteen in the Council of States (Gestion has seventeen, and Finance fifteen, in the National Council). Its importance is shown by the very high quality of the membership—the most politically powerful and the most economically influential of the Assembly. The quality of the membership rises, of course, when important decisions (such as alteration of tariffs) are in the wind. Membership is for six years.

This is the committee where one would expect vested interests to be most numerous and active.

10. Foreign Affairs
This has been discussed in Chapter XIV.

11. Military Affairs
So has this. Because the Swiss Army is more or less co-extensive with the Swiss electorate this committee has a special socio-political importance.

12. Posts and Telegraphs
This exists in the National Council only. The chief political importance of this committee is in the matter of personnel policy. Much the same remarks apply to it as to the two railways committees. Rural bus services come under the postal monopoly, and are provided either by the yellow 'post-autos' or under federal concessions.

AD HOC COMMITTEES

The line between *ad hoc* and standing committees is not a hard one. A law may sometimes be referred to the standing, and sometimes to an *ad hoc*, committee, and the choice may vary as between the Councils. There is likely, in any event, to be a strong personal union between an *ad hoc* and the permanent committee on any particular subject (e.g. the members of the Military Committee will be found in the *ad hoc* committee on military organization). It is natural for members to specialize, for example in foreign or in economic, or agricultural, or cultural, affairs, and to carry this specialization through their standing committee career. Such members will naturally be on their own 'fraction's' standing committee on that subject, and on the *ad hoc* committees that occur in their field of interest. An informal panel of available experts is an abiding feature of both Houses.

The typical *ad hoc* committees are those on draft laws. Two of these have been described in the chapter on legislation.

SELECTION OF MEMBERS

An important member will always be on one of the important standing committees and on any important *ad hoc* committee within his range of interest. Unimportant members have a fair share of the crumbs of important business, and of the unimportant standing committees. For the rising young man there is a ladder of minor committees leading to the important ones and to the offices of teller and then Vice-President and President of the Council. He may then move on to the States, or to the Federal Council if he is lucky. More often he is compelled to continue the treadmill of important party offices and presidencies of committees until he retires—meanwhile perhaps pursuing a parallel career in the cantonal executive, or in press or industry or *Verband*.

The *Règlement* of the National Council places a limit of membership of two permanent and two *ad hoc* committees 'as a rule' simultaneously. An idea of a committee career can be had from the example on page 172. The number of committees sitting at any one time can be gauged from the example illustrated on page 195.

The number of seats which each party has in a committee is determined by a 'key' formulated after each election.[1] This establishes exact proportionality with no generosity to the smaller parties. In consequence, the smaller parties simply do not get represented on the smaller committees at all. To qualify for representation on a committee a member must belong to a 'fraction', which is defined in the National Council as a group of five members. The Liberals have exactly five, the other minor parties combine in order to make fives. But the Communists are left out: this is not an accident, the number five is drawn so as to exclude them, and was raised from three for this purpose.

Taking this 'key' as a basis, 'election to the committees is by the bureau'. The bureau of each Council consists of the President of the Council, the Vice-President, and the eight tellers.

The tellers (*scrutateurs*) thus hold a very important position. They are elected for the whole legislature-period and may hold office for two consecutive terms, but are ineligible for a third consecutive term. In practice, each of the three main parties nominates two, and the Farmers one and the remaining member (often from the Landesring) has a general responsibility for the minor parties, which is sometimes exercised in a spirit of fairness and sometimes not. Because the offices of President and Vice-President change annually —the retiring Vice-President being elected President—in point of

[1] Illustrated on page 196.

fact the party composition of the bureau changes slightly from year to year. As the 'key' is laid down by the *Règlement*, the actual party proportions in the bureau do not matter much. The personal factor, however, is very important, and this is what gives a tellership its high place in the members' *cursus honorum*.[1]

Because nominations are, in practice, by the tellers of the fraction concerned for that fraction's vacancies, the over-all distribution of the interests or of the regions sometimes gets neglected. Each party may nominate its agricultural members, for example, to an agricultural committee where representatives of industry would be valuable. It might also happen by accident that none were from the Ticino or East Switzerland. An accidental disproportion can especially easily happen when there is not a physical meeting of the bureau, but only a series of telephone calls.

The Finance Committee, by law, is 'elected by the whole Council', by secret ballot. In practice the tellers instruct members whom to vote for: otherwise the proportions would come wrong.

The bureau members take it in turn to nominate the presidents of the *ad hoc* committees. A sort of proportionality between the parties is kept here also. It will be remembered that the president of a committee is almost always appointed Rapporteur by it (even if he represents the minority in the committee), and that occasionally the president virtually *is* the committee.

FUNCTIONS OF COMMITTEES

These have already been described incidentally. They may be said to be:

(i) 'Preparing the business of the Councils.' This is the function given in the textbooks. The whole House in practice never deals with any business without a committee report to hand.

(ii) Guiding the debate in the Council. The essentials of a debate are the report of the committee and the reply of the Federal Councillor to it if necessary. The committee Rapporteurs initiate the debate on *eintreten* (corresponding to the British 'Second Reading') and on the Discussion of Articles (committee of the whole House). They usually also reply and sum up if it is a long debate.

(iii) Linking the executive and the legislature. Committees always

---

[1] A teller recently informed the author that he had had fifteen informal approaches made for a single (chance) vacancy in his fraction's membership of an important committee. Many of the candidatures were impossible, the members knew too little or, being directly interested, too much. Between the remainder he used his personal preference. This is the substance of power.

work on the basis of a Federal Council draft, and prepare amendments of this for the Council. They are in formal and informal touch with Federal Councillors, and federal officials, and this contact works both ways.

(iv) Providing the channels of compromise between parties. The committee consideration of a project usually precedes the consideration by the fraction. Within the fraction, committee members take a lead, guiding their party more than they are bound by it, and doing the necessary horse-trading with other parties.

It should be added that they do NOT:
(i) directly *control* the executive, or
(ii) act as *masters* of their Council. The Council is often guided by the committee and its members. But very often it takes its own line, and
(iii) the members do not act as masters of their own fractions or *Verbände*.

Committees in fact may be a power in the land, an estate of the realm almost, but there is no feeling that the ultimate or the daily sovereignty resides in the Councils' committees. This might be the case, but it is not.

OTHER COMMITTEES

1. The Conference of Presidents

Before each quarterly session, the President of the National Council calls all the chairmen of National Council fractions together to fix the order of business, and the same Conference of Presidents (Präsidentenkonferenz) takes place as necessary throughout the session. For this purpose there is consultation with the Federal Council (for a Federal Councillor must be present at the debate and have the business prepared) and also, an unusual provision, there is consultation with the corresponding body in the Council of States. In the Council of States it is the bureau and the President of the Council who are responsible.

2. The Committee of Redaction

This has been described in Chapter X.

3. The Conference of Agreement (*Einigungskonferenz*)

Legislation is the work of the two Councils, sitting apart. There is thus the possibility of 'differences' (*divergences*, in French) between the two Houses. There are, in fact, four situations:

(i) The First Council rejects a project of the Federal Council, by refusing to 'enter upon the matter'. It must then send the project on, nevertheless, to the Second Council. If that also rejects it, the matter is finished with.

It is an interesting, but disputed, point what happens if the project rejected by the Second Council was not an official proposition of the Federal Council, but was one which arose from the ranks of the First Council. It would seem (under Article 93 of the Constitution) that the matter is finally rejected by the Second Council's first decision. In 1960–61 the matter was in controversy between the National Council and the Council of States, but since the question will probably be clarified under legislation that is pending while this chapter is being written, it does not seem profitable to speculate farther.

(ii) If the Second Council accepts the project rejected outright by the First Council, the matter comes back to the First Council. If the First Council still refuses to 'enter on the matter' then the project nevertheless returns to the Second Council. Whatever the Second Council does, the matter goes no farther.

Similarly, if the history of the project had been: 'acceptance by First Council, rejection by Second', the subsequent stages would be 'reconsideration by First Council, reconsideration by Second' and if neither changed their minds, the matter would be buried. This 'shortened procedure' is not laid down by law, but is a constitutional convention.

(iii) Outright rejection is rare. The usual situation is disagreement over details. Usually these are bandied about between the Councils and their respective committees, with the area of disagreement narrowed on each occasion, as in the example in Chapter X.

(iv) On rare occasions, however, having disagreed over details one Council refuses to move from its position, and the other Council insists upon a divergent view. It is in such an event that the official procedure laid down by the Law on the Councils of 1902 comes into operation. It is this situation (which, according to Dr Burkhard writing in 1952, has happened five times since 1903) that is the subject of this note.

The Law on the Councils stipulates a Conference of Agreement composed of the *ad hoc* committees of the two Councils on the disputed project of law. It will usually happen that the Council of States' committee will be smaller than that of the National Council, and in this case the smaller committee has additional members chosen to it, so that the two Councils each have the same number. The Conference is composed of the joint committees. If it makes a proposal, then this is to be accepted by both Councils outright—and if they do not both accept, then the matter is rejected and one must start anew from the beginning. It is a snake in the legislative game of snakes and ladders.

There is thus no procedure for forcing a deadlock between the Councils. In so far as this is a power of veto by the Council of States on proposals of the National Council (based on a report of the Federal Council), this is the basic principle which persuaded the cantons to sacrifice sovereignty in 1848. Since the linguistic minorities (French and Italian) *plus* the religious minority (Roman Catholics) command, if they join forces, a majority in the Council of States in terms of cantonal votes, it is also the basic principle of the whole federal compromise. The cantons, it will be remembered, have a similar veto in the referendum on constitutional amendments.

XVI

Interpretations

In the foregoing chapters I have tried to describe what I have seen in and read about the Swiss federal Parliament. But while watching and studying events I have had in mind three possible interpretations, and it is better to bring these into the open, rather than merely to hint at their presence. As a foreigner, I do not wish to refute totally any of these interpretations (which have all been adopted or hinted at by Swiss writers at various times). To the extent that the three interpretations can be held simultaneously, and only to that extent, I regard them all as valid. These three interpretations are:

(1) That the federal bureaucracy rules Switzerland from Berne, regardless of the Constitution or the people;

(2) That the *Verbände*, and in particular the *Vorort*, rule the country through the instrumentalities of party, Parliament and referendum—comprising perhaps, in all, a sovereign body of some four hundred persons;

(3) That the Federal Constitution of 1874 rules the country, and the People exercise sovereignty under it, through the intermediacy of Parliament, the cantons, the Federal Council and the Referendum.

The relative truth of these three theories is best examined with the aid of the description of the passage of a Law given in Chapter X. The following comments represent the argument on which I base my own interpretation.

(1) *The Bureaucracy Theory*

In its crudest form this is discredited by:

(a) the difference between the First Draft and the Seventh, which was the basis of the Federal Council's project;

(b) the successive influence of the committees of experts, the committees of the two Councils and of the Councils themselves; and

(c) the attitude of the Civil Service itself (until the committee stage in the Council of States) which was one of co-operation and of genuinely seeking help and advice;

(d) the lack of a common 'Civil Service will' (as opposed to the personal opinions of Berger and Fisch, which only crystallized into convictions at a late stage in the proceedings).

But the project remained in all its stages under the control of the civil servant who had initiated it. The strength he had was the strength of responsibility—which can only be borne and wielded by an individual. The influence of the bureaucracy in this case was not very far from the ideal one.

(2) *The Verband Theory*
In its crudest form this is discredited by:
(a) the limited *authority* of the committee of experts. The decisions were reserved to the civil servants, who retained responsibility, and the committee was instructed to debate the bill even if it decided upon rejection.

(b) The influential member of the committee was the one member not personally involved, Herr Iten.

(c) Both employers and agents were against inclusion of the insurance companies. Yet because one disinterested member of the first committee of experts spoke in favour of including them, the Civil Service decided that they should be included in the draft.

(d) In this case, the agents' representatives were overruled by the people they represented, and

(e) the insurance companies' representatives, a very powerful group indeed (with the backing of the *Vorort*), were compelled at pistol point to agree to their own inclusion in the law.

(f) The insurance companies were excluded from the operation of the law neither in the Federal Council nor in the National Council committee. Naïve though the statement appears, the National Council committee seems from the record at no time to have considered any other factor than the public interest.

(g) The consideration that the Committee of the First Council normally sits before the parties have taken up their positions.

On the other hand, the advice of the *Verbände* was taken at every stage, and statesmen made the greatest efforts to obtain their good will as the most desirable thing next to the public interest. The issues discussed throughout were principally the *Verband* issues, rather than the abstract merits of the reform as a reform of the Law of Contract.

Nevertheless, one has the impression that the genesis of the bill was a free decision of a civil servant, that a fresh decision (unbound by pressure) was taken by the responsible Federal Councillor, and again by the Federal Council as a whole, and again (though in a less degree) by the committees of the two Councils. My conviction that this was the case is derived from my impression of the integrity of those concerned, and the consideration that the 'fresh approach' is necessary to efficient administration. The *Verband* theory postulates a certain mental dishonesty, and, in its crude form, would lead to slovenly administration and muddle. It explains many things, but it is subjectively and objectively incredible as an explanation of the *whole* process.

(3) *The Law Theory*

In its simplest form this theory visualizes a statesman communing with the soul of a people, instructing an official to draw up a bill on that basis, then being advised by disinterested experts concerning the objective facts. The next stage is a mystic collegiate decision of the Federal Council in the public interest. Then the consciences of fifteen private persons, elected to the National Council for their merits, and to the committee for their objective knowledge, are added up. The parties then search their respective majority of consciences, and the same arithmetic of proportionally elected consciences is performed by the two-hundred odd deputies in the National Council, while the forty-four custodians of the personalities of the cantons deliberate the matter afresh in the Council of States. The law then awaits the chance of thirty thousand individuals being moved to send petitions against it, and the eventual verdict of the added-up consciences of the grown males of the nation.

Such a process would seem not merely to be improbable, but to be morally wrong. Things that are incommensurable, and in particular the consciences of individuals, are represented as being added together as simple arithmetical units. It is also anti-rational, as assuming that no solution can be arrived at through argument. As regards probability, it fails to account for the undoubted existence of *Verbände* and parties, it fails to give any reality to corporate life and to smaller loyalties and ambitions within the greater loyalty. Above all, it fails to square with what we know of human nature. Nevertheless, it is a theory which contains a great deal of truth: this book differs from its predecessors in the field of political sociology in the weight it gives to the juridical theory. It is especially valid in an old country of settled law such as Switzerland.

In fact the law, and the feeling for law, is the fixed point in the delicate and shifting relationships of social powers and administrative practice in federal legislation. It is the law which has called pressure groups into existence and made parties necessary—not explicitly, but by creating a system that could not work without them —and it is the law which provides a field (in proportional representation and the referendum) for their activity. It is the law which makes the Assembly at every point a 'toothless watchdog' and sets the Federal Council at the centre of the political process. Given the law, and the facts of Swiss society, then the way in which the Constitution actually works follows quite logically and, one could almost say, predictably. This is the importance of the law.

The conclusion to be drawn is that the three assertions limit one another. The power of the *Verbände*, for example, is limited by the independence of the executive and by the feeling for law that ensures that, at certain stages, a 'clean' decision is taken on the matter in hand.

IS THE SWISS PARLIAMENT WEAK?

The Parliament of Switzerland represents, not perhaps the Swiss people, but the forces that make up Swiss society. It embodies the ideas, not perhaps of the Swiss people, but of the Protestant urban upper-middle class—the *élite* of the Swiss people—and within the framework of Parliament the ideas held most strongly by effectively organized groups are heard, and find their outlet in action. How effective is this action?

The plenum, the whole National Council or Council of States in session, has been called 'toothless', and a limit has been set to the effectiveness of each of the (much more powerful) institutions which depend upon the plenum and would not exist without it—the standing committees or the meetings of the parliamentary parties, for example. The decisive power is never in the hands of the plenum, and seldom in the hands of the institutions depending on the plenum.

It does not follow from this, however, that the Assembly as a whole is weak. In any particular detail it will certainly be found to be rather weak, but over the years, and taken as a whole, it cannot be classed as 'a weak Parliament'. What is at issue is its total power, in legislation, administration and finance, together with the total power its members can bring to bear, in *Verbände*, at the polls, and in the cantons. This is a body no administration can ignore, with which the Civil Service must co-operate, and which (over the years) decides the personal fate of every Federal Councillor. No other theory than that the total power of the Parliament is very great fits the facts—the resignations of ministers, the respect of the Civil Service, and the personalities of the people who sit in Parliament. The roots of Parliament are deep in Swiss society, and draw nourishment from at least one aspect of every source of power in Switzerland—through party, *Verband*, and local administration. In the continuous process of legislation and administration its influence is rather that of a source of light which makes a plant grow in a particular direction, than that of a gardener who lops off a branch.

In examining this continuing process, however, one must think in terms of Herr Bringolf talking informally with Herr Condrau or Monsieur Chaudet—or 'Dr Berger'—rather than in terms of abstractions such as 'the legislature', 'the people', 'the executive'. The law of the Constitution is important, as the skeleton of a man is important and will survive him, but it is the flesh and blood and the ideas and emotions that make the skeleton dance.

The whole picture of the Swiss Parliament seems, to me, to be reassuring—the parts, and the immediate impressions, are disappointing. Compared with Britain, whose Houses of Parliament in full session are the most impressive political assemblies in the world (with the cantonal Landsgemeinden in Switzerland running very close in competition), the total picture, taking the dignified and the efficient together, 'adds up' to something rather similar. No Parliament wields a very effective power, but in their different ways, and working in a different material, the Swiss and the British Parliaments are equally impressive political achievements. In 1948 the final balance was perhaps, on the whole, a little in favour of the British solution, and in 1960 a little, even if a very little, in favour of the Parliament of Switzerland.

APPENDIX ONE

Swiss Foreign Policy

The following document seems of particular interest for understanding Swiss foreign policy and the limits within which it (and, therefore, each of the Foreign Affairs Committees of the legislature) works.[1] It is a translation of an Opinion in Administrative Law for the year 1954—these Opinions are now always published some five years in arrear. The original is in German only[2] and from its style it would seem to have been originally drafted in German (presumably by the Legal Branch of the Political Department) and to have been altered by several officials, some of them more accustomed to French than to German.

(Political Department, 26 Nov 1954)

The Concept of Neutrality

The Political Department summarized the ruling doctrine under the following heads:

I

A distinction must be made between 'ordinary' and 'permanent' neutrality.

Ordinary neutrality denotes the legal status of a state which does not take part in a war which has broken out between other states. Therefore its presuppositions are:

1. A war, as understood by the Law of Nations.
2. Non-participation of a state in the hostilities.

Permanent neutrality consists in a state taking upon itself the

---

[1] For further discussion of neutrality and neutralism the reader is referred to the unpublished (1961) thesis of my colleague, Dr Peter Lyon.

[2] Translation by the author of this book. The sentences in parentheses are so in the original. Those in square brackets are inserted by the translator.

The words 'oblige' and 'obligation' represent the German '*verpflichten, Verpflichtung*', which carry the meaning of '*Pflicht*', duty, rather than of external force. The word '*Vorwirkung*' is a nonce-word, difficult to render: its component parts mean 'pre-effects'. It is left in German.

In Section III (3) the first paragraph would appear from the style to have been originally thought in French, and the second paragraph in German. It looks as if the words 'apart from this' had been added so as outwardly to reconcile two divergent views. The concrete problem today concerns N.A.T.O., and the Common Market.

obligation to be permanently neutral. This may be combined with the express obligation taken by other states to respect that neutrality. Hence, the distinction must be made between one-sided permanent neutrality, and permanent neutrality arising out of treaties. Both these may be combined, as in the case of Switzerland.

II

Ordinary neutrality creates no rights and duties in time of peace. Only for a permanently neutral state do rights and duties arise even in time of peace. These may be described as:

1. The duty to begin no war.
2. The duty to defend neutrality or independence, as the case may be.
3. The so-called secondary duties of permanent neutrality, (*Vorwirkungen*).

These may be comprehensively summarized in the phrase, that a permanently neutral state must do everything to stop itself being involved in a war, and nothing which could get it drawn into a war. That is to say, it must, in general, avoid taking sides in a conflict between third-party states. It is obliged to follow a Neutralitaetpolitik. The carrying into effect of this policy of neutrality is a matter for its own judgement.

III

No further explanation is needed of the two chief duties (described above) of a permanently neutral state in time of peace. But investigation is needed concerning the so-called *Vorwirkungen*. What political, military and economic duties are implicit in them?

1. Political neutrality can be described as the obligation of the neutral state so to conduct its foreign policy that it can be drawn into no war. In particular, it should conclude no treaty that could lead to its being obliged to wage war, e.g. offensive alliances, defensive leagues with reciprocal effect, treaties of guarantee, collective security agreements. The obligation is, like all others, to be construed restrictively, and can only apply to foreign-policy acts properly socalled, and in any case not to other actions of the state (e.g. humanitarian activities in favour of the inhabitants of particular states, governmental explanations of the political situation to its own people, intra-state organization and arrangements, etc.). It need not be said that there is no obligation to a so-called moral neutrality. The individual is not a subject of duties of neutrality under the Law of Nations. (Hence, in principle, neutrality demands no restriction of the liberty of the Press.)

As regards participation in international conferences and organizations, the distinction must be made between whether they display a predominantly political or a predominantly economic, cultural or technical aspect. If it is a conference or organization of a political character, then the only possible question of participation arises if it displays a certain universality. The principal representatives of the political groupings in question must participate, and in particular both parties of a possible conflict. Here also Switzerland has to avoid taking sides.

As against this, neutral states have the right to offer 'good services' or 'mediation'—even during any hostilities; exercise of this right can never be understood by one of the conflicting parties as an unfriendly action (Art. 3 of the Hague Agreement for Peaceful Settlement of International Disputes, of 18 Oct 1907).

2. Concerning military neutrality, all one can say is that the permanently neutral state should in general conclude no military agreements with other states. The same applies as under No. 1 above.

3. There is only economic neutrality in so far as the permanently neutral state should conclude no customs or economic union with another state, through which it might affect in greater or less degree its independence in a political context also. This only applies when the neutral state is the weaker party and thereby falls into dependence on its stronger partner: in such a case even the legal possibility of denouncing the treaty by measures of its own economic policy or a special war clause would make no difference.

Apart from this, there is no such thing as economic neutrality, unless the neutral state expressly and intentionally supports either the armament or politically motivated economic measures of other states, directed against their adversary—so that the attitude of the neutral state would be pre-judged in a war and doubt arise as to its attitude.

In general the point must be made that the permanently neutral state should enter upon no ties with other states which in case of war would oblige it to un-neutral attitudes, i.e. to an attitude in conflict with the provisions of the ordinary law of neutrality (which applies only in war).

IV

When war breaks out, the duties of an ordinary neutral according to the general law of neutrality are added to the duties of a permanently neutral state.

In principle, the latter (the general law of neutrality) prescribes that the neutral should not intervene in war to the advantage of one party (prohibition of intervention, including political or economic measures). By the side of this the principle of equality of treatment applies; but positive law contains numerous exceptions from this rule.

Neutrality ends when the neutral state is drawn into a war (but not with the rebuttal by force of a breach of neutrality: Art. 10 of the Fifth Hague Convention).

Political and military obligations of neutrality can hardly be separated. In short, the following are involved:
1. Prohibition of hostilities against a belligerent.
2. Prohibition against sending troops.
3. Prohibition against handing over authority by the neutral state to a belligerent.
4. Duty to maintain the inviolability of the territory of the neutral state.

In particular the following are to be prevented: acts of war, passage of troops or convoys of food and munitions, handing over neutral territory as basis of operations, erection of agencies to encourage recruitment, maintenance of wireless stations, passage of aircraft over the territory.

These duties are to be fulfilled according to the measure of the means at the disposal of the neutral state. (Even if the Fifth Hague Agreement Concerning Rights and Duties of Neutral Powers and Persons in Event of War on Land does not contain any stipulation to this effect, such as Articles 3, 8 and 25 of the Thirteenth Agreement on the Rights and Duties of Neutral Powers in the Event of a War at Sea, nevertheless it is quite clear that a general principle of law is concerned here.)

Economic neutrality can only be spoken of in so far as the neutral state is obliged to afford the belligerents no financial support (by this is meant, of course, loans and financial payments intended for direct use for the conduct of the war: it does not exclude credits for trade-political purposes, more especially credits for the maintenance of normal trade relations) or to deliver weapons and munitions to them, and not even to do so if both parties are treated alike (absolute duty). As against this, it is not obliged to forbid private persons to export, for example, weapons, munitions and other war material. If, however, such prohibitions are issued, then the neutral must apply them equally to all belligerents.

Beyond this there is no economic neutrality. On the contrary, the neutral state has a right to trade with the belligerents. Switzerland has always represented this point of view (cf. Message of the Federal Council of 4 August 1919 concerning the entry of Switzerland into the League of Nations). The neutral state must only 'put up with' certain infringements on the part of belligerents (e.g. prohibition of contraband, blockade, etc.). The principles of *'courant normal'* and 'equal contribution to the mutual trade' followed by the Confederation in the last war are principles of trade policy chosen by the Confederation herself.

Nevertheless, it follows from the general duty of non-intervention in hostilities, that an exceptional and especially significant economc favouring of one party constitutes an infringement of neutrality.

V

In principle, all duties arising out of neutrality are to be interpreted restrictively, as being limitations upon sovereignty.

If a neutral state, and especially Switzerland, does more than the duties of permanent or ordinary neutrality demand, then this is done not in performance of a legal duty, but from political considerations, with the intent that the confidence of the belligerents in the maintenance of neutrality shall be strengthened.

Source: Verwaltungsentscheide der Bundesbehoerden. Jurisprudence des autorités administratives de la Confédération. *Heft*—Fascicule— 24. 1954. En vente au bureau des imprimés de la Chancellerie fédérale. 1. *Beziehungen zum Ausland:* Relations avec l'étranger (p. 9–13). The complete document, as published, is printed here. (Published 1959.)

APPENDIX TWO

The Committee Career of a leading National Councillor
(Dr Condrau, Catholic Conservative)
(Elected to the National Council, 1935)

A. Ad hoc Committees
(Chairmanships of Committees are *italicized*)

Swiss Civil Code	1936–7
Judicial Organization, amendment	1936
Transport of Goods in Lorries	1936
Promotion of Tourist Traffic	1936
Promotion of Exports	1936
Reorganization of Federal Railways	1936–43
Romansch Language	1937–8
Distressed Private Railways	1937–9
Transport of Persons and Goods	1937–8
Public Guarantee of Risk	1938
Swiss Chamber for Films	1938
Revision of Constitution: Finance	1938
National Defence	1938–9
Emergency Finance Legislation (temporarily)	1938
Cultural Defence of the Nation	1938–9
Provisional Financial Arrangements	1939–40
Popular Initiative for Election of Federal Council by the People	1940–1
Popular Initiative for Reorganization of the National Council	1941
Law Against Unfair Competition	1942–3
Purchase of Land at Oerlikon	1943
Votation on Economic Articles	1943–4
Experimental Station at Lausanne	1943
Agricultural Produce	1944
Amendment of Règlement of Federal Assembly (Joint Session)	1944
Economic Articles, Revised Draft	1945–6
Amendment of Règlement of National Council	1945–6
Revision of Statute Book (Recueil systématique)	1946
Initiative on Right to Work	1946
Economic Reform	1946–7
Press	1946–7

APPENDIXES

Purchase of a Sanatorium	1947
Rhone-Rhine Canal	1947
Refugees	1947
Law on Contract of Agency (see Chapter X)	1947–9
World Postal Congress	1947–8
Pro Helvetia ('Swiss Council')	1948–9
Opening of Inns	1948–9
Swiss National-Socialists	1948–9
Electricity Shortages	1949
Agricultural Produce	1949
Law on Trolley-Buses	1949–50
International Agreement on Air Transport	1949–51
Insurance Contributions	1949–50
Grants to those with Fixed Incomes	1949–50
Sickness Insurance	1950
Long Distance Planes for Swissair	1950
Assistance to Swissair	1950
Law on Agriculture	1950–
Rearmament	1950–
Aid for Railways	1951
Rearmament—Finance	1951–2
Federal Assistance for Television	1951–2
Promotion of Scientific Research	1951
Purchase of Armoured Cars	1951
Opening and Extension of Inns	1951
Initiative on Finance for Rearmament	1952
(Inter-Parliamentary Union, Berne)	1952
Federal Finance: New Regulations	1952–3
Rearmament	1953
Rheinau Project (see p. 43)	1953–4
Granting of Concessions. Hydraulic Power	1953–6
National Finance	1954
Freedom of the Press. Popular Initiative	1954–
National Finance—Executive Arrangements	1954
Dictionary of Dialects	1954–5
Report on Korea	1955
Television Experiments	1954–5
Reduction of Federal Taxation	1954–5
E.P.U. Prolongation of Membership	1956
Herr Duttweiler's Indictment of Federal Councillors	1956
Regulation of Lake of Lugano	1956
Wireless and TV, Constitutional Amendment	1956
E.P.U.	1956

Swiss-German Payments	1956
Finance, New Regulation	1956–8
E.P.U.	
Correction of a River in Ticino	1957
(*Inter-Parliamentary Union, London*)	1957
TV, Financial Aid	1957
Correction of a River (*Grisons*)	1957
Annual Contribution to Romansch League	1958
Dam on Rhone below St Maurice	1958
German Property in Switzerland	1958
Law on Agricultural Indebtedness, Amendment	1958–9
Subsidies to Cantons	1958–9
Agreement on Aeroplane Rights	1959
Law on Register of Aeroplanes	1959
Law on Air Transport. Amendment	1959
Law on National Motorways	1959–60
W.H.O. Loan	1959
Free Trade Zone: Membership	1959
Law on Councils, Revision	1960–
Law on Initiatives, Revision	1960–

B. Standing Committees

Validation of Mandates	1936–9
Gestion	1939–43
Customs Tariffs	1943–4
Full Powers[1]	1944–7
Finance	1947–53
Foreign Affairs	1954–9 (President 1955–7)
Customs Tariffs	1959–

C. President of the National Council 1956–7

---

[1] During the war, and immediately after it, this was a Standing Committee, and the most important one.

APPENDIX THREE

The Workings of Proportional Representation in a medium-sized Canton.
(Translation from the German of part of the Report of the Federal Council to the National Council on the Elections for the XXXVI Legislature, 19 Nov 1959)

CANTON LUCERNE
Number of Seats: 9

Number of Electors	69,773
Number of Votes cast	59,301
Spoiled Papers	185
Empty Papers	766
Valid Votes	58,351

Lists of Candidates
1. Christian Social Party [the left wing of the Catholic Conservatives]
2. Liberal Party [the local name of the Radical Party]
3. Social Democratic Party
4. Conservative People's Party [i.e. the Catholic right wing]

A. Total of Votes
Party Votes:

	All Lists	Connected Lists 1 and 4
1.	55,939	55,939
2.	203,944	—
3.	50,539	—
4.	214,607	214,607
Total	525,029	270,546
Divisor	52,503	

B. Allocation of Seats to the Lists or Groups of Lists

	First Allocation		Second Allocation	Electoral
Lists	No. of Seats	No. of Votes	No. of Seats	Quotient
1, 4.	5	270,546	5	45,091
2.	3	203,944	4	50,986[1]

[1] This is the so-called Final Quotient.

THE PARLIAMENT OF SWITZERLAND

Lists	No. of Seats	No. of Votes	No. of Seats	Quotient
3.	0	50,539	0	50,539
Total	8		9	

C. Allocation of Seats within the Connected Lists

Group of Lists 1, 4.   Party Votes 270,546.   No. of Seats 5.
Divisor 45,091.

Allocation

Lists	No. of Seats	Party Votes
1.	1	55,939
4.	4	214 607
Total	5	

D. Results
List 1. Christian Social Party

ELECTED

Votes

Wick, Karl,[1] born 1891, Dr jur., Chief Editor, of Lucerne
and Jonschwil (St. Gallen), at Lucerne   12,751

NOT ELECTED

1. Rogger, Hans, born 1913, Dr jur., Cantonal Councillor
   of State,[2] of Oberkirch, at Lucerne   6,975
2. Babst, Hans, born 1918, Commercial Agent, of Vilters
   (St Gallen), at Rothenburg   6,754
3. Waldis, Josef, born 1919, Parish Clerk, of Weggis, at
   Entlebuch   6,356
4. Vonwyl, Anton, born 1918, Parish Beadle, of Emmen,
   at Littau   6,300

---

[1] Dr Wick's name was 'cumulated' (printed twice). Had it not been, Dr Rogger would presumably have been elected. The two Catholic lists each only contain six names (instead of the nine names allowed). This is in the expectation that there will be cross-voting between the two lists. 'Of Lucerne' means that he held the bourgeoisie (citizenship) of that town. 'At' denotes his place of residence.

Note the *apparently* different value of a vote cast on one Catholic list to one cast on the other.

[2] Councillor of State is a cantonal minister (member of the cantonal Cabinet) but Councillor of States is a member of the Council of States.

APPENDIXES

List 2. Liberal Party

	ELECTED	Votes
1.	Ackermann, Alfred, born 1907, Merchant, of and at Entlebuch	24,714
2.	Malzacher, Fritz, born 1906, Trades Union Secretary, of and at Lucerne	23,693
3.	Honauer, Niklaus, born 1899, Manufacturer, of and at Root	23,179
4.	Kurzmeyer, Werner, born 1903, Cantonal Councillor of State, of and at Lucerne	21,831

NOT ELECTED
1. Meyer, Hans Rudolf, born 1922, Dr jur., Lawyer, of and at Lucerne — 21,047
2. Heller, Hermann, born 1919, Dr, Editor, of and at Lucerne — 21,007
3. Krummenacher, Albert, born 1919, Dr jur., Lawyer, of Hochdorf, at Emmen — 21,004
4. Gnägi, Armin, born 1916, Farmer, of Schwadernau, at Neuenkirch — 20,680
5. Amrein, Josef, born 1912, Merchant, of and at Uffikon — 19,913

List 3. Social Democratic Party

NOT ELECTED
1. Bratschi, Theo, born 1922, Dr jur., Lawyer, of Biel, at Lucerne — 6,246
2. Kistler, Max, born 1914, Dr jur., Lawyer, of Lucerne and Aarberg, at Lucerne — 6,203
3. Egli, Albert, born 1917, Locksmith, of and at Lucerne — 5,377
4. Wolfensberger, Fritz, born 1902, Secretary, of Bauma (Zurich), at Emmenbrücke — 5,374
5. Nyfeler, Fritz, born 1902, Beadle, of Gondiswil and Kriens, at Kriens — 5,287

List 4. Conservative People's Party

ELECTED
1. Leu, Josef, born 1918, Farmer, of and at Hohenrain — 27,669
2. Kurmann, Franz Josef, born 1917, Dr jur., Editor, of Alberswil, at Willisau — 27,248

3. Fischer, Hans, born 1901, Dr jur., Lawyer, of and at Grosswangen — *Votes* 27,101
4. Studer, Otto, born 1898, Parish Clerk, of and at Escholzmatt — 25,843

NOT ELECTED

1. Meyer, Otto, born 1910, Dr, Factory Owner, of and at Lucerne — 23,275
2. Brünisholz, Peter, born 1894, Tradesman, of Alterswil, at Reussbühl-Littau — 22,795

APPENDIX FOUR

Sources

Introductory Note and Chapter One
My own book, *The Federal Constitution of Switzerland*, Oxford, 1954, should be consulted. It contains a text of the Constitution, with a politico-legal comment on each Article of the Constitution; a discussion of parliamentary procedure, with the text of the Law on the Councils of 1902; the Full Powers *Arrêté* of 1939; the German Text of the Constitution; and a description of Swiss Constitutional literature and sources. The texts are indexed. Apart from some half-dozen details of an extremely minor character, I should like to stand by what I wrote then, with three exceptions: the social role of the Swiss Army is underemphasized, the degree of protectionism is exaggerated, and this book should be taken as replacing the commentary on the Law of the Councils. The latter contains some minor errors—none of them observed by reviewers. The description of a session of the National Council as seen from the gallery is true—as seen from the gallery—but I no longer wish to associate myself with the implied criticism of the Swiss Parliament.

In the Bibliography of that book I did not feel able to recommend *A Short History of Switzerland*, Bonjour, Offler and Potter, Oxford, 1952, because of the section on the nineteenth century. But this has been slightly amended in a second edition, and (on account of the first two sections by Offler and Potter) it is, really, the obvious book for the English reader.

The reader should be warned of the large number of uncritical books on Switzerland, or with a section on Switzerland. There are now so many of these that it is possible for one to quote from the other and thus derive a spurious authority.

Chapter Two
Of the English writers on this subject I need only mention Mr George Soloveytchik (*Switzerland in Perspective*) and Miss Wiskemann.

Swiss society is an unexplored territory, but we are on the threshold of a new era. I shall keep my eye on the following writers: Drs Kurt Eichenberger, Professors von Greyerz, Erich Gruner, Freymond, Behrendt, Dietrich Schindler—who may be expected to shed light on the sociology of politics.

The work by Dr Jürg Steiner cited is called *Die Beziehungen zwischen den Stimmberechtigten und den Gewählten in ländlichem und städtischem Milieu*, Berne, 1959. It concerns cantonal elections, but nevertheless is useful—a pioneer work in all Switzerland. The author also kindly showed me other work he was engaged upon.

I owe a debt to Dr Erich Gruner, who gave me offprints of his numerous studies, both for this chapter and the two following.

Much of the chapter is based on personal impressions. The National Library in Berne has a good folder on Max Huber.

Chapter Three

There are no objective studies of individual Swiss parties from the 'political science' point of view. There are memoirs, and apologies, and partial histories, and the publications of the parties themselves, but nothing to which I feel justified in calling the attention of an English reader. Swiss political standpoints are, of course, common to Western European Continental countries in general, and especially the party standpoints in Western Germany, France, Austria and Italy are comparable. For the Landesring there is the decennial party 'Handbuch' and an attack upon it, with the identical format. For the strike of 1918, and the use of cavalry, see *Das Oltener Aktionskomitee* by Willi Gantschi, Zurich, 1955.

The literature on pressure groups is either very general, almost all deploring the existence of sources of influence which were not foreseen in 1874 and which are, therefore, 'unconstitutional', or it is very specialized. I have found nothing on the '*Vorort*' in this century. Neither the 'armchair' literature (deploring pressure groups) nor the specialized literature is very relevant to questions which concern this book. One wants names and sums of money and an indication of quite which paragraph was altered and to what effect. One wants studies of particular referendums and of particular laws, elections and campaigns. These are not available.

François Lachenal *Le parti politique, sa fonction de droit public*, Basle, 1944, is a very remarkable and frank book on the organization of Swiss parties. But I am inclined to think that it conveys the wrong atmosphere as a description of present day party cohesion. It is very useful, nevertheless.

Chapter Four

This chapter is chiefly based on newspaper reports and oral tradition. The *Neue Zürcher Zeitung* has good articles on the parties and their history, and on the campaign in the various cantons, shortly before each election. The local papers have been also consulted.

APPENDIXES

The *Bureau fédéral de statistique* at Berne publishes—some three years in arrears—a statistical analysis of each election, which is of first rate interest on each occasion. The latest available at the time of writing was that for 1955, which is commented upon by U. W. Kitzinger in *Parliamentary Affairs*, Summer 1960, (pp. 335–45).

Ex-Councillor of States Emil Klöti very generously lent me a documentation concerning the Büro Büchi Agency. The biography of Dr Räber cited in the Appendix to the chapter is of exceptional interest.

For further information about the electoral law, see my *Federal Constitution of Switzerland*.

Chapter Five

I am grateful to the Secretariat of the Assembly for helping me to collect information about the committees on which the members selected have served. Much of the rest of the chapter relies on ocular inspection. For the *Rathaus des Auesseren Standes* (Messrs Christen's shop) see *Kunstdenkmäler de Schweiz vol. ii Stadt Bern*.

Chapter Six

There is nothing good on parliamentary procedure generally—Cron's dissertation *Die Geschäftsordnung der schw. Bundesversammlung* is not written from the political standpoint. There is a typescript commentary by Federal Chancellor Bovet on each article of the Standing Orders of the National Council (1943), which is also rather disappointing. The *Règlements* themselves are the best source.

Chapter Seven

(There is a list of Federal Councillors since 1848 in Soloveytchik's *Switzerland in Perspective*.)

The chief source of these narratives is again newspaper report and oral tradition. On the election of Wahlen there is a good note in *Reformatio*, 1959. An election in 1929 is described in *Die Schweiz* (annual of the *Neue Helvetische Gesellschaft*) 1931. It is an exception to the rule that articles in this publication—which often have the 'right titles'—are too discreet to be of any use.

Beyond this, it is a question of considering the election and retirement of each Federal Councillor in turn. There are adequate biographies of Motta (two), Schenk (two), Ador and Munzinger (and perhaps of others which I do not know) and there are two old collected biographies by Heer and Volmar. There is a modern one by Eugen Teucher, with biographies of all from 1848–1944, which serves to keep the Federal Councillors apart in one's memory. It is very difficult to find the facts in the bound volumes of the newspapers (to which there are no printed indexes) and oral tradition diverges widely. Often the obituary is the best source. There are no helpful works of reference. There is no usable history (in 1960) of the period after 1848.

The book by Ernst Laur, cited in the text, is a mine of indiscretions.

The dissertation by Akeret cited is excellent, with a strong sense of reality.

Chapters Eight and Nine

Numa Droz's *Études et portraits politiques (1896)* is still of interest and so is Theodor Curti's *Im Bundestratshaus* (1894). Georges Bovet's *Chemin Faisant*, unfortunately, tells nothing of his experience as Chancellor. Concerning the time before 1848, there is a good biography of Chancellor Mousson. I have used the '*Eidgenössische Abschiede*' for the years in question (i.e. before 1848).

The *Rapport de Gestion* has occasional items of interest concerning Federal Council, and there are the Reports and debates on the occasions when its conduct is criticized. The description of its proceedings on pages 95 and 96 is an account by the present Chancellor transmitted to a friend of mine, a Federal official, in September 1961.

Chapter Ten

Dr Kurt Eichenberger's brilliant thesis *Die Oberste Gewalt im Bunde* (1949) is the best, and indeed the only, description of the legislative process as it actually is. With the book by Burkhard on committees, and that by Akeret on the form of government, it can claim to be one of the best three books on the actual working of Swiss government. I follow his terminology. I follow a different method from his, however, and do not actually derive much from his book. Having gone over the same ground independently, I am pleased to confirm his findings, though in a few details I adopt a different interpretation. Like so many interesting books it derives its inspiration from Professor Hans Huber's seminar.

My source is the *Protokolls* of the Committees concerned, and the drafts of the bill and connected documents, and personal conversations with those concerned. The story of laws can often be pieced together from debates and reports (e.g. debate on Price Control in 1959–60), and the general truth of my picture has been confirmed verbally.

APPENDIXES

Chapter Eleven
Dr Briner's dissertation on Constitutional amendments is of no use in this context.
This is based on the *Stenographic Bulletin*, and anecdotes of parliamentarians and officials, and on observation.

Chapter Twelve
This is based on reports of debates (sometimes in newspapers) and on observation, and on documents made available by the Secretariat of the Assembly. The *Rapports de Gestion* since 1920 have been consulted, briefly. I have talked with 'both sides', members and officials.

Chapter Thirteen
I am most grateful to Dr Käser for his documentation of this subject. There are two theses on it and some minor literature, but my information is either from the legal texts laying down the procedure, or from officials of the Department. The *Feuille fédérale* has some information about the *Zentralstelle*, but most of my information is from its head, Dr Hongler. I have spoken to members of the Finance Committees and Delegation.

Chapter Fourteen
Most of this information is from the *Stenographic Bulletin*.

Chapter Fifteen
This, and other chapters, owe much to Dr Claus Burkhard's *Die Parlamentarischen Kommissionen der Schw. Bundesversammlung*, Zurich, 1952. The *Règlements* of the Councils have also been used. For the discussion of the Conference of Agreement I am indebted to the Debate in the two Councils on the International Labour Conference— which gave rise to an interesting debate on procedure in the last session of 1960 and the first of 1961. The remark about the significance of the procedure is from David Laserre *Étapes du fédéralisme: L'experiénce suisse:* Lausanne, 1954.

APPENDIX FIVE

Notes on the Illustrations

1. Party 'List' for the Federal Elections of 1951. Social Democratic Party, Canton of Berne.

This is an unofficial list sent by the Party to each voter in the envelope containing its electoral propaganda. The envelope itself was to be used (unofficially) to hand to the party observer at the polling station to enable him to check the list of voters of his own party. The pamphlet enclosed contained photographs of all the candidates and a brief manifesto. Enclosed also was an invitation *not* to vote for the Landesring.

The unofficial list can (in this case) be used as a vote. The voter crosses out and inserts names—for which no space is provided—or, in the more usual case, hands in the unaltered list. In either event the vote is counted (i) as a 'party list' of the S.D.P., and (ii) as a collection of personal votes for the candidates.

Before inserting the vote into the box it must be stamped by the 'electoral bureau'—representatives of the parties who control the electoral act.

The word '*bisher*' indicates the sitting members. The sitting members are first listed in alphabetical order, then the new candidates in alphabetical order, then, in alphabetical order, the four leading candidates who are cumulated (i.e. whose names are already on the paper, and who thus get two votes if the list is handed in unaltered).

2. How to vote. The *Neue Zürcher Zeitung* assists its readers on how to vote at a Federal and a communal referendum, and whom not to vote for as schoolteachers, and whom to vote for as notary.

Note how much a local newspaper Switzerland's leading daily is.

3. The personal invitation sent out to each member of the National Council before the summer session of 1960.

Though the list of the order of business is determined by the Conference of Presidents, i.e. by parliamentarians, it in point of fact depends on the readiness, and the availability, of Federal Councillors to be personally present during the discussions, and on whether the Report or Message of the Federal Council is to hand. The order of business is thus *apparently* fixed by Members of Parliament, but actually by the executive.

Article 18 of the Law on the Relations between the Councils

APPENDIXES

(Hughes, *The Federal Constitution of Switzerland*, p. 159) provides for this letter of convocation. It is sent by the Chancery on the instructions of the Federal Council, but the session is held on the statutory date and in pursuance of the resolution of the Councils themselves at their previous session. Here, therefore, the action is *apparently* that of the Federal Council, but in actuality that of the Parliament.

4. The name of a candidate for election as a Deputy Judge of the Insurance Tribunal has been agreed between the Presidents of the parliamentary parties—no doubt on the proposition of the party whose turn it was to nominate a candidate (strict proportionality being the rule).

This paper was distributed to all members, at the Federal Assembly in Joint Session. The candidate was duly elected.

5. Reproduction of the original copy of a postulate. This is the piece of paper on which the member (National Councillor Suter) has collected signatures. It has been prepared for printing by the Secretariat, who have added a number, a date, and a French translation of the title, and have underlined the words that are to be the title of the German version, and counted the signatures (18).

The daily list which members sign so as to testify their presence—and qualify them for their daily honorarium—forms the key whereby the Secretariat decipher the signatures.

The postulate is translated and further discussed on page 120.

6. The Committee of *Gestion* of the National Council.

This is the proposition of the President of the Committee as to how the committee will divide into sections. The proposition was not actually followed in every case.

7. The same committee for the same session. Division of the *Rapport de Gestion* (*Geschäftsbericht*) among the Rapporteurs (*Referenten*) of the 'sections'. This is the first of two pages—the second not being reproduced here.

8. The same committee again. The letter of invitation sent to the members of the section (on the instructions of its President) by the Secretariat of the Assembly. This is the section on the Political Department. The 'special questions' are those decided by the whole committee at its plenary session, to which the Department has provided written replies (enclosed with the letter). Copies are sent to the members of the section, the President of the whole committee, and

to the Federal Councillor who is to attend—with fourteen copies for himself and the divisions of his Department.

A German-language version is on the obverse of the letter: only the French version is reproduced here.

9. List of Committees in session during a typical period of about six weeks, before the autumn session of 1960.

The first column shows which Council's committee is to deal with the business (N, National Council, S, States). The second is the official number that accompanies the item of business during its whole parliamentary career. The third column indicates the Council that had 'priority'. The fourth is the item of business. (Note that the session of the Conference of Presidents, and of the Bureau of the Council of States are included in the list.) The fifth is the Department concerned (I., Interior. E.V.D., Public Economy. F.Z.D., Finance. P.E.D., Posts. J.P.D., Justice. Pol., Political. E.M.D., Military).

The sixth column indicates the place of session. Some of the ones outside Berne indicate a session in an agreeable resort, but in three cases it represents a voyage of personal inspection of the place chiefly concerned. There is little evidence of sprees by committees in this example.

10. The 'key' (*Schluessel*) determining how many members of each party sit on a committee of any given number, for the National Council of 1959–63.

The first column gives the names of the parties, and the second their numbers of members (which remains constant throughout the session, as there are normally no by-elections). The three Communists are listed as 'without party', since five members is the minimum to form a party, and no one will join with them. The twenty-one members of the small parties ('*Uebrige Fraktionen*') divide the seats allotted to them according to their proportional entitlement within this heading. Only in a committee of twenty-seven members are all of these groups represented.

Committees always have uneven numbers of members. In committees of nine and of seventeen members one seat has to be shared between the Radicals and the Socialists. Because the Law on Proportional Representation in Elections to the National Council applies (by analogy), in theory it should be decided for each committee by lot which of the two parties nominates a member: this is what happens in case of a tie in Federal elections. In practice (in the present instance) the parties agree among themselves, i.e., the members of the bureau agree how the seat is to be alternated.

☛ **Gilt als Wahlzettel** — *Vaut comme bulletin de vote* ☚

Kanton Bern — *Canton de Berne*

Nationalratswahlen — 1951 — *Elections au Conseil national*

Ausseramtlicher Wahlzettel — *Bulletin non officiel*

Sozialdemokratische Partei des Kantons Bern
Parti socialiste du canton de Berne

LISTE Nr. 8

1. **Aebersold Ernst**, Schulinspektor, Biel (bisher)
2. **Bratschi Robert**, Generalsekretär des Schweiz. Eisenbahnerverbandes, Bern, Präsident des Schweizerischen Gewerkschaftsbundes (bisher)
3. **Fawer Albert**, Gemeinderat, Biel (bisher)
4. **Freimüller Eduard**, Dr., Gemeinderat, Bern (bisher)
5. **Geissbühler Karl**, Zentralsekretär SAS, Köniz (bisher)
6. **Grimm Robert**, Direktor BLS, Bern (bisher)
7. **Grütter Fritz**, Präsident der Sozialdemokratischen Partei des Kantons Bern, Bern (bisher)
8. **Meyer Fritz**, Gemeindepräsident, Roggwil (bisher)
9. **Roth Hans**, Sekundarlehrer, Interlaken (bisher)
10. **Schmidlin Fritz**, Gemeinderat, Bern (bisher)
11. **Steiner Arthur**, Vizepräsident des Schweizerischen Metall- und Uhrenarbeiterverbandes, Bern (bisher)
12. **Stünzi Walter**, städtischer Fürsorgeverwalter, Thun (bisher)
13. **Weber Max**, Dr. Prof., Präsident des Verbandes Schweizerischer Konsumvereine, Wabern (bisher)
14. **Aeschbacher Karl**, Maschinensetzer, Zentralpräsident des Schweizerischen Typographenbundes, Bern (neu)
15. **Bircher Ernst**, Zentralpräsident des Verbandes der Bekleidungs-, Leder- und Ausrüstungsarbeiter der Schweiz, Bern (neu)
16. **Felser Max**, Sekretär des Schweizerischen Bau- und Holzarbeiterverbandes, Nidau (neu)
17. **Geyer Jakob**, kaufmännischer Angestellter, Burgdorf (neu)
18. **Häusler Gottfried**, Lehrer, Büetigen (neu)
19. **Michel Oskar**, Gemeindepräsident, Bönigen (neu)
20. **Müller Fritz**, Spengler-Installateur, Belp (neu)
21. **Müller Hans**, Lehrer, Herzogenbuchsee (neu)
22. **Müller Richard**, Dr., Sekretär der PTT-Union, Bern (neu)
23. **Rubi Christian**, Geschäftsführer des Schweizerischen Skischulverbandes, Wengen (neu)
24. **Sägesser Fritz**, Stationsvorstand, Heustrich-Emdtal (neu)
25. **Schneider Erwin**, Sekretär der Sozialdemokratischen Partei des Kantons Bern, Bern (neu)
26. **Stähli Walter**, Mechaniker, Stettlen (neu)
27. **Staub Werner**, Zentralsekretär des Schweizerischen Textil- und Fabrikarbeiterverbandes, Gemeindepräsident, Duggingen (neu)
28. **Steinmann Fritz**, Kupferschmied und Gemeinderatspräsident, Langnau i. E. (neu)
29. **Zingg Karl**, Sekretär des Gewerkschaftskartells des Kantons Bern, Bern (neu)
30. **Bratschi Robert**, Generalsekretär des Schweiz. Eisenbahnerverbandes, Bern, Präsident des Schweizerischen Gewerkschaftsbundes (bisher)
31. **Grimm Robert**, Direktor BLS, Bern (bisher)
32. **Grütter Fritz**, Präsident der Sozialdemokratischen Partei des Kantons Bern, Bern (bisher)
33. **Steiner Arthur**, Vizepräsident des Schweizerischen Metall- und Uhrenarbeiterverbandes, Bern (bisher)

Unmittelbar vor Einwurf in die Urne vom Wahlausschuss auf der Rückseite abstempeln lassen
Faire timbrer au dos par le bureau électoral immédiatement avant la mise dans l'urne

1. Party 'List' for the Federal Elections of 1951. Social Democratic Party, Canton of Berne

Abstimmungen und Wahlen

vom 2. März 1952

1. Eidgenössische Volksabstimmung:

Bewilligungspflicht für die Eröffnung und Erweiterung von Gasthöfen (Hotelbauverbot)	**Stimmfreigabe**

2. Kantonale Volksabstimmung:

PdA-Initiative über die Ermäßigung der Staatssteuer für 1951 („Rabattgesetz")	**Nein**

3. Bestätigungswahl der Primarlehrer: **Gemäß den Anträgen der Schulpflegen**

Mit Ausnahme von:
Schulkreis Uto:

Nr. 60	Gujer Felix	**Nein**
Nr. 113	Meier-Senn Frieda	**Nein**

Schulkreis Limmattal:

Nr. 82	Meier Max	**Nein**
Nr. 96	Rüegg Fritz	**Nein**

4. Notarwahl in Höngg: *Paul Isler*

Freisinnige Partei von Kanton und Stadt Zürich

---

2. Advice on how to vote at a Federal and a communal referendum—printed in the *Neue Zürcher Zeitung*

A MESSIEURS LES DEPUTES AUX CHAMBRES FEDERALES

BERNE, le 28 mai 1960

Messieurs les députés,

Conformément à votre décision du 17 mars 1960, l'Assemblée fédérale se réunira à Berne, pour la session d'été, le mardi 7 juin 1960.

Nous vous prions de vous rencontrer ce jour-là, à 18 h 15, dans la salle des séances. Ci-inclus, nous vous remettons

1° la liste des objets en délibérations de l'Assemblée fédérale (session d'été 1960);
2° la liste des objets à traiter par votre Conseil dans la session;
3° la liste des motions, postulats et interpellations, auxquels le Conseil fédéral est prêt à répondre;
4° le programme chronologique provisoire de la session pour votre Conseil.

Veuillez agréer, Messieurs les Députés, les assurances de notre haute considération.

PAR ORDRE DU CONSEIL FEDERAL,
Le chancelier de la Confédération:

Annexes

Ordre du jour pour le mardi 7 juin 1960

CONSEIL NATIONAL

- - Eloge funèbre.
1/ - - Vérification des pouvoirs et assermentation.
45/8029 n Régie des alcools. Budget pour 1960/1961.

CONSEIL DES ETATS

- - Eloge funèbre.
1/ - - Communications des cantons et assermentation.
16/8027 é Rectification de la frontière franco-suisse. Conventions.

3. The invitation sent to each member of the National Council before the summer session of 1960.

VEREINIGTE BUNDESVERSAMMLUNG
Assemblée fédérale (Chambres réunies)

Sommersession
Session d'été
1960

Ersatzmann beim Eidg. Versicherungsgericht

Suppléant au Tribunal fédéral des assurances

Vorschlag der Fraktionen
Proposition des groupes

K o r n e r , Hans Dr., Rechtsanwalt, Luzern

4. Candidate proposed by 'Committee of Presidents' for election to the Insurance Tribunal

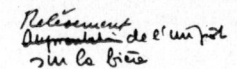

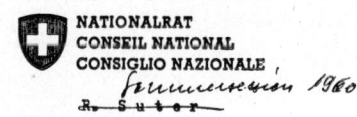

NATIONALRAT
CONSEIL NATIONAL
CONSIGLIO NAZIONALE

Postulat Suter
vom 30. Juni 1960

Der Bundesrat wird eingeladen, den eidgenössischen Räten Antrag für eine Erhöhung der Biersteuer auf den früheren Stand von Fr. 12.- pro hl zu stellen. Der Mehrertrag der Biersteuer soll für die Förderung der Volksgesundheit, insbesondere durch die Popularisierung von Trinkmilch und Milchprodukten, verwendet werden.

5. Reproduction of the original copy of a postulate

NATIONALRAT
Geschäftsprüfungskommission

Sektionen für 1960
(Vorschlag)

Allgemeine Verwaltung
   Grandjean (Président)
   Eisenring (2)

Politisches Departement
   Leuenberger (Präsident)
   Büchi
   Vontobel (3)

Departement des Innern
   Fischer (Präsident)
   Arni
   Berger-Neuchâtel
   Eisenring
   Etter
   Guisan (6)

Justiz- und Polizeidepartement
Gerichte
   Huber (Präsident)
   Berger-Neuchâtel
   Büchi
   Guisan
   Tenchio (5)

Militärdepartement
   Eisenring (Präsident)
   Bratschi
   Brechbühl
   Guisan
   Revaclier
   Tenchio (6)

Finanz- und Zolldepartement
   Revaclier (Président)
   Brechbühl
   Brochon
   Huber
   Jacquod (5)

EVD-Verrechnungsstelle
   Arni (Präsident)
   Etter
   Fischer
   Jacquod
   Leuenberger
   Vontobel (6)

Post- und Eisenbahndepartement
   Brochon (Président)
   Bratschi
   Grandjean
   Vontobel (4)

6. Sub-divisions of the Committee of Gestion of the National Council, as proposed by the President of the Committee

NATIONALRAT
Sommersession 1960

8028 Geschäftsbericht des Bundesrates, des Bundesgerichts und des Eidg. Versicherungsgerichts für 1959

	Geschäftsbericht Seite	Referenten HH.
Allgemeine Verwaltung	1	Grandjean Eisenring
Politisches Departement:		
Einleitung	149	Berger-N'burg
I. Politische Angelegenheiten	153	" "
II. Internat. Organisationen und Hilfswerke	179	Vontobel Büchi
III. Verwaltungsangelegenheiten	210	"
IV. Atomenergie	214	"
Departement des Innern:		
Motionen und Postulate	219	Fischer
I. Abteilung für Kultur, Wissenschaft und Kunst		
A. Departementssekretariat	222	Eisenring
B. Zentralbibliothek	235	"
C. Bundesarchiv	235	"
D. Schweizerische Landesbibliothek	236	"
E. Eidg. Technische Hochschule	237	Guisan
F. Annexanstalten der ETH	245	"
G. Materialprüfungs- und Versuchsanstalt	248	"
H. Meteorologische Zentralanstalt	248	"
J. Landesmuseum	249	"
II. Oberbauinspektorat	250	Fischer
III. Baudirektion	255	"
IV. Inspektion für Forstwesen, Jagd und Fischerei	260	Arni
V. Gesundheitsamt	278	Allemann
VI. Statistisches Amt	289	Etter
VII. Bundesamt für Sozialversicherung	292	"
Justiz- und Polizeidepartement:		
Motionen und Postulate	299	Büchi
I. Departementssekretariat und Rekurssektion	301	Tenchio Huber
II. Justizabteilung	302	Guisan
III. Polizeiabteilung	311	Huber Büchi
IV. Fremdenpolizei	323	Tenchio
V. Bundesanwaltschaft	328	Berger-N'burg
VI. Versicherungsamt	336	Büchi
VII. Amt für geistiges Eigentum	339	Berger-N'burg
VIII. Beschwerdedienst	341	" "
Bundesgericht	545	" "
Eidg. Versicherungsgericht	556	" "
Militärdepartement:		
I. Einleitung	343	Eisenring Tenchio
II. Motionen und Postulate	344	Guisan
III. Militärverwaltung	347	Revaclier

7. Division of work amongst Rapporteurs of various sub-sections of the Committee of Gestion (National Council)

193

CONSEIL NATIONAL
Commission de gestion
1ère section: Département politique

L.

Berne, le 13 avril 1960

Monsieur le Conseiller national,

D'ordre du président de votre section, M. Claude B e r g e r, j'ai l'honneur de vous convoquer à la séance de votre section qui aura lieu

jeudi 28 avril 1960, à 9 heures,

à Berne, palais du Parlement, dans la salle du Conseil fédéral.

Ordre du jour:

A. Questions spéciales:
1° De quelle façon les questions d'intégration sont-elles traitées entre le département politique et le département de l'économie publique?
2° Comment ont été utilisés les crédits suisses en faveur des pays en voie de développement? Quel contrôle le Conseil fédéral exerce-t-il dans ce domaine? Que se passe-t-il sur le plan bilatéral?
3° A quoi en sont nos relations avec les pays asiatiques et africains? - Situation des Suisses dans les pays en voie de développement.
4° La question des traitements des chefs de missions a-t-elle été réglée à nouveau?
5° Qu'a-t-on fait pour tenir compte des critiques que la commission de gestion a formulées l'année dernière au sujet du règlement protocolaire?
6° L'activité de nos attachés culturels et sociaux est-elle profitable?

B. Autres questions concernant le rapport de gestion du département politique.

Vous trouverez sous ce pli les réponses préparées par le département aux questions spéciales énumérées ci-dessus. Le rapport de gestion vous est déjà parvenu.

D'ordre de la commission de gestion, M. le chef du département est prié d'assister personnellement aux délibérations de la section. MM. les chefs de division sont priés de se tenir à la disposition de la section pour être appelé en séance ou pour donner dans leur office à l'issue de la séance, des renseignements plus détaillés aux membres de la section.

Veuillez agréer, Monsieur le Conseiller national, l'assurance de ma considération distinguée.

Le secrétaire
de l'Assemblée fédérale:

Annexes
Aux membres de la section:
MM. Berger-Neuchâtel, Büchi, Vontobel (3)
A M. Grandjean, président de la commission de gestion
Au chef du département politique, pour lui et les divisions (14 expl.)

8. Letter sent to committee members (Gestion, National Council) by the Secretariat of the Assembly

SEKRETARIAT
DER BUNDESVERSAMMLUNG

KOMMISSIONSSITZUNGEN

August - September 1960

Rat			Geschäft	Dep.	Ort	Zeit		
N/S	8056	n	Verbauung des Nietenbaches	I	Schwyz, Wysses Rössli	8. Aug.		18.00
S	8057	s	Treibstoffe. Zollzuschlag	I	Bern, Zimmer IV	23.	"	10.00
N	8101 8102	n n	Zolltarifkommission	EVD/FZD	Scuol/Schuls, Hotel Engadinerhof	23.	"	08.30
S	8101 8102	n n	Zolltarifkommission	EVD/FZD	Scuol/Schuls, Hotel Belvédère	23.	"	17.15
N	7992	s	Internat. Fernmeldevertrag	PED	Bern, Zimmer IV	24.	"	09.00
N	8054	n	Schweizerschulen im Ausland	I	Bern, Zimmer IV	25.	"	15.15
S	8058	s	Panzerbeschaffung (Mil.Komm.)	EMD	Bern, Zimmer IV	27.	"	08.00
N	7994 7995	n n	Geschäftsverkehrsgesetz. Revision) Initiativengesetz. Revision)	JPD	Davos, Hotel Central	29.	"	08.15
N	7986 7987	n n	Militärorganisation. Aenderung) Truppenordnung)	EMD	Sils-Maria, Hotel Waldhaus	30.	"	08.15
S	8055	n	Kinematographische Filme. Einfuhr	I	Bern, Grünes Zimmer	30.	"	15.00
N	7993	s	II. Juragewässerkorrektion	PED	Bern-Murten-Solothurn	30.	"	11.30
N	7991	s	Schweiz. Verkehrszentrale	PED	Oberhofen, Hotel Moy	31.	"	08.00
S	8060	s	Hotelgewerbe. Aufhebg.d.rechtl.Massn.	EVD	Bern, Grünes Zimmer	31.	"	10.00
S	7727	s	PTT-Organisationsgesetz (Diff.)	PED	Bern, Zimmer IV	31.	"	14.00
S	7979	s	Abzahlungs- u. Vorauszahlungsvertrag	JPD	Bern, Zimmer IV	1. Sept.		08.30
S	7031	n	Landwirtschaftspolitik	EVD	Bern, Zimmer IV	2.	"	15.00
S	-	-	Petitionskommission	-	Oberhofen, Hotel Moy	3.	"	08.30
S	8061	s	Geschützte Warenpreise	EVD	Bern, Zimmer IV	5.	"	08.30
S	8065 8066	s s	Atomenergie. Zusatzvertrag m.USA) Halden-Abkommen)	PED	Bern, Grünes Zimmer	5.	"	11.00
N	8065 8066	s s	Atomenergie. Zusatzvertrag m.USA) Halden-Abkommen)	PED	Bern, Zimmer IV	7.	"	10.00
N	8043	n	Krankenkassen. Zusätzl. Beiträge	I	Bern, Zimmer III	8.	"	08.15
N	-	-	Fraktionspräsidentenkonferenz	B'präs.	Bern, Zimmer d.N'ratspräs.	9.	"	15.30
S	-	-	Bureausitzung	-	Bern, Zimmer d.S'ratspräs.	9.	"	15.30
N	8064	n	Rohrleitungsanlagen	PED	Martigny, Hôtel de Ville	12.	"	08.30
N	8055	n	Kinematographische Filme. Einfuhr	I	Bern, Zimmer IV	12.	"	10.00
S	8058	s	Panzerbeschaffung (Mil.Komm.)	EMD	Bern, Zimmer III	13.	"	08.00
S	8063	s	Preiskontrollmassnahmen. Durchführg.	EVD	Bern, Zimmer IV	13.	"	08.15
N	8046	s	Bekämpfung d.Maul- u.Klauenseuche	EVD	Liestal, Rathaus	14.	"	08.00
N	8059	n	Int.Bank für Wiederaufbau	FZD	Bern, Zimmer III	14.	"	09.00
N	8053	s	Komm. f. auswärtige Angelegenheiten	Pol.	Bern, Zimmer IV	14.	"	09.00
S	8053 8046	s s	Komm. f. auswärtige Angelegenheiten	Pol.	Bern, Zimmer IV	15.	"	08.30
N	8057	s	Treibstoffe. Zollzuschlag	FZD	Lausanne, Hôtel de la Paix	16.	"	14.00
N	-	-	Wahlprüfungskommission	-	Bern, Bundesratszimmer	19.	"	18.00

Beginn der Herbstsession: Montag, den 19. September 1960

9. List of Committees in session during a typical period of about six weeks before the autumn session of 1960

195

NATIONALRAT
36. Legislaturperiode

Vertretung der Fraktionen in den Kommissionen

(Berechnet nach dem für die Nationalratswahlen geltenden Proporzverfahren; kleine Fraktionen zusammengefasst)

Fraktionen	Zahl der Fraktions-Mitglieder	Mitglieder der Kommissionen												
		5	7	9*)	11	13	15	17*)	19	21	23	25	27	29
Sozialdemokraten	53	2	2	2	3	4	4	4	5	6	6	7	7	8
Radikaldemokraten	51	2	2	2	3	4	4	4	5	6	6	7	7	8
Konservativ-Christlichsoziale	47	1	2	2	3	3	4	4	5	5	6	6	7	7
Bauern, Gewerbe und Bürger	23	–	1	1	1	1	2	2	2	2	3	3	3	3
Uebrige Fraktionen 1)	21	–	–	1	1	1	1	2	2	2	2	2	3	3
Zusammen 2)	193	5	7	9*)	11	13	15	17*)	19	21	23	25	27	29

1) Landesring 10, Liberaldemokraten 5, Demokraten und Evangelische 6.
2) Ohne die 3 Fraktionslosen.
*) Der 9. bzw. 17. Sitz müsste gemäss Art.18, Al.3 des BG über die Wahl des Nationalrates durch Losentscheid den Sozialdemokraten oder den Radikaldemokraten zugeteilt werden.

10. The 'key' determining party representation on committees, in the National Council

INDEX

(The more important references are in **bold figures***)*

Abbreviations: C. of S.—Councillor of States
Fed. C.—Federal Councillor
Nat. C.—National Councillor

Aargau, Canton, 5, 9, 45, 47, 72
Accounts, Federal, 131, 136, 145, 153
Adams and Cunningham, 93
Administrative Law, 67, 96, 134, 167
Ador, Gustave, Fed. C., 19, 77, 85–6, 92, 181
Agreement, Conference of, 159–161, 183
Akeret, Dr Erwin, Nat. C., viii, 83, 182
Amnesties, 154
Amrhyn, Fed. Chancellor, 88–9
Anderwert, Fridolin, Fed. C., 80
Annuaire des autorités fédérales, 54
Anregung, 103. See also Postulate
Appenzell, Canton and Village, 5, 41, 79
Arbeitsfrieden, 28
Aristocracy, 1, 2, 5, 8, 14–16, 24, 31, 148
Army, 1, 27, 35, 50, 53, 81, 91, 114, 149, 156, 179, 195. See also Committees, of legislative Councils, of Military Affairs
Arrêtés, Federal, 101; Emergency Powers A., 150, 179
Austria and Switzerland, v, 10, 180

Basle, Canton and City, 3, 15, 25, 30, 31, 72, 74, 78, 106
Bauernsekretariat, 29, 44, 79, 94

Baumann, Johannes, Fed. C., 79–81
Bentham, J., v, 66
'Berger' (pseud.), 103 seq., 166
Berne, Canton and City, 59, 66, 92, 107 seq., 184, 186–7; Council of States and, 55; Election in, 44–7; Federal Council seat, 71, 74–5; History of, 4, 8, 44–5; Parties in, 24, 29
Bernese Jura, 4, 45
Bicameralism. *See* Council of States, Divergences, Priority
Bienne (Biel), Town, 6, 45
B.I.G.A., 103 seq.
Bill (*Entwurf*). *See* Legislative Procedure
Bommeli, Herr, 126–7
Bonjour, Offler, Potter, their *Short History of Switzerland*, (11), 179
Books on Switzerland, 179–83
Borel, Georges, Nat. C., 126–7
Bovet, Fed. Chancellor, 60, 181–182
Bracher, Prof. K. D., 12
Bringolf, Walther, Nat. C., viii, **43–4**, 57–8, **73–4**, 78, 110, 142–143, 151, 166
Brühwiler, Dr, viii. *See* Secretariat of Federal Assembly
Bryce, Lord, 93
Büchi, Büro, 50, 181
Büchi, Traugott, Nat. C., viii, 192, 194
Budget (Estimates), 124, 130–1, 136 seq., 153

197

INDEX

Buildings of Parliament, 58 seq.
Bundeshaus-West, 59, 95, 97
Bundesrat. *See* Federal Councillor, Federal Council
Bureau fédéral statistique, 25, 180
Bureaux of Councils, 141, 152, 157–9, 195
Burkhard, Dr Claus, 152, 160, 183

Calonder, Felix, Fed. C., 76, 86
Cantonal democracy, 6, 8, 51, 137, 148, 188
Cantons. Citizenship of, 2, 75, 78; Constitutional amendment and, 161; Consultation of, 105; Executive Council (Regierungsrat) of, 55, 69, 74, 86, 100, 105, 176–8; Great Councils of, 16, 42, 52, 154–5; Proportional Representation and, 41 seq.
Career of Federal Councillor, 57–8, 78
Career, Parliamentary, 18, 52, 140, 142, 150, 158, 172–4
Catholic Party (Conservative People's Party, Christian Socialists, Catholic Conservatives), 21–2, **24–7**, 29, 31–2, 42 seq., 71 seq., 89, 196
Celio, Enrico, Fed. C., 81
Challet-Venel, Jacques, 80, 82
Chancellor, Federal, viii, 61, 68, 84, **88–90**, 96, 129, 132, 145, 171, 185, 189
Chaudet, Paul, Fed. C., 57–8, 72–3, 78, 166
Chuard, Ernest, Fed. C., 79
Civil Service (Beamtentum), viii, 13, 22, 53, 56, 61, 73–4, 89–90, **96**, 98, 103 seq., 114, 126, 138–140, 145–6, 159, 162–4, 186; Appointments to, 96, 155–6. *See also* the various Departments
Clavadetscher, Christian, C. of S., 47–9

Code of Obligations, 102 seq., 113, 119, 163
Committees of Experts, 104 seq., 125, 162–3
Committees of legislative Councils, 56, 172, 183; Ad hoc, 109, 117, 156, 158, 163, 186, 195–6; Functions of, 158–9
Committee of Redaction, 119
Committees, Standing:
 in general, 123, 174, 186, 195–6
 Alcohol, 153–4, 189
 Finance, 57, 58, 124, **140–2**, 151, 174. *See also* Delegation, Finance.
 Foreign Affairs, 57, 148–51, 154, 167, 195
 Full Powers, 57, 148, 150, 174
 Gestion, 153. *See also* Gestion
 Military Affairs, 57–8, 145, 151, 156
 Pardons, 154
 Petitions, 154
 Posts and Telegraphs, 156
 Railway Concessions, 153, 155
 Railways, Federal, 153, 155
 Trade and Tariffs, 57, 155
 Verification of Mandate, 57, 152–3, 174, 189, 195
Common Market, etc., 125, 167, 174
Communes. Citizenship of, 2, 176; Councils, 18, 148, 155
Communist party, 21, **31–3**, 96, 196
Condrau, Dr Joseph, Nat. C., viii, 56–8, 74, 78, 109, 166, 172–4
Conference of Agreement, 159–161, 183
Conference of Presidents (of Councils), 90, **159**, 184, 186, 195
Constitution, Federal:
 1813–48, *see* Diet, Federal
 1848, 10, 85, 161
 1874–present day, 10, 162

Constitution (*cont*):
  Economic Articles, 101, 172
    Art.32, 101–2
    Art.74, 37
    Art.85, 136, 149
    Art.89 *bis*, 101
    Art.92, 70
    Art.93, 160
    Art.96, 69–70
    Art.102, 128, 149
Contrôle des finances, 139–40, 143, 146
Control of Executive, 56, 65, 136 seq., 159
Co-operation of Parliament and Executive, 65, 141, 158
Council of States, 3, 21, 40, 43–4, 47, 54 seq., 62–3, 105, 118, 153, 159–61, 189
'Cumulation', 38, 49, 52–3, 176, 184, 187
Customs duties, 29, 155, 174, 179

Decoppet, Camille, Fed. C., 81
Delegation, Finance, 142–3, 146; Secretariat of Joint Finance Delegation, 140, **143–4**, 147
Democracy, 3, 6, 12, 14, 17, 147–8
Democratic Party, 21, 32, 196
Devaluation of Franc, 94
Dicey, A. V., 23, 93
Diet, Federal, 5, 6, 8, 10, 58–9, 68, 88, 115
Discussion of Articles, 116, 158
'Divergences', 118, 159–61, 183
Doyen d'âge, 152
Droz, Numa, Fed. C., 85, 86, 97
Dumont, Etienne, v, 66, 67
Duttweiler, Gottlieb, Nat. C., viii, 30–1, 63, 120, 173, 190

East Switzerland, 29, 33, 73, 78, 158
Eichenberger, Kurt, 99, 116, 182
Eintreten, 107, 110, 111, 115, 158

Emmental, 16, 29, 45, 46
Etter, Philipp, Fed. C., 99
Evangelical Party, 21, 32, 196
Experts, 133. *See also* Committees of Experts
Extraordinary Military Tribunal, 84
Extraordinary Public Prosecutor, 84

Farmers' Party, 21, 28–30, 42 seq., 71 seq., 196
  See also Peasantry, *Bauernsekretariat*
Federal Assembly, 'a toothless watchdog', 131, 137, 165–6
  Joint Session, 67, 154, 185, 190
  Elections of Federal Council, 64, 69–80
  Other Elections by, 84–91
Federal Chancellor, *see* Chancellor, Federal
Federal Council, v, vi, 59, 65–6, 181, 184, 189; as College, 94, 98, 105, 128; Committees, delegations, 97; Description of meeting, 95; Work of, 92–100. *See also* Gestion, Message, Responsibility
Federal Councillors, and Cantons, 95; and Parties, 94–5, 114; and Plenum, 61, 99, 115, 123, 163–4; Election of, 64, 69–80; Resignation of, 34, 80–83, 94, 130, 165
Federal Insurance Tribunal, 84, 91, 130
Federal Tribunal, 24, 84, 90, 103, 104, 130. *See also* Judges
Feldmann, Markus, Fed. C., 71, 75
Feuille Fédérale, 68, 95, 109, 129
Final Quotient, 39, 175
Final Vote on Bill, 119
Finance Delegation, 57, **142–4**
Finance Department, 94, 104, 124, 145–7; *Mitbericht*, 95

INDEX

Finance, federal, 65, 70, **136–47**; and Gestion, compared, 137, 141, 144, 153, 156. *See also* Committees, Standing—Finance
'Fisch' (pseud.), 103 seq., 166
Food Office, 71–2, 95, 100
Foreign Affairs Committee, *see* Committees, Standing—Foreign Affairs
Foreign Policy, Swiss, 33, 90, 92, 121, 174; Neutrality, 167–71
Forrer, Ludwig, Fed. C., 81
'Fractions' (parliamentary party), **21 seq.**, 32–3, 93, 110, **114**, **156–8**, 163, 186, 190, 196
France and Switzerland, 8, 66, 67, 180
Fribourg, Canton and City, 25–26, 55, 73, 76
Full Powers Committee, 57, 148, 150, 174. *See also* Urgency
Furrer, Jonas, Fed. C., 84

Gadient, Nat. C., 33
General, The, 81, **91**, 95
General Strike of 1918, 27, (35)
Geneva, Canton and City, 4, 6, 15, 31, 55, 66, 78
Germany, and Switzerland, 2, 4, 5, 10, 14, 28, 36, 43, 79, 91, 93, 102, 149, 180; (C.D.U.), 25, 32, 77
Gestion, 57, 65, 66, 70, 97, 124, **128–35**, 141, 146, 151, **153**, 156, 174, 183, 185–6, 192–4
Glarus, Canton, 41, 75
Giacometti, Prof., viii
Gnägi, Rudolf, Nat. C., 72
Gonzenbach, A. von, 88
Gotthelf, Jeremias, 16
Grandjean, Jules, Nat. C., 133, 192
Greyerz, Prof. H. von, viii, 179
Grimm, Robert, Nat. C., 149, 187

Grisons (Graubünden), Canton, 6–8, 73, 76
Gruner, Prof., 49, 179–80
Guisan, General, 81, **91**

Haab, Robert, Fed. C., 74
Häberlin, Heinrich, Fed. C., 82, 99
Hague, Agreement, Court, 19, 169–70
Hammer, Bernard, Fed. C., 74, 82
Helvetic Republic, 8, 88
History, **1–11**; sense of, 1, 2–3; teaching of, 1, 12
Hoffmann, Arthur, Fed. C., 19, 81, 85, 86, 87
Hongler, Dr., viii, 183. *See also* Zentralstelle
Huber, Prof. Hans, 182
Huber, Prof. Max, **19–20**, 171, 180
Hughes, Prof. C. J., 67, 179, 181, 185, 150*n*.

Incompatibility, 55, 63
Industry, 16, 34, 54, 82, 100, 116
Initiative, Constitutional, 31, 34, 69, 125, 146
Initiative, of Legislation. 103. *See also* Postulate
Inner Switzerland, 3, 6, 7, 9, 48. *See also* Urschweiz
Insurance Companies, 19, 107 seq., 111–12, 117, 163
Insurance Tribunal, Federal, 84, 91, 185, 190
International Post Bureau, 82
Interpellations, 65, **121** seq., 189
Interpretations of Swiss Institutions, vii, 14, 37, 56, 69–70, 98, 122, 125, 128, 130, 134, 137, 145, 148, 151, **162–6**, 179; Bureaucracy Theory, 162–3; Conspiracy Theory, 34–5, 104, 163–4; Law Theory, 35, 138, 164

INDEX

Iten, Alphons, C. of S., 106, 107, 116 seq.
Jews, 5, 36, 79
Judges, 34, 53, 185, 190. *See also* Federal Tribunal
Jürg Jenatsch (novel: C. F. Meyer), 7
Justice and Police Dept., viii, 103, 129

Käppeli, Herr, 100
Käser, Dr, viii, 183. *See also* Delegation, Secretariat of Joint Finance
Kelsen, Prof. Hans, 23
'Key', for Committees, 157–8, 186, 196
Kitzinger, U. W., 181
Klöti, Dr Emil, Altständerat, viii, 77, 181
Knüsel, Melchior, Fed. C., 82
Kobelt, Karl, Fed. C., 78, 81, 99
Küssnacht, 50–1

Labour, 16, 17–18, 23
Lachenal, Adrien, Fed. C. and C. of S., 82
Lachenal, F., his *Le parti politique*, 180
Land, the, 15–17, 23, 26–7, 35
Landesring, of Independents, 21, **30–31**, 43, 72, 184, 196
Landsgemeinde, 3, 55, 166
Language, 10, 45, 62, 73, 76–7, 106, 111, 115, **161**, 167
Laufental, 46
Laur, Ernst, 79, 94, 182
Laws:
   on Army Reform, of 1960, 114
   on Contract of Agency, of 1949, 102 seq., 162–4, 173
   on Organization, of 1914, 88, 96, 97
   on Proportional Representation, of 1919, 37
   on Relations between the Councils, of 1902, 60, **67**,
101, 120, 154, 158, 160, 179, 184–5, 195
   on Responsibility, of 1958, 131
Legislation, procedure, 64, 66, 93–4, **101–19**, 156, 182; Interpretations of, 162–5
Leimgruber, Oscar, Fed. Chancellor, 26, 89
Leu, Josef, Nat. C., 48
Liberal Party, 9–11, 21–3, 30–2
Lieb, Ernst, C. of S., 44
Lötschental, 6
Lucerne, Canton and City, Election in, 47–9, 175–8; History of, 8, 26, 88–9; Insurance Tribunal, 91; Parties in, 24–5
Ludwig, Carl, 36, 79–80, 96
Lyon, Peter, viii, 167

Maillefer, Nat. C., 79
Mathys, Herr, 103
Mediation Constitution, 8, 85
Message (Report) of Federal Council, 107, **109–10**, 121, 125, 170, 184
Meyer, Albert, Fed. C., 94
Meyer, C. F., his *Jürg Jenatsch*, 7
Middle-class, 13, 14, 24, 27, 31, 33, 98, 104, 165
Military Committee, *see* Committees, Standing — Military Affairs
Minger, Rudolf, Fed. C., 77, 94
Moos, Ludwig von, Fed. C., 62, (73)
Motions, 65, 120 seq., 129, 189
Motta, Giuseppe, Fed. C., 15, 19, 81, 87, 99, 149, 181
Mousson, Chancellor, 88, 182
Müller, Eduard, Fed. C., 85
Munzinger, Fed. C., 80, 99, 181
Musy, Jean Marie, Fed. C., 12, 77, 81, 99

Näff, Wilhelm, Fed. C., 80, 84
Nationalrat, *see* National Council, National Councillors

201

INDEX

National Council, building, 61 seq.; clerkship of, 89; General Election, 37–51
National Councillors, Character of, 52 seq., 109; pay of, 54, 185. *See also* Career, parliamentary
N.A.T.O., 167
Nebelspalter, 50
Neuchâtel, Canton and Town, 31, 55
Neue Zürcher Zeitung, 19, 20, 31, 38, 180, 184, 188
Neutrality, **167–71**
New Helvetic Society, 35, 181
Nidwalden, 3, 41
Nobs, Ernst, Fed. C., 15, 29, 75, 77, 85

Obrecht, Hermann, Fed. C., 94
Obwalden, 3, 41
Ochsenbein, Ulrich, Fed. C., 80
Old Confederation, 1–7; as a political programme, 10–11. *See also* Diet, Federal Organization and Methods. *See Zentralstelle*

Panachage, 38, **40**, 52
Papal Nuncio, 26
Pardons, 154–5
Parties, political, **21–36**, 76–8, 82, 164, 180; Organization of, 49–51. *See also* Catholic, Communist, Democratic, Evangelical, Farmers, Fractions, Landesring, Liberal, Radical, Religion, Socialist
Patriotism, 1, 10, 35
Peasantry, **15–17**, 23, 26, 27, 35. *See also* Farmers' Party, *Bauernsekretariat*
Péclard, Ulysse, Nat. C., 111
Petitpierre, Max, Fed. C., 74*n*., 87, 99
Petitions, 154, 195

Pilet-Golaz, Marcel, Fed. C., 81, 87, 99
Political Department, vi, viii, 74*n*., 85, 86, 95, 96, 129, 136, 167, 192–5
Posts and Telegraphs, 156
Postulates, **120** seq., 129, 154, 185, 189, 191
President of Confederation, 74, 82, **84–8**, 92, 96–7, 145
President, of Committees, 109, 132, 172–4
President, of Council, 61, 67, 78, 157–8, 174. *See also* Conference of Presidents
Press, 31, 50–1, 53, 62, 68, 71, 89, 93, 133, 168. *See also Neue Zürcher Zeitung*
'Priority', 109, 131–2, 186
Procedure, parliamentary, vi, **64–68**, 69, 70, 130, 147, 148, 181. *See also* Legislation, Motions, etc.
Promulgation of Law, 119
Property, right to, 23–4
Proportionality, 37, 109, 148, 157–8, 185, 190
Proportional Representation (National Council), 22, 28–9, 33, **37–41**, 152, **175–8**, 184, 186–7, 196
Public Relations, 50–1, 150
Publicity of Debate, 61, **68**

Question Hour, 65, 93, 120
Questions, written, 65, 122
Quorum, National Council, 117

Räber, Dr, C. of S., 50–1, 181
Radical party, 14, 21–4, 29, 42 seq., 196
Railways, 153, 155, 172–4
Rapporteurs, 61, 111 seq., 133, 144, 158, 185–6, 192–3
Rathaus des äusseren Standes, 59, 181
Red Cross, 19

INDEX

Referendum, 31, 34, 45, 51, 68, 77, 81–3, 101, 104, 146–7, 149, 161, 180
Règlements (Standing Orders), of Committees, 141–2; of Councils, **66–7**, 101, 120–2, 152, 157–158, 181, 183
Religion, 5, 7, 9, 13, 18, 23, 34, 51–2, 58, 72, 77–78; Politics and, 14, 89, 98, 161, 165
Report of Federal Council, *see* Message
Responsibility, **130–1**, 153
Rheinau Scheme, 43, 173
Romansch Language, 7, 76, 172, 174
Ruchonnet, Louis, Fed. C., 76, 98
Rütli, 3, 62

Sachlichkeit, 63, 98, 100
St Gallen, Canton and City, 5, 6, 47, 55
Savoy, 85
Schaffhausen, 29, 73, 110; Election in, **41–4**
Schaffner, Herr, Fed. C., 73–4
Schenk, Carl, Fed. C., 88, 181
Scherrer, Carl, Nat. C., 43
Schiess, Ulrich, Fed. Chancellor, 89
Schobinger, Josef, Fed. C., 86
Schoch, Dr Kurt, C. of S., 43–4, 118
Schools, 12, 34, 188; Gymnasium, 13, 18
Schulthess, Edmund, Fed. C., 85–6, 94, 99
Schwyz, Canton, 3, 41, 48, 50–1
Secretariat of Federal Assembly, viii, 61, 68, 90, 120, 123, 181, 183, 194–5
Secretariat of Joint Finance Delegation, *see* Delegation
'Secretary of State', plan, 100
Separation of Powers, 64, 134
Separatists (Jura), 45

Social Democrat Party, 21–2, **26–28**, 42 seq., 72 seq., 89, 94, 120, 121, 126, 127, 148, 153, 184, 187, 196
Society, Swiss, v, 12–20, 33, 56, 164–5
Solothurn, 25
Soloveytchik, George, 87, 179, 181
Sonderbund, 9–10, 47, 77, 88
Speiser, Nat. C., C. of S., 116–18
Sprecher, Colonel von, (7), 91
Ständerat, *see* Council of States
Stämpfli, Jakob, Fed. C., 60, 81
Stampfli, Walter, Fed. C., 99
Standing Orders, *see* Règlements
Steiger, Eduard von, Fed. C., 110 seq.; Election, 15, **79**; Resignation, 71
Steiner, Dr Jürg, 16, 36, 179–80
Steinmann, Ernst, 85, 87
Steinmann, Paul, Nat. C., 127
Stenographic Bulletin, 68, 127, 133, (182), 183
Streuli, Hans, Fed. C., 77
Suter, R., Nat. C., 120
Swiss National Bank, 94, 139

Tariffs, 29, 155, 174
Tell, William, 50, 60
Tellers, 61, 78, **157–8**
Tenchio, Ettore, Nat. C., (73), 76
Tettamenti, Cantonal Councillor, 98
Thurgau, Canton, 6, 29
Ticino, Canton, 5, 98, 158
Trades Unions, 28, 53, 103 seq.
'Trumpf Buur', 50
Tschudi, Prof. Peter, Fed. C., 57, 74

United Kingdom, comparisons with, v, 36, 56, 64, 82, 90, 97–99, 104, 108, 116, 120, 122, 128, 134–6, 138–9, 141, 145, 154, 166

INDEX

U.S.A., and Switzerland, 10, 67, 146
Universities, 13, 18, 19, 22, 96, 106
Urgency, 57, 88, 101, 148, 150, 174, 179
Uri, Canton, 41–2
Urschweiz, 3, 73

Valais, Canton, 6–8, 26, 73
Vaterlaus, Dr Ernst, C. of S., 38
Vaud, Canton, 16, 47, 55, 58; Federal Council Seat, 71, 74–75; History, 4, 9, 45; Parties in, 24, 31, 33
Verbände (Lobbies, pressure-groups), 29, 33, **52–4**, 98, 124, 134, 145, 156–7, 159, 162–4, 180; Federal Council and, 103 seq., **112**
Vice-Chancellor, 89, 95
Vice-President of Federal Council, 57, 61, 84
Vice-President of Council, 157–8
Vorort (Capital of Confederation before 1848), 9, 59, 88
Vorort (Federation of Swiss Industry), 19, 31, 33–4, 50, **104** seq., 124, 162–3, 180
Votum, 115

Wahlen, Prof. Friedrich, Fed. C., 57, 74*n*., **71–2**, 80, 87, 127, 181
Walther, Nat. C., 27, 79
Weber, Prof. Max, Fed. C. and Nat. C., viii, 75, 77, 81, 82, 121, 187
Welti, Emil, Fed. C., 60, 81
Wick, Dr Karl, Nat. C., 48, 176
Wireless, 57
Women, 40, 55

Zemp, Josef, Fed. C., 76
Zentralstelle, 90, 145–7, 183
Zug, 41
Zurich, Canton and City, 4, 8, 15, 19, 20, 24, 30, 44, 66, 106; Federal Council Seat, 71–2, 74–5; Radical Party in, 24, 31, 38